A POLITICIAN
GOES TO WAR

Lieutenant Colonel John W. Geary

A POLITICIAN GOES TO WAR

*The Civil War Letters of
John White Geary*

Edited by
William Alan Blair

Selections and Introduction by
Bell Irvin Wiley

The Pennsylvania State University Press
University Park, Pennsylvania

Library of Congress Cataloging-in-Publication Data

Geary, John White, 1819–1873.
    A politician goes to war : the Civil War letters of John White Geary / edited by
    William Alan Blair ; selections and introduction by Bell Irvin Wiley.
        p.   cm.
    Includes bibliographical references and index.
    ISBN 0-271-01338-9 (alk. paper)
    1. Geary, John White, 1819–1873—Correspondence.   2. Generals—United
States—Correspondence.   3. United States.   Army—Biography.
I. Blair, William Alan.   II. Title.
E467.1.G29A4   1995
978.1'02'092—dc20   94-6497
                                                                                              CIP

Published by The Pennsylvania State University Press,
Suite C, Barbara Building, University Park, PA 16802-1003

It is the policy of The Pennsylvania State University Press to use acid-free paper for the first
printing of all clothbound books. Publications on uncoated stock satisfy the minimum
requirements of American National Standard for Information Sciences—Permanence of Paper for Printed Library Materials, ANSI Z39.48–1984.

Frontispiece: Lieutenant Colonel John W. Geary. Courtesy of Ron Palm Collection, U.S.
Army Military History Institute, Carlisle Barracks.

Contents

Preface

by William Alan Blair

A Union officer may seem an unlikely subject for Bell Irvin Wiley, who spent most of his career reclaiming the lives of ordinary people. Yet the final project of the historian's life focused on a general who served as governor of the Kansas Territory before the Civil War and of Pennsylvania afterward. Upon absorbing the letters of John White Geary, a reader can guess at the fascination they held for Wiley, the quintessential scholar of the common person. These letters of an uncommon man reveal ordinary concerns about children, money, home, and religion that linked Geary to many on both sides of the war.

Bell Wiley viewed Geary as an admirable example of a soldier whose duty to country and attention to family reflected the best of the American spirit. However, the historian failed to finish the project before his death in 1980, and the material lay dormant for more than a decade before being passed to a co-editor. It is perhaps inevitable that someone a generation removed from Wiley would view the subject differently, interpreting Geary as a political general whose greatest talent was the ability to enhance his own reputation through self-promotion. These portraits do not necessarily conflict, for the general's multifaceted character included bravery and duty, on the one hand, and a more-than-ample ego, on the other.

Sometime in the late 1970s, Wiley selected these roughly 200 letters for publication, wrote an introduction, and began editing. The manuscript was discovered in 1992 after the death of his wife, Mary Frances, by one of the two surviving sons, George Wiley. Because the historian had retained correspondence concerning the project, George knew that his father intended to publish the work with Penn State Press. Although the manuscript was incomplete (it had not yet been annotated or checked against the original letters for accuracy), the Press remained interested in publication for at least two reasons. First, the letters revealed the private mind of a Union

general who saw action in major campaigns of both the Virginia and Tennessee-Georgia theaters. Second, and equally important, the project represented the last known work of a major historian of the Civil War.

Well before the new social history of the 1960s and 1970s made it
standard to focus on the lives of ordinary people, Bell Wiley had staked out
this historical turf. A native of Halls, Tennessee, he earned his doctorate at
Yale in 1933, taught at several Southern institutions, and then in 1949
settled into a position at Emory University at Atlanta, where he remained
until retiring in 1974. A popular scholar, Wiley also could be a critic of
the section he loved, claiming he was "neither a partisan nor an apologist
for the South. And I have never found an occasion to be."[1] He wrote or
edited twenty-four books, many of them providing insight into the lives of
common people and advancing our understanding of what motivated civilians and soldiers to support the Union and the Confederacy. Among his
most popular works are the classics *Billy Yank* and *Johnny Reb*, which
opened inquiry into the attitudes of the common soldier that historians still
pursue. But he also wrote a study of the Southern homefront during the
Civil War that contains cogent insights into the relationship of battlefield
action to civilian morale.[2]

Although his study of the common folk broke new ground, Wiley's
overall theme—that the experiences of soldiers gave them a profound com-
monality—mirrored the interpretive trend of his generation. Scholars during and after World War II often focused on the distinctiveness of American society and looked for the characteristics that all Americans shared. In
Civil War terms, this translated into viewing the similarities between
Northerners and Southerners as more important than sectional traits. Wiley
observed about the soldiers of both sections that "the similarities of Billy
Yank and Johnny Reb far outweighed their differences. They were both
Americans, by birth or by adoption, and they both had the weaknesses and
the virtues of the people of their nation and time."[3] Through this frame-
work, Geary's ego and other less attractive traits could be overlooked.
"Love of country, combined with a lofty idealism reflected in his repeated
references to honor, duty, sacrifice, and nobility," Wiley concluded in his
introduction to the letters, "helped to make Geary a devoted husband, a

---

1. *Atlanta Constitution and Journal*, April 6, 1980.
2. Bell Irvin Wiley, *The Road to Appomattox* (Memphis, Tenn., 1956). See also Wiley's *The Life of Johnny Reb: The Common Soldier of the Confederacy* (Baton Rouge, La., 1943) and *The Life of Billy Yank: The Common Soldier of the Union* (Baton Rouge, La., 1952).
3. Wiley, *Billy Yank*, 361.

loving father, a loyal friend, a great American, and a thoroughly admirable man. To him and his kind the nation owes an enduring debt of immeasurable gratitude."[4]

Possibly because he had not finished the research—and because of the questions that informed his inquiry—Wiley ignored the less appealing side of Geary's character, which emerges in a close reading of these letters and in the private comments of officers. Geary was first and foremost a politician, which often caused him to exaggerate achievements in a naked attempt at self-promotion. His career began in 1849 with a patronage appointment by President James K. Polk to serve as postmaster of San Francisco. The Pennsylvanian quickly rose to prominence in that frontier community, becoming the first mayor of the town. National reputation waited until President Franklin Pierce appointed Geary governor of the Kansas Territory in 1856. He handled himself competently, although his fiery personality did not help a volatile situation. Unable to resolve matters as he wanted, Geary resigned just as James Buchanan, the first and only Pennsylvania president, had established himself in the White House. This left Geary outside the currents of state and national power. On January 23, 1865, the general reminded Mary that the couple had married in 1858, when his fortunes looked bleak and when friends feared his "political contagion as they would have been of one who had the small pox or more contagious disease."[5]

While the former governor volunteered to lead a regiment in the Civil War partly from his sense of duty to nation, he also knew that military service could translate into public office. It had worked once before. His political career was launched by the Mexican War, in which Geary gained a reputation for bravery in the charge of American soldiers at Chapultepec. At the end of that conflict, Geary rose to colonel of the 2nd Pennsylvania Militia while serving as military governor of the city of Mexico.

Evidence suggests that Geary finessed the promotion. Richard Coulter, who served in the 2nd Pennsylvania, wrote his father in Westmoreland County that Geary achieved the colonelcy through political rather than military skill. Coulter's comments might have been tainted; after all, he

---

4. See Wiley's "Introduction" to Geary's letters, following.

5. Biographical material on Geary is from William C. Armor, *Lives of the Governors of Pennsylvania, with the Incidental History of the State, from 1609 to 1872*, new ed. (Philadelphia, 1873); *Dictionary of American Biography* (New York, 1931), 7:203–4; John N. Boucher, *History of Westmoreland County, Pa.*, 2 vols. (New York, 1906), 1:658–60; and Harry Marlin Tinkcom, *John White Geary: Soldier-Statesman* (Philadelphia, 1940).

probably supported a man who failed to win the promotion. Yet the political behavior he attributed to Geary fits a pattern noted by officers in the Civil War and resembles efforts by the general himself to win promotion to major general in that later conflict. In Mexico, Geary concealed an order from General Winfield Scott to schedule the requisite election for officers until rival Captain S. H. Montgomery left town. He also followed a common practice in the political culture of the time by courting the "hard scrabble of the regt whom liquor would buy and who were so tickled by the attention and notice of a *Lieut. Col.* that they considered their support as the least return they could make for his condescension."[6] To gain support of officers, he apparently promised commissions or promotions and got them to send letters to Pennsylvania newspapers praising his abilities in exchange for his doing the same for them. Geary easily defeated two other candidates hastily offered by soldiers who disliked the lieutenant colonel but could not agree on a replacement for Captain Montgomery.

Coulter also insisted that the new colonel misrepresented his conduct in the attack at Chapultepec. Although the toll in colonels had been heavy at the gate along the causeway, "our Col regardless of his situation as commander of the largest Regt in the action only sought to preserve his cowardly carcass at the expense of his own." Geary marched to the gate, where he found the fire "too heavy for his weak nerves" and fell back roughly twenty arches down the causeway. A vexed Coulter concluded about Geary's promotion: "It is the only circumstance which has yet caused a regret during the campaign that we are compelled to serve under a Col[onel] who is the laughing stock of the whole regular service and a man who is more despised the better he is known."

Coulter's assessment of his colonel's bravery may have been too severe. The judgment does not describe what happened during the Civil War, although it was not clear which Geary would emerge when it came time to face the enemy. His letters to Mary in the beginning revealed an anxious person who consistently exaggerated the enemy's threat—a tendency that contributed to an ignominious flight from ghost troops created by rumor during "Stonewall" Jackson's Valley Campaign of 1862. He eventually settled down, and although he never became tactically adroit he displayed courage under fire at Cedar Mountain, Chancellorsville, and Wauhatchie Station in Tennessee.

6. This and subsequent quotations are from R[ichard] Coulter to "Uncle," Nov. 27, 1847, Geary Papers, Westmoreland County Historical Society, Greensburg, Pa.

To publicize his actions for future constituents, Geary relied on two tools: the newspaper correspondents who followed the armies, and the official reports of operations required of all officers. Through correspondents he gained credit not only for what he did himself but also for the achievements of others. While Geary may not have been exceptional in using these outlets, he was among the most proficient. Brigadier General Alpheus S. Williams observed about Geary: "We have had one division commander who, I judge, has kept a corner in the notes of every correspondent in the army, besides keeping his staff busy at the same work. He claims [to have done] pretty much everything." A major in the 28th Regiment Pennsylvania Volunteers also noted his general's tendency to exaggerate: "Gen. G. saw 8 rebels, so he says. I did not see them. In next week's paper there will no doubt be an account of 'A Dash' into the enemy's lines. The 28th in the field. Flight of the enemy. Geary at work, etc., etc.'" Finally, a staff officer wrote home in November 1862 about a recent expedition near Shepherdstown, Virginia: "I see the correspondent at Harper's Ferry of the *New York Herald* puts it down to the credit of General Geary who had nothing whatever to do with it or with us in any way."[7]

Reports of operations undergirded Geary's efforts to publicize his activities. These reports constituted a principal source for correspondents needing news of the war for the people at home. The general absolutely excelled at crafting long, detailed accounts that turned minor engagements into epic contests. For instance, Geary's report of the Atlanta campaign ran thirty-five printed pages—five more to describe one division's experience than William Tecumseh Sherman needed to write about the entire army. The general also filed his reports promptly, which helped his reputation inordinately at Gettysburg because his version was available when Union commander George G. Meade compiled the overall report of the battle. Geary thus had a prominent role in forming Meade's interpretation of the defense of Culp's Hill on July 3. Geary had fought well enough, and no one should deny him just acclaim. However, as the letter to Mary of July 4 indicates, he made it appear as if he planned and coordinated the entire defense against the Confederate Second Corps. Alpheus Williams, who temporarily commanded the Twelfth Corps, deserved the recognition for establishing the line, placing troops where needed, and reacting to the exigencies of the moment. When Williams saw Meade's report crediting Geary, he com-

---

7. Alpheus S. Williams, *From the Cannon's Mouth*, ed. Milo M. Quaife (Detroit, 1959), 330; Gertrude K. Johnston, ed., *Dear Pa, And So It Goes* (Harrisburg, 1971), 202; and John C. Gray and John Codman Ropes, *War Letters, 1862–1865*, ed. Worthington Chauncey Ford (Boston, 1927), 31.

plained to his daughter: "Save me from my friends!"[8] He subsequently per-
suaded Meade to issue a correction in February 1864. Geary also avoided
censure for a truly lackluster effort on July 2, when his division lost its way
in the rear of the Union army and the general ordered the men into bivouac
instead of trying to sort through the difficulty and make them available.

Gettysburg thus highlights the abilities and limitations of Geary as a
soldier. He displayed bravery and followed orders well. He sometimes coordinated offensives adequately—provided they were not too complicated and
involved an enemy of inferior strength, as at Lookout Mountain on November 24, 1863. Like many officers, he was most effective when attacked,
tenaciously defending against superior numbers at the battle of the Wauhatchie on October 28, 1863, and against the Confederate assault on Culp's
Hill on July 3, 1863. But Geary displayed little ability to think beyond his
orders and blundered into situations that better scouting, not to mention
judgment, would have avoided. At Bolivar in 1861 he nearly lost part of
his command left across the Shenandoah River because he had no idea how
many rebels were in the vicinity. Geary compounded these shortcomings
with an unforgiving personality, quick anger, and an obsession with discipline, which caused one young soldier to write: "Gen. G[eary] has such a
reputation for severity that every poor soldier does not like to approach
him."[9]

Officers from other units sometimes reacted strongly against Geary, but
soldiers and officers who benefited from his patronage overlooked their general's faults. The politician knew how to court common soldiers as well as
superiors. He does not appear to have "treated" them with liquor, as during
the Mexican War; in fact, he developed temperance sentiment and criticized drinking habits of a subordinate officer. Possessing strong adminis-
trative skills, Geary won soldiers over by paying attention to their needs.
Some wrote home about how well the general fed and supplied them; more-
over, they ignored Geary's obvious hunger for advancement because of admiration for his love of Union. "Gen. Geary has our utmost confidence &
respect," wrote a commissary for the brigade. "He is not aristocratic

8. Geary's report is in U.S. War Department, *The War of the Rebellion: A Compilation of the Official Records
of the Union and Confederate Armies*, 128 vols. (Washington, D.C., 1880–1901), ser. 1, vol. 38, pt. 2, 112–
47. See also Albert Castel, *Decision in the West: The Atlanta Campaign of 1864* (Lawrence, Kans., 1992), 132.
For Coddington's assessment that Geary let his pen run away in describing his accomplishments, see *The
Gettysburg Campaign: A Study in Command* (New York, 1968), 470; Williams, *From the Cannon's Mouth*, 271–
72.

9. Quoted in Joseph T. Glatthaar, *The March to the Sea and Beyond: Sherman's Troops in the Savannah and
Carolinas Campaigns* (New York, 1985), 25.

enough to suit some tastes and is rather petulant, but the latter results from his disgust at every thing that evinces other than *'pure patriotism'* a virtue little known or shown in our army. He suspects everyone of a desire to shirk duty or make profit on the countrys ruin. This makes him exceedingly arbitrary with all evil doers—with the enemy or with a traitorous citizen he has nothing in common. He looks upon them as persons who have forfeited all rights they ever possessed."[10]

The politician's touch did not always work. The delay in his promotion cost Geary some of his greatest effort and frustration during the war. Despite leading a division, he remained a brigadier general until January 1865, and then achieved the rank of major general only through brevet, or honorary, designation. In late 1863 and early 1864 he mounted an impressive campaign to promote his own cause—a fact ignored in the letters to Mary. He caused 173 officers serving under him to sign a petition requesting their general's promotion, and packaged this with letters of recommendation from Governor Andrew G. Curtin and more than fifty members of the Pennsylvania legislature. This effort failed because he did not have the ultimate backing of Ulysses S. Grant. The general-in-chief advanced Geary's name on a preliminary list for promotion in early 1864, but the field of candidates exceeded the number of vacancies. Geary failed to make a second list of officers who Grant believed deserved advancement.[11]

It should come as no surprise that Geary remained a brigadier until late in the war. Although no comments on the general's aptitude could be found, it appears that superiors recognized he had risen to an appropriate level. A lack of West Point training may have worked against him, but it seems more likely that William Tecumseh Sherman recognized that Geary's talents lay with administration. The Pennsylvanian served as commandant of Murfreesboro, pulled garrison duty in Atlanta, and performed well as the military governor of Savannah. An assessment of Geary's service as governor of Pennsylvania unintentionally captured the essence of his generalship: "He was naturally a man of executive ability and of great energy rather than a man of brilliant intellectual powers."[12]

10. James [Gillette] to "Mother" [c. October 1862], James Gillette Papers, Civil War Times Illustrated Collection, U.S. Army Military History Institute (MHI), Carlisle, Pa. For other comments from subordinates, see Levi L. Smith diary, August 7, 1861, Alexander R. Chamberlin Collection, MHI; and Joseph Addison Moore, "Rough Sketch of the War as Seen by Joseph Addison Moore," p. 3, Moore Family Papers, MHI.

11. For Geary's campaign to win promotion, see Letters Received, Commission Branch of Adjutant General's Office, National Archives, M1064, roll 93, G720; and U.S. Grant to Maj. Gen. H. W. Halleck, February 20, 1864, ibid., roll 91, G108.

12. Boucher, *History of Westmoreland County*, 1:660.

All this means that the letters written to Mary contain hidden agendas that affect their value. The politician composed these thoughts with the knowledge that someone might read over Mary's shoulder. In this correspondence, Geary counseled her when not to speak of certain matters and noted that he burned all of her letters immediately after reading them, probably to destroy anything that might carry postwar consequences. These concerns shaped the content of letters. Unlike most officers, Geary only infrequently criticized leaders, fellow officers, or strategy in his letters home. With rare exception, he censored himself in such areas. This reticence leaves readers hungering for more.

The same hunger to know more also occurs with Mary Geary. Because John burned her letters, she exists as a rather murky figure. The public record fills only a few gaps. Mary grew up in Cumberland County, the daughter of Robert R. Church, who ran a lumber business in partnership with Benjamin F. Lee and V. Feeman, both of whom John refers to in the letters. The family had minor political connections: the father married a relative of William Bigler, who was elected Pennsylvania governor in 1851 and U.S. Senator in 1855. During the 1850s, Mary's father died and she married a man named Henderson, bore two children, and probably was widowed. In 1858, she married John White Geary in a ceremony at Philadelphia. The remainder of her life after the governor died in 1873 remains unreported.

A reader nonetheless receives hints of a woman's life on the Civil War homefront. The family lived comparatively well, although most of the finances were tied up in nonliquid real estate. Mary had to manage money tightly, depending on how often the general received pay—something that became more haphazard with his transfer to the western theater. Like many women during the war, her household duties expanded as she negotiated and collected rents on the family's farm in Westmoreland County. John at times also coached her at writing checks and conducting banking. She lived a restless but not uncomfortable existence for the first two years of the war, boarding in New Cumberland and a Philadelphia hotel before purchasing a house in early 1863. That year also brought a new member of the family, as Mary's pregnancy ended in November with the birth of Margaret. During her pregnancy, Mary at times became depressed, although the cause is uncertain. She had reason enough with a husband away at war. The Confederate army provided more cause for concern as it nearly came to the doorstep of the Geary home during the Gettysburg campaign. Her impressions of this time would have been invaluable, particularly for comparison with those of Southern women who faced similar circumstances, although more frequently. More revelation of Mary's life awaits a future researcher who will coax more details from standard and less conventional sources.

Although the letters overall contain little that would startle, they are well worth reading. It is rare to have a consistent flow of letters from a person in significant engagements in the two principal theaters of war. One can contrast attitudes between soldiers of the eastern and western armies, or be struck by how early a hard brand of war was waged in northern Virginia. This supports recent work modifying standard notions that the Civil War was waged in two distinct styles: limited in the early stages and more vicious later.[13] As mentioned above concerning Mary, readers also can glimpse pieces of life on the Northern homefront and how relationships between men and women changed. Finally, if used with caution, the descriptions of army routes and campaigns enrich understanding of the western campaign.

The correspondence also reveals the mind of a War Democrat who hated slavery but did not like African Americans. Geary viewed the "peculiar institution" as preventing Southern whites from recognizing their true potential and creating an aristocracy that led the ignorant masses into war. The general's staunch Presbyterianism contributed to his antislavery opinions and fortified him with an appreciation for industry and thrift that he saw lacking in the poorer whites of the South. His religious views offer food for comparative thought with Southerners who shared the same faith but differed with one another about slavery. As Lincoln noted in his Second Inaugural, both sides prayed to the same God for different ends: "The prayers of both could not be answered; that of neither has been answered fully."[14]

Ultimately, the letters may be most valuable in showing how a political general plied his trade. In doing so, they also remind us of the complexities of analyzing any historical actor, much less one more than a century beyond our experience—for Geary had both the admirable qualities of loyalty to Union and the less attractive need to exaggerate his abilities. Parts of his character justifiably attracted Bell Wiley. A reader would have to be less than human not to sympathize with the general's writing of the death of his son, Edward. At the same time, Geary could be mean-spirited, egotistical, and self-serving. It is tempting to dismiss him as nothing more than a

---

13. For a brief overview, see Mark Grimsley, "Conciliation and Its Failure, 1861–1862," *Civil War History* 39 (December 1993), 318.

14. Roy P. Basler, ed., *Abraham Lincoln: His Speeches and Writings* (Cleveland, 1946), 793.

politician. However, he had enough military capacity to make the assessment hasty, but too little to rank him among the best divisional commanders in the army.

To help these complexities come through, the editing attempts to remain as faithful as possible to the original letters. Spelling, punctuation, capitalization, and grammar of the general have been preserved. More literate than many Northerners and Southerners, Geary nonetheless employed usage and construction that underscore the flexibility of nineteenth-century grammar and punctuation in the hands of even an educated man. Capitalization served as a device through which Geary emphasized matters and concepts important to him. Hasty, incomplete sentences at times reveal when the general was writing hurriedly while facing the distractions of command. I have added comments in brackets to assist comprehension or clarify the current spellings of cities, towns, and proper names. The usual caveat must be added that scholars still might want to consult the original letters in the Geary Family Collection of the Historical Society of Pennsylvania in Philadelphia. Readers should know that the selection of letters is Bell Wiley's; mistakes in their handling belong to the co-editor.

Finally, as all editors know, few projects of this kind come together without help from others. I wish to thank Marilyn Moorehead at the Family History Center of the Church of Jesus Christ of the Latter-Day Saints for her help in tracing the Geary family in Westmoreland County; Edward H. Hahn of the Westmoreland County Historical Society; Dr. Richard J. Sommers and Pamela Cheyney at the U.S. Army Military History Institute in Carlisle for information on the 2nd Division and the 28th Pennsylvania; Michael Winey for photographs of Geary in the archives at the Carlisle Barracks; Virginia Evans for accommodations that provided access to the Historical Society at Philadelphia; George F. Skoch for producing the maps; Dr. Gary W. Gallagher for support and advice that can never be repaid; Peter S. Carmichael for ideas, encouragement, and government connections; and most of all Mary Ann Blair, without whom life would be far poorer.

Introduction

by Bell Irvin Wiley

On June 24, 1863, Brigadier General John White Geary wrote his wife concerning his young son, Willie, who was about to join forces being marshaled to defend Pennsylvania against Lee's invading army: "Tell him to be manly, brave and true, to cast away boyishness, and whatever he does, to be sure he is right and do it with all his might." This advice reflected well the principles that had guided the general in his own long and distinguished career.

John W. Geary was born on December 30, 1819, at Mount Pleasant in western Pennsylvania. He attended Jefferson College but was compelled to leave school prematurely, owing to the death of his father and inheritance of a considerable debt. He taught school, studied civil engineering, invested successfully in Kentucky lands, read law, and was admitted to the bar. An early interest in military affairs led him to join the militia, and at age sixteen he became a lieutenant. During the Mexican War he rose from captain to colonel in the 2nd Pennsylvania Infantry Regiment. He distinguished himself in the assault on Chapultepec and served as an officer in the occupying force of that city.

Geary was a Democrat and a strong supporter of James K. Polk. In January 1849, President Polk appointed him postmaster of San Francisco, but he soon had to vacate the position in favor of a Whig designated by President Zachary Taylor. Geary stayed on in San Francisco and in 1850 became the first mayor of that city. In 1852, owing to the failing health of his first wife, Margaret, whom he had married in 1843, he returned to Pennsylvania.

In 1856, President Franklin Pierce appointed Geary governor of the strife-ridden Kansas Territory. The Pennsylvanian tried very hard to steer clear of partisan politics, but his efforts at impartial administration brought him into conflict with extreme proslavery elements, an aggressive minority seeking to take control of the territory and convert it into a slave state. Threatened with assassination, and denied effective support by the U.S. government, Geary deteriorated in health. He resigned on March 4, 1857, and headed for Washington, where he reported to President James Buchanan. The Kansas experience embittered Geary against slaveholders and slavery, and the memory of the Southerners' highhanded tactics lingered on throughout his Civil War career. Shortly after the murder of President Lincoln, Geary wrote: "The cowardly assassins are only exhibiting the same *phases* which so greatly embittered me towards them ever since the Kansas affair, and no one understands better than I their nefarious designs."

During the years 1857–61, Geary farmed and practiced law in western Pennsylvania. His first wife had died in 1853 after bearing him two sons, Edward and Willie. On November 2, 1858, he married a widow, Mary Henderson, and by her he had two daughters, Mary, born in 1859, and Margaret, born in 1863. When the Civil War broke out, the Gearys moved to the vicinity of Mary's relatives in New Cumberland, Pennsylvania [just across the Susquehanna River from the state capital, Harrisburg], and this remained their home throughout the war.

After Fort Sumter, Geary took an active part in recruiting the 28th Regiment Pennsylvania Volunteers and soon became colonel of that organization. In August and September 1861, he and his regiment participated in skirmishes in the vicinity of Harpers Ferry. They were part of the command of General Nathaniel P. Banks, of whom Geary wrote: "Genl. Banks is a c-----d or something worse . . . else he would sustain my precarious position better." He came to like Banks personally, but he never rated him highly as a combat commander. One of the qualities manifested early by Geary was pride in the unit he commanded. On September 5, 1861, he wrote: "I have every reason to be proud of my Regt, and so I am. I consider it the noblest in the service."

During most of his first six months in the service, Geary had both of his sons with him. Willie, the younger, served as drummer boy, but he was allowed to carry a rifle and to participate in target practice and skirmishes. Eddie, the older, who was only sixteen, was a second lieutenant in Knap's Battery of artillery, which in September 1861 was attached to Geary's command. Willie was sent home early in 1862, but Eddie remained in the service and in the summer of 1862, at age seventeen, was promoted to first lieutenant and given command of a section (two guns) of his battery. He was an exceptionally attractive person and a highly competent officer. Geary rejoiced at his son's success, and in letters to his wife he often commended the lad for his valor and nobility of character.

Late in September 1861, Geary, while still a colonel, was given command of a brigade, but not until April 1862 was he commissioned a brigadier general. The tardiness of his promotion cannot be attributed to poor performance. He led his brigade ably in several sharp encounters with Confederates in the vicinity of Point of Rocks, Maryland, in the fall and winter of 1861–62. He was wounded in the leg on October 16, 1861, but continued in active command. On December 9, 1861, he wrote his wife: "God bless the noble hearts of my men. Wherever I command, they will go." His officers and men demonstrated their esteem by presenting him with a sword, sash, hat, and saddle on the occasion of his promotion to brigadier general.

During the late spring and early summer of 1862, Geary's duty consisted largely of guarding and maintaining more than fifty miles of the Manassas Railroad. He chafed at this unglorious assignment, which denied him participation in the Shenandoah Valley campaign and the Seven Days battles. He wanted to fight. His desire for combat was abundantly realized on August 9, 1862, at Cedar Mountain. There he received a painful wound in the elbow that sent him home for several weeks of recuperation. So, he missed the bloody fight at Antietam, but his old regiment, the 28th Pennsylvania, was there, and so was Eddie's battery; both gave a good account of themselves.

When Geary returned to duty near Harpers Ferry on September 30, 1862, he found himself in command of the 2nd Division, which was destined to become the famous White Star Division of the Twelfth Corps. He commanded this division for the remainder of the war, and with distinction. But for some strange reason he was not promoted to major general until January 1865, and then only by brevet. He was greatly disappointed at his failure to win the recognition he felt he fully deserved, but he never expressed bitterness.

Apparently, Geary missed the battle of Fredericksburg, but he was at Chancellorsville. It is interesting that he makes no mention of that battle in his correspondence. At Gettysburg on the third day he and his division played a distinguished role in repelling Ewell's attack on the Union right. On July 4 he wrote proudly to his wife: "Yesterday I had the honor to defeat Gen Ewell's [Second] Corps. . . . They attacked my command at 3 oclock a.m. and we fought until ½ past 11. . . . I repulsed his command with a loss [Ewell's] of about 1000 killed and 3000 wounded. We also took about 500 prisoners, about 5000 stands of arms. My loss is 110 killed, 584 wounded. The whole fight was under my control, no one to interfere. *Thank God for so glorious a victory.*"

Geary was appalled by the bloodshed of Chancellorsville and Gettysburg. July 5, 1863, he wrote: "I have seen so much death and suffering this month that I am perfectly sick of the times. My very clothes smell of death. The stench of the battle fields was horrible and beyond description." Yet he was proud to be in the forefront of action. On August 22, 1863, he wrote: "It is now over 4 weeks . . . [that] my 'White Star' Division has occupied the most advanced position of the army. . . . It sometimes seems queer to me that during nine-tenths of the time I have been in the service, I have been face to face with the enemy & consequently have been in the front."

In October 1863, Geary and his division moved to the Chattanooga area with General Hooker's other troops to assist Grant in the campaign against Bragg's Confederates situated on Lookout Mountain and Missionary Ridge. Geary, like others from the eastern army, was shocked by the poor appearance and loose discipline of the western forces. On October 25, 1863, he wrote his wife: "We find every thing very different in the Army of the Cumberland from that we have been accustomed [to] in the Army of the Potomac. Discipline, the pride of that glorious body, is unknown here." In the desperate battles that occurred a month later, the easterners were to learn that the shabby-looking westerners fought with as much determination and valor as any troops in the Northern armies.

In the meantime, on the night of October 28, a portion of Geary's command, engaged in trying to open a route by which Grant's beleaguered troops in Chattanooga could be supplied, was attacked at Wauhatchie by Confederates of Hood's Division. The Southerners were repelled, but only after severe fighting and heavy casualties. Geary's jubilation over the victory was offset by grief over the loss of his beloved Eddie, who died in the thick of the fighting. On November 2 the sorrowing father wrote his wife: "A portion of my command numbering 1200 men . . . [was] attacked at midnight by that celebrated Hood's Division of Longstreets Corps numbering over 5,000 men. They came upon us in three heavy columns with great rapidity and with the most demoniacal yell. I instantly brought my men into line. . . . They [the Confederates] were . . . thoroughly defeated. . . . I have gained a great victory. . . . But oh! how dear it has cost me. My dear beloved boy is the sacrifice." Geary concluded his official report of the action with a poignant statement: "Numbered with the honored dead were the only two officers attached to . . . [Knap's] battery present, Captain A. C. Atwell and Lieut. E. R. Geary, who fell in the midst of their command, zealous in execution of their duty. . . . In the latter named, I may be permitted to remark I experience in conjunction with the keen regrets of a commanding officer for a worthy officer, the pangs of a father's grief for a cherished son, whose budding worth in wealth of intellect and courage was filling full the cup of paternal pride." Geary's sorrow was enhanced by the fact that Eddie, who recently had celebrated his eighteenth birthday, was at the time of his death awaiting orders for transfer to the Army of the Potomac, where he was to be promoted to captain and placed in command of a battery of artillery. The father's grief was deep and enduring. Henceforth he campaigned with increased ferocity, as if to wreak vengeance for the slaying of his son.

On December 4, 1863, Geary wrote his wife that he had requested and been granted the privilege of leading the Federal assault of November 24 on Lookout Mountain. "I stormed what was considered the impossible and inaccessible height," he stated. "I captured it, turned the . . . flank of Bragg's army and drove him from his position. This feat will be celebrated until time shall be no more." He added: "I burnt the town of Ringgold [November 27] because the enemy fired upon us from the houses. . . . I have won promotion over and over, and it has come not, such may be the case again. I am indifferent upon that subject."

In January and February 1864, Geary enjoyed a month's leave with his family in New Cumberland. En route back to his command, he spent a day and a night in Nashville. There he talked with Ulysses S. Grant. He liked Grant, and he strongly approved of the general's statement that he would eschew politics and devote himself fully to crushing the rebellion, which he thought he could accomplish in six months. In Nashville, also, Geary called on the widow of James K. Polk, who told him that President Polk had always regarded Geary as one of his best friends in Pennsylvania.

On March 21, Geary wrote his wife: "Do not trouble yourself about my promotion, if I act well my part as a Brigadier General, it will be as honorable as if 'twere done by a Maj. Genl." But his spirit was low. In this letter he complained of the "moral malaria of an army" and in his next, that of March 31, he admonished: "I desire that you *not* breathe the subject of my contemplated resignation to any one."

It seems exceedingly unlikely that Geary seriously considered leaving the army. Certainly, renewed activity with his troops restored his morale. In April 1864, he led some far-reaching reconnaissances in force into northern Alabama, and his success in these activities won the commendation of both General George H. Thomas and General Grant and contributed to Geary's continuation as commanding general of the White Star Division, now a part of the Twentieth Corps.

During the campaign for Atlanta, May–July 1864, Geary experienced the most strenuous service of his Civil War career. On June 25 he wrote: "My command has participated in ten battles during the present campaign without dimming the lustre of its glorious emblem, the 'White Star.'" In several instances during the campaign in north Georgia, he wrote letters amid the roar of artillery and the rattle of musketry, with his knee serving as writing desk.

Geary's division bore the brunt of Hood's attack on the Union right at Peachtree Creek, July 20, 1864. At the critical point of this fight he was almost surrounded. But his division changed front and fought off the Confederates. His casualties numbered 476 in killed, wounded, and missing. On September 3 Geary wrote proudly to his Mary: "The 20th Corps . . . [was] the 1st to enter [Atlanta]. And the flags of the ever-ahead and glorious old White Star Division were the first to wave from the town Hall." He added, with a bit of Yankee bias: "The city is a very pretty place, built much in northern taste and stile. . . . There is scarcely a house that does [not] exhibit in some degree the effects of the battle. . . . Many of the best are utterly ruined."

In November and December 1864, Geary participated in Sherman's famous march to the sea, an experience greatly enjoyed by both the general and his troops. Not until after he reached Savannah, on December 23, did Geary learn of Lincoln's victory over McClellan in the presidential campaign of 1864. He expressed great satisfaction over the results, but neither here nor elsewhere did he reveal any great enthusiasm for Lincoln. He was outraged by the assassination of the President, but his reaction suggested more of anger at the assassins than sympathy for the deceased. Perhaps his attitude was affected by his long-standing ties with the Democratic party.

On December 23, 1864, Geary wrote his wife: "I am now the *Commandante* of the City [of Savannah], in honor of its capture by me, and of the surrender to me. My command was in the city five hours earlier than any other troops. We captured by ourselves about 75 Cannon with ammunition, 30,000 Bales of cotton, 400 prisoners, and liberated many of our own soldiers [from Confederate prisons]." Geary remained in command of Savannah until late January 1865.

In February, March, and April 1865, he led his White Star Division in the campaign through the Carolinas. In March he applied for and received a second lieutenancy for his son Willie and made arrangements to have the boy detailed as his aide. "[It] will please him to ride and be a gentleman," Geary wrote, "more than to [be] a foot soldier."

After the final Confederate surrender, Geary proceeded with his division to Washington, where in mid-May they participated in the great victory parade. He then left the army and returned to his home in New Cumberland. He soon became a Republican, and as a candidate of the Cameron faction he was elected governor of Pennsylvania. During his two terms as governor, 1867–73, he followed a course largely independent of the Cameron machine and, motivated in part by aspirations for the Presidency, he sought to build up a personal following. He sympathized with the plight of workingmen and opposed legislation favoring large business establishments, such as the Girard National Bank and the Pennsylvania Railroad. During his second term, he successfully supported a convention for revision and reform of the state constitution. He died on February 8, 1873, shortly after vacating the governor's office.

During his Civil War service, Geary wrote frequently to his wife and children. A total of 289 of the wartime letters were preserved by his descendants, and in 1978 they were donated, along with other family papers, to the Historical Society of Pennsylvania. I am indebted to Colonel Richard M. Ludlow and other descendants of General Geary, and to the Historical Society of Pennsylvania, for permission to edit and publish the letters. Owing to a desire to eliminate some of the repetition resulting from the frequency of Geary's writing, and in order to meet necessary limitations of space, I have selected for publication roughly 200 letters that I regard as the best and most informative.

What do the letters reveal of the man who wrote them?

First, they confirm the impression based on his prewar career that he was a person of integrity. He deplored corruption. As leader of foraging parties and as commandant of the occupied Confederate towns of Murfreesboro and Savannah, he had opportunities to enrich himself, but this he did not do. In a letter of March 26, 1865, after marching with Sherman through Georgia and the Carolinas, he stated: "My hands are perfectly clean." There seems to be no doubt that he was telling the truth.

Second, he was deeply religious. Almost every letter contains a reference to his reliance on Divine Providence. He attributed his survival in battle to God's mercy and care. In the dark days following Fredericksburg, he professed abiding faith that God would bless the Union cause and bring the imperilled nation safely through the war. In the extreme and prolonged grief following the death of his son Eddie, reliance on spiritual support helped him to accept his loss, maintain his emotional balance, and cope with his continuing responsibilities.

His bravery was attested by his repeatedly exposing himself to enemy fire. He seemed to be thrilled by the rough-and-tumble of battle, and he provided a shining example of gallantry for those whom he led.

He was deeply devoted to his family. One of the most valuable aspects of his letters is the rich information they provide concerning the attitudes and relationships of an upper-middle-class family in the crisis of separation and war. The currents of mutual affection were very strong, and family ties were consistently close. Geary's love for his wife was based on a profound respect for her ability and her character. He entrusted to her the discharge of business and responsibilities and commended her for the efficiency she demonstrated in meeting them. He was unfailingly solicitous of the well-being, happiness, and constructive development of his children. In March 1864, he wrote: "There is no happiness comparable to the domesticity of a cherished home."

Geary's letters reveal a great ambition for himself and his children. He delighted in his achievement as a military leader and demanded excellence of those for whom he was responsible. He often encouraged his son Willie Geary and his stepson Willie Henderson to excel in their studies. In October 1862, he severely rebuked Eddie for acquiescing in the promotion over him of a fellow lieutenant whose claims to advancement the general regarded as inferior to those of his son. The general's wrath at his son's failure to press his claims for preferment was so great that he ordered Eddie from his tent. Later he apologized for his flareup of temper, but he did not change his position. He was exceedingly desirous that his son rise in the military hierarchy.

General Geary had a well-developed aesthetic appreciation combined with an exceptional gift of being able to express himself. He often commented on the natural beauty of his surroundings, and his descriptions of flora and fauna, while sometimes grandiloquent, were marked by poetic eloquence. In March 1864, he wrote from near Chattanooga: "The Climate is very mild, the frogs are chirping in every pond. The birds are carolling most delightfully from every tree and rendering the valley vocal. The buds are bursting forth on every tree and many of them will be in bloom in a fortnight." Geary often apologized for the haste in which he had to compose his letters, but even the hurriedly written missives are clear, well-phrased, and informative. His superiority in clarity of communications was also demonstrated in his official reports.

Geary was highly critical of Southerners and their customs and institutions. He once referred to Stonewall Jackson as a "cold-blooded rascal," and of Jefferson Davis, whom he blamed for much of the suffering experienced by lowly Southerners, he wrote: "If there is one spot in hell hotter than another why should it not be reserved for him who has brought such evils on his fellow man." In January 1864, while suffering the freezing cold of northern Alabama, he wrote: "The whole idea of the 'Sunny South' is exploded and much of the idea of Southern beauty. . . . It is a humbug and a falsehood and a lie which the war has fully exploded. Southern greatness was always a humbug in my opinion, and more so now than ever before." Some of Geary's most disparaging comments were about the rank and file of Southern civilians. In December 1862, he wrote from near Fairfax, Virginia: "The people are so ignorant that they may be with truth stiled *natural 'Know-nothings'* and the depravity of the youthful portion of the community is monstrous." In September 1863, he wrote from Ellis Ford, Virginia: "The meanest, lowest, vilest people on earth, purporting to be civilized, is to be found here. . . . The more . . . the local affairs of Virginia are examined into, the more desperate and rotten we find its society." Geary was especially critical of South Carolinians. On March 26, 1865, he wrote: "The people of South Carolina are the meanest, lowest, most contemptible, whining curs I have ever seen in any state. . . . They seemed anxious only for their lives and all said it was not they who brought this accursed war upon the nation, but somebody else was always to blame." The general attributed much of the poverty, ignorance, and depravity that he observed among Southerners to the blighting effects of slavery.

Geary loathed Northern Copperheads almost as much as he hated Southern slaveholders. On August 7, 1863, he wrote: "There seems so little patriotism among the people at home, the country appears scarcely worth preserving."

One of Geary's most resplendent qualities was his deep and abiding love for his country. He repeatedly demonstrated his willingness to endure any hardship, however great, to save the imperilled Union. Near the end of the war he wrote: "I have labored long and hard, but not grudgingly, for my country. . . . I love my country so much that I am still willing to honor 'Old Glory' our starry banner, as long as I possess the power to do so . . . and in the future remind all traitors of their everlasting infamy." Love of country, combined with a lofty idealism reflected in his repeated references to honor, duty, sacrifice, and nobility, helped to make Geary a devoted husband, a loving father, a loyal friend, a great American, and a thoroughly admirable man. To him and his kind the nation owes an enduring debt of immeasurable gratitude.

Guarding the Potomac
July 1861–February 1862

{When war came, the Geary family moved from Salem Township in Westmoreland County to New Cumberland, Mary's native area on the west bank of the Susquehanna River across from Harrisburg. The colonel proceeded to Philadelphia to organize the 28th Regiment Pennsylvania Volunteers, consisting of 1,500 soldiers from Philadelphia and the counties of Luzerne, Westmoreland, Carbon, Cambria, Allegheny, and Huntingdon. The Federal defeat at First Manassas on July 21 prompted officials to order the 28th to the front with ten of its fifteen companies organized. The rest joined in August, reporting to the District of the Shenandoah, where the unit spent most of 1861 guarding the Potomac. Although service in the Mexican War should have taught him better, Geary poorly screened reports of enemy strength, which caused him to overestimate the Confederate threat. For this he received a mild rebuke from Banks.

The colonel's staff included in-laws from his previous union with the Logan family in Westmoreland County and his current marriage to Mary Henderson, a widow and member of the Church family of Cumberland County. Adding to the family flavor of the camp were Geary's sons from his first marriage: Edward, about sixteen at the time, and Willie, about thirteen, who remained as unofficial staff and members of the regimental band. (Edward later gained a commission in an artillery unit.) The couple maintained their farm in Westmoreland by renting it to *tenants while Mary attempted to establish a new household, first by boarding. It would be a year and a half before the couple established a home in New Cumberland.}*

*   *   *

Camp "Geary" Near Harper's Ferry Maryland   July 30th, 1861

My Beloved Mary,

I have telegraph[ed] you three times since my departure for Phila. and now I will write you a few lines. You can scarcely imagine my feelings when I left you and our dear little ones. I thought my heart-strings would be torn assunder, but still I managed to maintain my composure and firmness—some of course would call this stoicism, but call it what they may, there was every impulse of love in my nature only restrained by the necessity of the case and the surrounding circumstances. Nothing particular happened on our march from Phila. to Baltimore, except the falling of one of the men from the platform of one of the cars, the only injury received was a slight bruise on the head. The fellow sprang to his feet, ran after the cars, and jumped on again. At Baltimore we formed, distributed ammunition, and marched through the streets in which the various attacks and insults had been offered the northern troops in their transit through the city.[1] We felt that the blood of the Pennsylvanians had moistened the streets, that it was yet *unavenged*. My determination was, if there had been the slightest insult offered to my regiment, to have resented it instantly, and if necessary would have fired the city, but luckily we received nothing but respect and kindness. However, at the depot we were obliged to compel the agents of the B&O R.R. Co. [Baltimore & Ohio Railroad] to furnish additional cars and another locomotive, which they did, but very reluctantly. At 3 o'clock p.m. we arrived at Harper's Ferry, where we found the whole army retiring from Virginia to the Maryland side. Helter skelter men, horses, cannon, wagons, &c., &c. "ad infinitum." I never saw more confusion. I thought the army was again defeated, but was soon informed that that was the way the three months men[2] done the thing up. They are leaving for home—the service will not lose much—but of course this is for your own eye only.

1. On April 19, 1861, a mob attacked the 6th Massachusetts Regiment—the first fully equipped Northern unit to respond to Lincoln's call for troops—as it made its way through Baltimore. Soldiers fought their way to the train, leaving four of their number and twelve citizens dead.

2. Soldiers who had enlisted for ninety days—which was more common at the start of the war, when people on both sides anticipated a short conflict.

I reported immediately after my arrival to Major Genl [Nathaniel P.] Banks[3] and from him had a very gracious reception. To-day I have had orders to report to Col Thomas of the Regular Army, who is the commander of our Brigade.[4]

The condition of affairs is somewhat doubtful. We cannot tell any thing definite about the movements of [Confederate] Genl [Joseph E.] Johnston. But we are ready and I think from our present condition we can defy any force the enemy can or dare bring to molest us.

Willie is well and is getting along very contentedly. He is much delighted and seems to relish hardships. He has already gained much confidence in himself and I think the campaign will be of service to him. I hope Eddie will come on when Maj Tindale[5] comes.

My Dear Mary I cannot tell you how much I miss you. Your kind attentions and caresses, the sweet little prattler too comes in for a share of my loss.[6] Were I not so filled with business I would not know what to do. God bless you all and preserve you in health and strength is the sincere prayer of your husband. Ever devoted and true,

Jno. W. Geary

* * *

Camp "Geary"   Pleasant Valley   July 31st 1861

My Dear Wife

I drop you a hasty note by [Lieutenant] Col [Gabriel] De Korponay [of the 28th Pennsylvania] to inform you of my welfare. Willie and myself are

---

3. On July 19, Banks replaced Major General Robert Patterson as commander of the Department of the Shenandoah.

4. Colonel George H. Thomas rose to prominence as a major general in the western theater. Here, Thomas commanded the 2nd U.S. Cavalry and a brigade of infantry.

5. Major Hector Tyndale had remained in Philadelphia to organize five of the fifteen companies that had not been organized when Geary received the order to report to the front. Tyndale would earn promotion to brigadier general for his performance at Antietam in 1862. When illness forced his resignation on August 26, 1864, he had risen to command of the 3rd Division in the Eleventh Corps.

6. The "prattler" was the couple's youngest daughter, Mary C. Geary. John and Mary had children from previous marriages which, when the households combined, created a situation in which five people shared two names. Wife Mary had a daughter named Mary Lee, age three in 1860. The youngest Mary—also called the "baby" or "Pet"—was the first child of the new marriage. Because both Mary and John had sons named William, the couple designated them Willie G. (Geary for John's son) and Willie H. (Henderson for Mary's).

both in the enjoyment of good health and send our kindest, truest, and best love. The Col will tell you all the news.

Kiss the Baby a dozen times for me. Give my love to Eddie and Willie, and Mary Lee. I have [not] heard a word from Pennsylvania since I left it. Write soon

Ever your faithful husband
Jno. W. Geary

*   *   *

Camp "Geary" Near Sandy Hook, Md   Augst 3rd 1861

My dear & Beloved Wife

Your esteemed letter was received this morning, and although a "pile" of others accompanied it, I of course gave it my immediate consideration. Thank you, my love, for the many expressions of affection. Thank you for the many kind remembrances it brought to the mind in one, who though absent in the body, is nevertheless with you in spirit. I wish I could see you all a few minutes just now, everything is quiet in Camp—it is high noon. The soldiers are slumbering around me, enjoying the genial coolness of the shade. The scenery around Harper's Ferry is majestically Grand, and such as bears an Almighty impress, and although all the magnificent works of art for which this valley has been so long famed have been destroyed by ruthless hands, still the hand of man is impotent in defacing its natural beauty. Large numbers of troops are daily arriving—the three months Reg'ts are nearly all gone home. The Army is [in] good spirits and anxious to redeem the honor of our nation.

Willie is a good, obedient boy—shoots marks with men, and sometimes excels them. He seems to enjoy the martial life. He wishes for Eddie's presence. He sends you and all his love with kisses to Mary. As an evidence that he thinks of home I observe his scribbling about the tent the name of "Mary C Geary."

My dear wife, the Bugle Call has sounded. I must close and drill with my Regt. Write soon. May God bless you and our dear little ones is the prayer of your absent and loving husband

Jno. W. Geary

Tell Eddie to get every [thing] right at home and come on.

*   *   *

Camp "Geary"   Sandy Hook, Md.   Augst 6th 1861

My Beloved Wife

Time passes rapidly amid the hurry and bustle of camp life, with its drills, parades, etiquette, and routine of duty. To say nothing of the "Alarums" by night and by day. The latter are not unfrequent as we are in the immediate presence of the enemy. Yesterday a skirmish occurred at Point of Rocks, a few miles below us, the result of which was, the killing of 5 of the rebels, the capture of 15 prisoners and *twenty* horses. The prisoners are all Virginians, all old acquaintances of mine. Some of them employees of mine when I was at Point of Rocks managing the Furnace.[7] The first inquiry they made when they came into camp was for me, they were fearful they might be maltreated, and thought I would benefit them.

We had an *alarum* yesterday & one last night. During that of yesterday, one of my men was accidentally shot, by the premature discharge of a gun. He was killed instantly. I have sent his remains to his friends in Philadelphia, with an escort of two men.

The Country is filled with secessionists, but I think that the Union feeling is on the increase.

Willie is well and so am I, both burnt brown with the sun. His health seems more robust than when at home. I think camp life will do him good.

I miss you very much my love. I place all confidence in your love and lasting affection, and I trust that ere long, God will bless this hitherto favored land with the benign influences of peace, when we shall again be permanently united in each others presence and love. God bless you and my dear babe and Willie, and make you all as happy as you deserve to be.

---

7. The prewar experience with Virginians represents a gap in biographical accounts about Geary. Just before the war, Geary apparently served as an officer on the Baltimore & Ohio Railroad, staying in Loudoun County with a family named Dawson while managing Potomac Furnaces. In the case of the prisoners mentioned here, Geary negotiated with the Confederate War Department to exchange them for Union soldiers. One of the Confederates was Arthur Dawson, son of Sarah A. Dawson, whose antebellum hospitality Geary remembered. See J.W.G. to Dearest Mary, June 1, 1859, Geary Papers, Historical Society of Pennsylvania, Philadelphia; U.S. War Department, *The War of the Rebellion: A Compilation of the Official Records of the Union and Confederate Armies*, 128 vols. (Washington, D.C., 1880–90), ser. 2, 2:1480, 3:755 (hereafter cited as *O.R.;* unless noted, citations are from series 1).

I trust we shall not need the proffered assistance of our Hungarian friend.[8]

Ever & truly,
your loving husband,
Jno. W. Geary

* * *

"Camp Geary" Sandy Hook, Md. August 11th 1861

My Dear Beloved Wife

Your kind letter is just received and I hasten to reply. This is the holy Sabbath day and I do not know that I can devote a portion of it more advantageously than to write to the woman of my heart's truest, warmest, and most devoted affection. I miss your many kindnesses very, very much, but it is a great solace to have Willie with me. He seems delighted with the army and is quite contented. You would laugh to see how he struts along with his drum on parade.[9] He is learning to beat rapidly, and can beat many of the men shooting.

To-day Col. Painter & Thomas G. Stewart[10] were here, they witnessed one of our parades and were highly delighted.

The Enemies pickets have [been] in sight of the surrounding heights this afternoon, I do not think they will dare to attack us in our present position. We have eleven thousand fighting men here. The last of the three month's troops will leave here tomorrow morning, viz: the "First City Troop." My Regt. is to escort them at their outset a short distance. Frank[11] is in good health and says he is stronger and more able to endure labor and

8. A reference to De Korponay, a member of an artillery unit who was referred to as "an old Hungarian soldier wearing seven medals on his breast and as we learned was the hero of 7 wars." See James P. Stewart, "Knaps Penna Battery," James P. Stewart Papers, Civil War Times Illustrated Collection, U.S. Army Military History Institute, Carlisle, Pa. (hereafter cited as MHI), p. 4.

9. William Geary served in the band attached to the 28th Pennsylvania.

10. Thomas G. Stewart, age thirty-eight in 1860, was a merchant in Derry Township, Westmoreland County. The Painter family was a rather large one in that area, making a definite confirmation problematical. An atlas from the time, however, reveals that a "P. Painter" lived in Salem Township near Geary's former home.

11. Benjamin F. Lee, whom Geary called "Frank," was in the lumber business with Henry Church, Mary Geary's eldest brother. Lee performed commissary duties for the regiment. After the war, Governor Geary appointed Lee grain measurer for Philadelphia, and then as a private secretary during the governor's second term. Lee went on to serve as an Indian agent under President Ulysses S. Grant.

Enquire at P.O. for letters to Mrs. Mary C. Geary & Mrs. Jno. W. Geary. fatigue than he has ever been. [Second Lieutenant] John B. [Church] is well and is in good spirits. He gets along very well, and his promotion is the best thing that ever happened [to] him.[12] Frank, John, & Willie all send their kindest love to you.

I wish you had the house [in Westmoreland County] rented, but I would not stay there a day longer than I desired, regardless of what the Needles might say. Where will you store the furniture? If that is done, I hope you will not confine yourself any longer to housekeeping. I know how irksome it must be for you to be alone, by my own experience. Try and rent the house as soon as you can get to boarding, and write cheering letters to me, and I will endeavor to reciprocate.

Bless my little Baby! How is She? How I would love to fold my beloved ones again to my bosom. But for the present honor says this cannot be—for we are in the immediate presence of the enemy, and I cannot without censure leave my command. God in his own good pleasure will bring this about I trust in time when He thinks best. In Him will I trust for a future. He foreknows all things, and will doubtless cause all things to work together for his own glory.

His Almighty hand can shield as well in the storm of battle as elsewhere, and in Him will we put our trust.

Eddie can come with the detachment, or if he desires to come sooner, he can come via Baltimore. But in my opinion he had better come with Maj. Ty[n]dale. I trust his abolitionism will not hurt him.

Ever & truly
your affectionate husband,
J.W.G.

---

12. Mustered in as a private on July 4, 1861, John B. Church was promoted to second lieutenant of Company H on July 12, 1861. The brother of Geary's wife, Church resigned his commission as a first lieutenant on February 14, 1863, to continue in the family's lumber business in New Cumberland. The 1860 census for New Cumberland identifies him as a lumber merchant, age twenty-seven, with $1,200 in real estate and $4,400 in personal estate.

Fig. 1. John W. Geary sits for his portrait as colonel of the 28th Pennsylvania Volunteers. "The stern realities of war are upon us," he wrote on August 15, 1861, "and I thank God I am embued with strength and courage to meet its emergencies." (Ron Beifuss Collection, U.S. Army Military History Institute, Carlisle Barracks)

*   *   *

Camp Korponay   Point of Rocks, Md.   Aug 15th 1861

My Dear Wife

You will observe from the date, my change of location— At 10 oclock at night of the 13th I was ordered to strike my camp and proceed to this place, which was done, and after marching all night we arrived here yesterday too late for the mail. I am in command of this post, and have 1 Company U.S. Cavalry, Rhode Island Battery and my own Regt with me. So you see I am already almost a general.

My health and that of Willie is first rate, and the health of my command is generally good.

Frank and John are well. The Enemy is vigilant, and is in near proximity. The moment they appear in sight I will send my compliments to them from the mouths of the guns of the R.I. Battery.—[13]

The stern realities of war are upon us, and I thank God I am embued with strength and courage to meet its emergencies. Pray God to sustain me in the trying adversities to which we are subjected as a nation, and that I may be instrumental in turning the tide of its affairs.

My heart yearns in love to my dear wife and babes. I hope you are all well.

I set out this morning with an escort of cavalry to reconoitre the position of the enemy.— I will also extend my command several miles down the River. After my return I will again write to you.

My kind love to you, Eddie & Willie. Kisses to Willie and Mary.

> Ever your faithful husband
> *Jno W Geary*
> Col 28th Regt P.V
> Comdg Post.

P.S. Our march was 16 miles on foot, wet weather & bad roads.

---

13. From early in the war, Geary showed a fondness for using artillery. Alpheus S. Williams, who rose to major general and periodically led Geary's corps, wrote in December 1862: "Every now and then we could hear Geary's guns shelling the woods in his advance, a favorite mode he has of skirmishing with artillery." See Alpheus S. Williams, *From the Cannon's Mouth*, ed. Milo M. Quaife (Detroit, 1959), 155.

*   *   *

Camp De Korponay   Point of Rocks, Md.   Aug 17th 1861

My Beloved Mary

You complain of not receiving my letters in proper time. I fear there is something wrong in the intermediate Post Offices. I have written almost every day since I left home, if they do not reach you, I cannot be responsible for the malfeasance of the mail carriers.

My health is good and so is that of Willie. The condition of my command is good.

The enemy is hovering about us in considerable strength, perhaps three times as great as that of my command. Notwithstanding their insolence I will resist any attack from that side at all hazards. —and I think I will whip them badly if they attack me in position— Being in command I am engaged in active duties night and day, as I am determined not to be surprised.

Yesterday about 1200 of the enemy were visible crossing the Catoctin mountain Eastward. They appeared, however, more like plunderers than a fighting party. They had with them a large drove of cattle.

The enemy since the battle of Manassas Gap, has become exceedingly insolent—they are preparing to burst through our lines and cross the Potomac for the purpose of carrying Baltimore, Washington, &tc. This game may look well on paper but they run against some obstacle in the shape of a snag.

My Dear Wife I have not time to write you a love letter as I would like to do, but will tell you all when I get to see you, which I hope will be soon.

You see I am in the post of danger—therefore in that of honor.

I will write you every day or cause Willie to do so.

I have just captured a secession spy laden with important letters. I will send him to Genl Banks. The letters fully disclose the plans of the enemy.[14]

Love & kisses to all the babies.

My kindest love to you & Eddie—

Your ever true husband
Jno. W. Geary

---

14. Geary made no mention of this in his reports. He was, however, in contact with a Francis L. Buxton of the U.S. Secret Service, who slipped across the Potomac via Geary's position during the fall to estimate enemy troops and report on their movements. Through Buxton, Geary gained the impression that he faced a potential 27,000 Confederate soldiers concentrated at Leesburg who looked for an opportunity to cross the Potomac.

* * *

{Because he inflated enemy numbers, Geary grew increasingly anxious over what he believed to be his exposed position. His impatience with Banks's refusal to send more troops brought on a mild rebuke issued through Adjutant Robert Williams: "The general {Banks} instructs me to say that, having selected you to fill a very difficult and exceedingly important position, on account of qualities he believed you possessed, he is surprised at the feeling you evince at the first approach of an enemy in any force."[15] *Banks promised to send reserves should Geary's fears materialize, although the general expected the subordinate to hold the position against at least 3,000 of the enemy. Union high command acted appropriately, although the decision produced a rare outburst in Geary's next letter home.}*

* * *

Camp De Korponay   Point of Rocks Md.   Aug 22nd 1861

My Beloved Wife

I have been very busy here for several days and indeed sometimes I began to think that we are in a pretty tight place. My Regt is extended as guard from Harper's Ferry to Monocacy, distance 18 miles.

Genl. Banks is a c-----d or something worse, (but this is only for your own eyes), [Notation at side of letter at this point: "Dont speak of this."] else he would sustain my precarious condition better. If the enemy attacks my lines, we will make it a Thermopilae, for we have no support, and unless I am ordered to do so I will not retreat.

The Evening Journal[16] you should get at once and if possible a few daily back numbers, you will find much about the Regt in it.

Last night I sent away the baggage of the Regt and put everything in fighting trim. The Regt is now at home wherever our arms are.

Yesterday I expected a fight, but the enemy would not give us battle. We captured five small boats from the Virginia shore, right under the guns of their Pickets.

My health is good. Willie is well, and really enjoying the excitement.

Your kind letter of yesterday is duly appreciated. William also recd a letter from Eddie.

15. *O.R.*, 5:593.
16. Geary likely meant the *Philadelphia Daily Evening Bulletin*, which referred to the 28th Pennsylvania on August 3, 12, and 23.

As soon as you have rented the house I will give orders about Eddie.
He will not require much money to come here.

Love to all—kisses to all—and "papie's baby" particularly.

When Eddie comes don't forget my big boots. I need them.

Ever your affectionate husband

Jno W Geary

My last letter was by Lieut. Wolffe—[17] contents $100—

＊   ＊   ＊

Point of Rocks.   Sept 5th 1861.

My Dear Wife

Your kind and loving letter from New Cumberland was received to-day.
It contained little Mary's offering of love which is duly treasured. The dear
little pet would scarcely know me now, with my bearded face, all bronzed
as I am, and perhaps something fatter than when I left home, at least much
more muscular. It would keep you busy to recognise me yourself. On Sunday three additional companies of my Regt arrived, numbering 300 men &
Officers. They are a fine vigorous set of soldiers— We gave them a grand
reception, for our need of them was very sore. I also ordered forward Major
Tyndale & [Assistant Surgeon] Dr. [Samuel] Logan.[18] Eddie has not yet
arrived—I expect him with Capt Wilson's Company and the Brass Band
which I have ordered forward. The Band contains 24 instruments, and is
said to be very fine.

My Regt now here numbers over 1300 men, when the other two companies arrive it will be about 1551 men, which is equal to any two of the
three month's regiments.[19] Besides my own Regt I have 3 companies of the
13th Massachusetts Regt under my command— My authority is undis-
puted from Harpers Ferry to Monococy junction 20 miles on the Potomac,
besides I have a company stationed at the Monococy Bridge where the B&O
RR crosses that stream, about 2½ miles from Frederick City. I control the
Rail Road, Post Office, and Telegraph Office, at this place. —The inhabit-

17. First Lieutenant John M. Wolff, Company K.

18. Dr. Samuel Logan of Greensburg, younger brother of Geary's first wife, Margaret.

19. The 28th Pennsylvania was an oversized regiment; 1,000 troops was the normal limit.

ants here are rotten to the core with secessionism, and if my lines are attacked and forced by overwhelming numbers I will burn this town—

The capture of the 39 cattle is regarded here as a gallant affair. It showed that some things can be done as well as others.[20] Some of the more insolent of our foes have been made to bite the dust by the unerring aim of our sharp shooters. I have every reason to be proud of my Regt, and so I am. I consider it the noblest in the service. Genl Banks' (division) is safe. —This latter is a great consolation.

Willie says you owe him a letter perhaps he will send you one in the morning. He is well and sends much love to you, Willie, & the baby.

Remember me very kindly to Mrs. Church and Sister Comfort.[21] I am delighted to learn that she is convalescent. Give my love to them both, to John's wife,[22] John Lee & lady,[23] Col Feeman & lady[24] & all our kind friends in N[ew] C[umberland].

Accept my kindest & most devoted love to you my much beloved wife. Kiss our mutual pledges of love, and believe and know me your

Ever faithful husband
Jno. W. Geary

Qr Master Lee & Lieut Church are well.

*   *   *

Near Harper's Ferry   Sept 15th 1861

My Beloved Wife

I am sitting on the Bank of the Potomac just [at] the point of confluence of the Shenandoah river with it. The Potomac is at present a clear beautiful stream, its resistless tide rushing headlong over the rocky surface of the channel and roaring with "the voice of many waters.["] The Shenandoah is very muddy at present, and rolls its waters along with equal haste, into the

---

20. Geary's men raided cattle from across the Potomac. A member of the 28th Pennsylvania noted that there "was thirty head of Beef Cattle brought over from Virginia to Day and drove through Berlin towards the Point of Rocks" (Levi L. Smith Diary, September 1, 1861, Alexander R. Chamberlin Collection, MHI).

21. Geary's mother-in-law, Catharine Church, lived with daughter Comfort in New Cumberland.

22. Elizabeth Brenneman Church, referred to as "Lizzie" in subsequent letters.

23. Brother of Benjamin F. Lee, Geary's commissary. The 1860 census identified his wife as H. Lee.

24. V. Feeman, a lumber merchant in New Cumberland worth $3,300 in real estate and $4,000 in personal estate, according to the 1860 census. He had been in business with Mary's father, Robert R. Church.

same channel with the Potomac, but the waters seem to refuse to commingle and become one. The clearness and limpidity of the Potomac is discernable for miles, and the muddyness of the Shenandoah equally so in the distance, refusing to join their waters and mingle into one grand kindred stream. I cannot help thinking it resembles the condition of our country; the clear waters of the north refusing to mingle with those from the south. —But what firing—yes the rattling of small arms—I must to horse and try the fate of battle once more. The enemy is upon us—To arms my voice has already resonaded—The heavy, solemn but rapid tread of men preparing for action. Good bye my much loved wife duty calls to the field—I go—if I ne'er come back, then goodbye on earth, but I trust we shall meet in heaven. Kiss my babe. Good-bye.

Four hours ago I bid you good bye. But by the providence of God who has always protected me amid dangers, I am here to announce myself alive and well. Quite fatigued after three hours amid the whistle and blaze of battle. Our victory is complete. The enemy scattered like the wind. Eight or ten killed of the enemy—a number wounded. Our loss *one killed*. The moral effect of this victory is important here.[25]

May the God of battles continue to protect me. May He protect the wife and children of my house & bless them, is the prayer of your devoted husband, who ardently loves you.

                                                                Jno. W. Geary

Lieut Jno B. Church is well he was in the thickest of the fight.

*   *   *

Encampment 28th Regt Pa. Vols.   Point of Rocks Md.
Sept 29th 1861—

My Beloved Mary

During the last two weeks I have been in the saddle night and day. I have hardly had time to eat or sleep, much less to write you or any body

25. According to Geary's report, Union and Confederate soldiers traded fire across the Potomac at Pritchard's Mills for a little more than two hours that day. A small number of Geary's men sparked the fighting by trying to learn more about the enemy's position and numbers. The skirmish involved about 130 Union soldiers, who found cover in dry basins along the Chesapeake & Ohio Canal bed known as the Maryland Ore Banks. Geary estimated the enemy's losses at eighteen killed and twenty-five wounded, although he admitted he could not know for sure because the river separated the two. See *O.R.*, 5:198–99.

else. It is almost a constant skirmish here, even now the guns of my Pick-etts are being discharged in the darkness of the night at some object either fancied or real. It is now ten oclock at night & the troops are marching past my tent door, Enroute for the purpose of defending a portion of our line which is threatened by the enemy. I leave at 3 oclock in the morning with the artillery for the same point, and before I return it is probable we shall be in a fight. It is cold I cannot write. Good bye my dear beloved wife. If spared I will write you more fully when I return. Your devoted husband.

J.W.G

Gen Johnston is in command of 27,000 men with[in] 12 miles of me and I must thwart him if he attempts to cross the river. I have but 2,200 under my command. I think I am enthusiastic enough in the cause not to flinch from the work. I have only 4 pieces of artillery. My own Battery has not yet arrived. I will be glad to see it.

Your faithful husband.

Love to all. Ed & Will join me in it

*   *   *

Encampment 28th Regt P. V.   Point of Rock M'd,
Sept. 29th 1861   11 oclock P.M.

My Beloved Wife,

I have just returned from Berlin 6 miles above this place whither I was about to depart when I wrote to you last. I left here this morning at 3 A.M. and proceeded by a back road, travelling 12 miles to get to a place 6 miles distant. I arrived at Berlin about 7 oclock, and immediately opened on the rebel batteries which frowned from the Va side of the Potomac over the town of Berlin. My guns and men were soon enveloped in a dense cloud of smoke, now & then the wind lifting the curtain and exposing to view the havoc upon the works of the enemy which our guns were making. I need not give you any more particulars about the fight. Enough to say we were successful and the enemy once more scattered to the winds, like chaff before the storm. Edward was with me. He is well. I will attend to his case in the Battery but these things must take a little time, and great deal of address to accomplish. I do not desire to be defeated in any thing I under-take. Matters of this kind must not be done by brute force.

Willie is well. We are all very sorry to hear of poor Pitt's decease, and

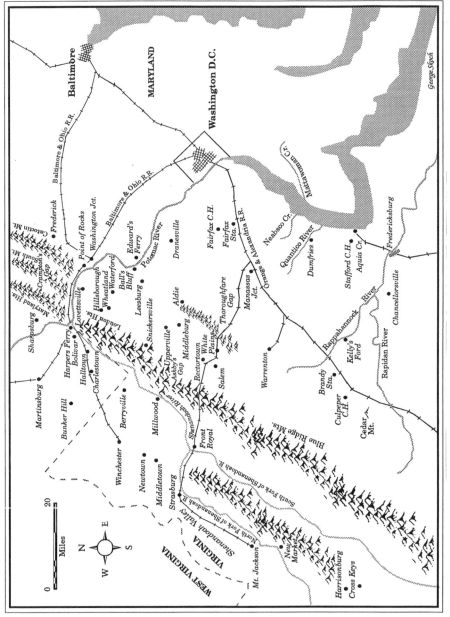

Map 1. Northern Virginia

the more especially so, as he came to his end by the violence of a fellow, who must certainly be a Border ruffian.[26] We are pleased you gave him a decent burial. I feel as though I cannot quit the subject without giving you a part of a dogeral composed some years ago.

> Oh! had Pitt live longer,
> He might have grown stronger,
>   And somewhat older I trust.
> Let the curtain be drawn to,
>   I hope he has gone to,
> The land which other dogs must.

Give my kindest love to Mrs. Church & Comfort, John's wife and Juliana[27] & all the others. They are too many to be mentioned by name. — Kiss Willie & Mary for me.

My dear wife, I would like to pay you a visit but situated in the immediate presence of the enemy as I am, I cannot—dare not leave, and I know you would not desire me to do so. For it might dishonor me, and I do not want my command to have a fight without me.

The paymaster has not reported here. I'll have no *funds* until I see him. You must get along until I can get it. And even then with as much economy as possible. For if it pleases God to bring me out of this campaign with life, I wish to have a little over and above our expenditures.

Accept my warmest and most devoted love to you—my dear wife. My most ardent prayers are for your health and happiness, believe me ever and truly your loving husband

J.W. Geary

*   *   *

Camp Tyndale   Point of Rocks Md.   October 2nd 1861

My Dear Wife

I received a letter from you yesterday, and am pleased to hear of your continued health and that of the children. This is an awfully wet day. The

26. Pitt was the family's dog. The reference to "border ruffians" comes from Geary's experience as governor of the Kansas Territory. The term described proslavery people from Missouri who came into the area to stuff ballots or conduct reprisals.

27. Juliana Church of New Cumberland, widow of Mary's brother, Henry.

river is foaming high, and as I do not apprehend a "passage at arms" with
Genl Johnston & his rebels to-day we are all resting quietly in Camp.

My force has been increased by the addition of the 12th Indiana Regt,
and my entire command consists of the following troops, viz:—

28th Regt Pa	Vols	14	companies	present
12th Indiana	"	10	"	"
Part of 13 Massachusetts	"	3	"	"
4 pieces of artillery and 50 men				

Numbering in all about 2500 men of whom 2200 are effective.—

I am daily expecting my 15th company from Phila, numbering 100 men.

Thus you see I am in command of a Brigade as Senior Col. Gen Johnston's command opposite to me on the Virginia side, numbers 27,000—
We fear them not, and in every collision thus far we have whipped his
advance, and with God's assistance, the 28th "will never surrender".—

Eddie & Willie join me in love to you and all our friends.

Believe me ever your
true & faithful husband
Jno. W. Geary

*   *   *

Point of Rocks Md   Oct 18th 1861

My Beloved Mary

This will be handed to you by brother John who goes home on leave.

Another glorious victory has perched upon our banner, and that too on
Va. soil against a force 6 times greater than my own. John [Church] will
give you particulars.[28]

28. Geary refers to the skirmish at Bolivar Heights, which occurred over wheat that Banks wanted seized from Confederates across the Potomac. Ten companies, numbering 600 soldiers and supported by two pieces of artillery, crossed the river on October 15 and withdrew, leaving about 100 men from the 9th Massachusetts on the Confederate side overnight. At 7 A.M. on October 16, an enemy column pushed Union pickets back into the town of Bolivar and brought on an engagement. The action resulted in little for either side to brag about. Geary's men nearly became trapped in Bolivar, with Confederate guns shelling them from Loudoun Heights, protected by three regiments under Nathan G. Evans. But the Confederates were equally raw. Lieutenant Colonel Turner Ashby led a motley force of 300 militia armed with flintlock muskets, two companies of a regiment with rifle muskets, and about 230 cavalry. After charges on both sides, the Union soldiers flanked the Confederate left, forcing a withdrawal. The axle of a twenty-four-pound gun broke, and the piece fell into Union hands. Geary reported four dead, seven wounded, and two prisoners; Ashby reported one killed, nine wounded. Geary placed overall Confederate losses at roughly 150, but no Southern estimate confirmed this. See *O.R.*, 5:239–43, 247–48.

Write me affectionately. Kiss our babies a hundred times—love to all friends—Accept my most devoted love
Your faithful and devoted husband

Jno. W. Geary

* * *

Encampment 28th Regt Pa Vols　　Point of Rocks Md.
Oct 20th 1861

My Dear Wife

Your letter informing me of your arrival at the St Lawrence[29] is just received. I am happy to learn that you are so comfortably situated, and that Mary, Willie and Yourself are so well.

My own health was never better than now—although I perform much hard work. Four fights in one month are about as much as any people can attend to without other business, but God has blessed me with an excellent constitution and I am always where duty calls me.

Our fight of the 16th inst has not yet had justice done to it in the papers.[30] It was one of those in which the finger of God was visible for our deliverance. I had only 600 men, and the enemy over 3000—I had 4 cannon— They had 7.—

The forces of the enemy consisted of the 13th and 19th regiments of Mississippi Vols, 8th Regt Virginia Vols, Col. Ashby's cavalry regt. & some raw militia. Also Roger's Richmond Battery of 6 pieces & 1- 32 pounder Columbiad—on which I wrote my first despatch to Genl Banks a few minutes after it was captured. The rebel loss is reported to be 150 in killed and wounded, and 4 prisoners, among [whom] is a celebrated Chaplain of the rebel army.[31]

Our loss 4 killed and seven wounded—2 prisoners—

I was struck with a piece of a shell in the early part of the action just

29. St. Lawrence Hotel on Chestnut Street near Tenth Street, Philadelphia. On October 10, Geary sent Mary $150 and suggested that she stay in the hotel, which he had used on visits to the Quaker City before the war.

30. Geary's men shared the notion that the engagement held greater significance. A member of the 28th Pennsylvania called this action "a Second Bulsrun" and became agitated when Confederates apparently quartered the body of a Union dead soldier. Geary also complained of this mutilation in his report. The incident fed the desire of Union troops to seek vengeance whenever they crossed the Potomac. See Licert P. J. Hughes to Peter Russel, October 17, 1861, Michael Winey Collection, MHI.

31. The Rev. Nathaniel Green North, a chaplain in Ashby's command.

below the knee in the front of the leg, which cut to the bone.— I did not let it be known until after the victory was won, it is healing rapidly and will soon be well.

You will see my official report in a few days.

Give my respects to Mr. and Mrs. [William S.] Campbell[32] & other friends. Kiss our babies. Believe me your true and faithful husband

> Affectionately
> *Jno. W. Geary*

*   *   *

> Camp at Edwards' Ferry, Md.   Oct. 24th 1861

My Beloved Wife

I live to write you from this point. I wrote you last as I left the Point of Rocks. That night we made a forced march to join the army at this place, distance about 20 miles, it rained very hard all the time and was exceedingly muddy and cold, but some 30,000 or 35,000 men of the army got themselves in a scrape here, and the glorious "28th" had to come down to the rescue. Under illy advised arrangement, an attempt was made to cross the Potomac in which at least 400 men were either killed[,] wounded or drowned. 'Tis too horrible to contemplate. You will know the truth from the papers.[33]

My Regt is one-half at Point of Rocks and the other half here, that is 760 of us are here, all well. Willie is here mounted on a horse I captured some time ago from the enemy.

Kiss our babies. Respects to Mr. & Mrs. C[ampbell]. My most devoted love to yourself.

> God bless you,
> Your husband *J.W.G.*

---

32. Proprietors of the St. Lawrence Hotel, in which Mary Geary stayed while in Philadelphia.

33. At the Battle of Ball's Bluff, October 21, 1862, poor reconnaissance resulted in a Union embarrassment. Troops under Colonel Edward D. Baker pushed across the Potomac and blundered into Confederate soldiers under Brigadier General Evans. The disaster cost 49 Union dead, 158 wounded, and 714 missing. A sharpshooter killed Colonel Baker, a former Congressman and personal friend of President Lincoln. This stimulated the Radical Republicans, who wanted a more aggressive prosecution of the war, to create the Joint Committee on the Conduct of the War to investigate causes of the defeat.

*   *   *

Point of Rocks, Md.   Nov. 9th 1861

My Beloved Wife,

Your kind letter was received to-day. I thank you for the many assurances of love and confidence contained in your present and former ones.

I have had so much to do the last few days that I have not had time to write you as frequently as I desired.

I have not heard from Eddie for several days. He is getting a little careless since he is a "Tenente." But I excuse him on the grounds of his close studies and attentive practice.

Willie and myself are well. I have a "bile" on the point of my nose which renders my personal appearance not quite natural. This prevents me from having my likeness taken. I hope I will be more comely in a day or two.

Mrs Tyndale is with the Major at Harper's Ferry. She was shot at the first day, by a rebel. My opinion is she ought to be at home.

The Rebels are threatening an attack at Harper's Ferry every other day. And just now I hear the cannon of the rebels belching away at my troops in that direction, and of course I must go to their aid.

I have nothing to say concerning my commanding officers. But I think some of them *slow* & *slack in the twist.*

Accept my most devoted love for you & the children. Kiss the little ones for me, and tell Willie to be a good boy.

Affectionately your
devoted husband
Jno. W. Geary

*   *   *

Encampment 28th Regt P. Vols.   Point of Rocks, Md.
Nov. 15th 1861

My Beloved Wife

This will be handed to you by Lieut John B. Church who goes to Phila. in charge of Capt Thos. McDonough [of Company I] who has ceased to be a member of the 28th Regt.

This of course you might have anticipated from his conduct before you in

Phila. I gave him his choice to resign or be dismissed by order of a court martial. He chose the former and so it is. I mention this, you not to speak of it, for every [word] you say will be quoted as Gospel, and therefore let others speak, and you & I can hear.

I am well, and Willie is growing finely. John will give you all the news. Eddie is at Washington.

Accept my most devoted love

> Ever your affectionate husband
> *Jno. W. Geary*

*   *   *

Encampment 28th Regt Pa. Vols.   Point of Rocks Md.
Nov 25th 1861

My Beloved Mary

I received your welcome letter to-day, and although it was not a very long one still it was pleasant to hear you were all well. How pleasant it would be to step into the St. Lawrence and spend an evening with you and the babies, to Sport a little while with my Marys and Willies, but stern, grim visaged war will not admit of such luxuries, and I am compelled by duty to remain in the deep recesses of our secluded home. About ten days ago I had my Camp removed from the beautiful and airy spot we occupied during the Autumn to a piece of woodland a few hundred yards distant from it. We are thus screened from the sharp blasts of winter in depth of the forest, which affords inexhaustible supplies of fire wood. During the live long day the loud sounds of the axe and the falling of sturdy oaks are familiar sounds to our ears, and roaring, cracking fires, enliven, *enlighten* and diffuse their genial warmth to all concerned. The first [snow] whitened our camp last night and bids us prepare for approaching winter.

I have been detailed by Maj Genl [George B.] McClellan [General-in-Chief of the Armies] as a member of the Board of Examiners for the officers of Maj Genl Banks Division.[34] I leave here to-morrow morning to attend to that duty at Darnestown, a distance of 25 miles from here. My next letter

---

34. Congress established the board of examiners in the Army Act of July 22, 1861, to screen the qualifications of current and future officers. See *O.R.*, ser. 3, 1:349, 380–83.

will probably bear date at that place. How long I may be absent I cannot say, but I hope it will not be long.

Willie will remain here and I will instruct him to write to you daily.

Enclosed you will find another "type"[35] with Co.

May God bless & keep you in health and strength is the prayer of your affectionate husband

J.W. Geary

*   *   *

Point of Rocks   December 7th 1861—

My Dear Wife

I have just returned from Harper's Ferry, where I have been on a tour of inspection in company with Maj Genl Banks. I gave the Genl a handsome reception along the line, and he was much pleased with his visit. Every thing is tolerably quiet along the river. The health of the Regt is generally good. We expect the paymaster to-day, after which I will pay Mr. Campbell and send you money. High expectations among the soldiers exists, hoping for a forward movement soon. I am not yet able to say whether we will go into Winter Quarters or not.

One Section (2 guns) of our battery arrived here last night. We gave them a grand reception. The other Section to which Edward is attached is at Frederick City. I expect them in a few days.

The boys and myself are hearty and well. All send much love to you and Willie and Mary.

Enclosed I send you a *type*.

I hope you will excuse my negligence in writing during the last few days. I will make amends for the future.

You were correct about Taggart. He is a man without *moral reputation.* To be seen perambulating with him would throw suspicion on Mrs. Caesar, Virgin Mary, or any body else. You need not treat him disrespectfully, but I would rather not hear of you walking with him.[36]

35. Daguerrotype, an early photographic process.

36. John Henry Taggart enjoyed a long career in newspapers in Philadelphia. Before the war, he owned half interest in the *Sunday Mercury*. He served in the Pennsylvania Reserve Corps, then as a war correspondent for the *Philadelphia Inquirer*, and finally as a recruiter for U.S. Colored Troops in the city.

I have every confidence in my beloved wife's virtue and patriotism. I commend her to the guidance of God who alone can deliver us from evil and temptation.

Kiss the babies for me and believe me, Ever faithfully and lovingly your

husband

Jno. W. Geary

*   *   *

Point of Rocks Md.   Dec. 9th 1861

My Dear Beloved Wife,

I have to write you a hasty note this morning. We were under arms a considerable portion of the night and I feel a little drowsy, which I trust will be a sufficient excuse for a prosy letter. The weather during the past three days has been exquisitely beautiful, and the only drawback upon active movements is the mud on the roads.

I just now sent Mary E. Logan a check on the Bank of Pittsburg for $150, and Hetty one for $30, making $180.[37]

Mary is to be married in a short time to Dr. [Robert] Brown of Greensburg. I have given my *consent*, I think the match is a *good one.*[38] Please look in my Account Book for the accounts of the two ladies & charge them respectively. [Notation at side of letter: "If you cannot find the books, preserve this letter."]

I expect Edward and the section of Battery to which he is attached here this morning. The troops are generally on the move, and some stirring times may be anticipated. God grant it may be in success to our arms.

My health is very good, and all our friends are equally so.

God grant you health, and keep you in safety during the perils of the war, and through life.

Bless and kiss the babies at home. We have not yet been paid off. As usual the paymasters do not like to come among "danger's paths," and consequently the 28th still holds the front rank in the column.

37. Mary E. Logan and Hetty A. (Logan) Moore were sisters of Geary's first wife, Margaret. Mary lived in New Salem with Eliza Logan, Margaret's mother; Hetty had married Robert F. Moore, a steamboat clerk, but remained in the neighborhood. Geary served as administrator of the estate of James R. Logan, a storekeeper and husband of Eliza.

38. Geary served as legal guardian of Mary and Hetty Logan. The marriage between Dr. Brown and Mary Logan took place on January 14, 1862.

God bless the noble hearts of my men. Wherever I command, they will go.

Ever and truly
your devoted husband
Jno W. Geary

* * *

Encampment 28th Regt   Point of Rocks Md.   Dec. 13th 1861

My Beloved Mary

Your three letters were received only yesterday, by some "hocus pocus," the mails are detained in Baltimore at least three days in a week.

I regret exceedingly the illness of Willie Henderson, but as it [measles] is one of those diseases which can come but once, I trust he will soon be convalescent. Great care will be necessary that he does not take cold for some time. If Mary takes them, she will not have them as severe as Willie. I hope she will not take them now.

We are all well. Both sections of the Battery are now under my command. *Two* Guns are here, & *two* at Harper's Ferry. Eddie is here. The Enemy keeps at a very respectful distance from us, for they are not safe within 2 miles of us, since we got our new "Parrotts" (I mean the guns).

The Government is extending telegraph lines up the river and have connected my camp with Washington City by a special line. The office [is] in the camp.

Yours of the 13th inst is this moment received, announcing the convalescence of Willie. I do not think Mary will take the measles, nor will she have them very badly if she does.

I think it would be imprudent for you to take Willie on a journey so soon as Christmas and if you wish to enjoy the city, the holy days season is the cream of the year. You had better stay in the city and enjoy it, and then go to the country. Enclosed you will find draft for $125. on the Western B[an]k of Phila. You can use Eddie's money. Pay Campbell's bill.

With my most ardent love I remain your true and faithful husband

Jno. W. Geary

Eddie and Willie join me in love to you and the children.

Mr. Campbell will draw the money for you—you sign across the Back of the check.

*   *   *

Frederick Md.   Dec.   18th   1861

My Dear Wife

I am here as a member of the board of Examiners, which meets tomorrow morning at 10 o'clock A.M. for the examination of such Officers as may be brought before it. This city is literally filled with soldiers, and as one of the Brigades is in motion tonight the streets are more than usually lively.

The Rebel, Genl [Thomas J. "Stonewall"] Jackson, is marching upon Williamsport with 10,000 men, and the movement mentioned above is intended to prevent it.[39] It is probable I will be ordered forward in that direction tomorrow morning with 600 men & 4 pieces of artillery. My men have just received their new uniforms, which is a blue frock coat, and blue pants and cap. They look exceedingly well in their new dress.[40] From the movements of the enemy I think a collision will take place soon in this quarter, if somebody is not afraid.

Eddie & Willie are well & send their kindest love to you.

My Brother Edward arrived in New York yesterday. I have not seen him for upwards of 10 years.[41] He may call upon you as he passes through Philadelphia. He says he will be here in a few days. Kiss the babies.

Ever your faithful husband
Jno. W. Geary

39. Thomas J. "Stonewall" Jackson had fewer than 10,000 men scattered throughout the lower Shenandoah Valley. In early December, he sent only a portion of his command—not all 10,000, as Geary suggests—to destroy Dam No. 5, seven miles above Williamsport. The Federals used the Chesapeake & Ohio Canal to ship coal, grains, and other goods from the west. The first attempt failed, but a second effort, begun on December 17, created a small breach that did not check the flow of Union supplies.

40. Securing these uniforms provided a way for Geary to boost morale in his unit and keep soldiers on his side. A soldier writing to his father indicated that when the regiment had still not received their uniforms by early November the colonel promised to make every effort to get them. He succeeded in about a month. See R[obert] M. Irvin to "Father," November 3, 1861, Jay Luvaas Collection, MHI.

41. The second son of Richard Geary, Edward was a Presbyterian minister for nearly twenty years in Oregon. He was the namesake for Geary's oldest son.

* * *

Encampment 28th Regt Pa Vols   Point of Rocks, Md.
December 22nd 1861

My Beloved Mary

In the multiplicity of business which surrounds me, a small interstice in the meshes of time occurs to-day, and I embrace it as a fitting opportunity to write my loved one a few affectionate lines.

Imprimus. The Boys and myself are in the enjoyment of good health and spirits. Edward made his maiden effort on the enemy, and sent the messengers of death into their ranks with unerring aim and with great effect. He is a gallant boy. Willie was every where with his short Sharp's rifle[42] in hand during the conflict, and so did no person any discredit by his conduct during the recent fray. I was not present, being at Frederick attending a meeting of the Bd of Examiners. The result you have had in the Inquirer & Press.

The weather is cold, and we are putting up log cabins for men. The enemy are in motion in front of our line almost constantly. After having annoyed my line in every way they could, they passed in force to Williamsport, to which place 5 Regts. are sent to meet them. You can draw your own inferences. We (the 28th) meet them single-handed. When others have to do so, multitudes are sent to help them.

Away with this, I will talk to you. I received your picture and handed Edward the one you intended for him. I do not think the artist flattered you very much, however, I will keep it and look at it. It will serve as a remembrance of the happy hours we have spent together, and of the joy I hope is still in store for us. God bless you, my dear Mary. I hope He will preserve us for many pleasant years of life and the unsullied enjoyment of each others society.

I am situated here as you know in the front rank, in the post of danger, I do not know what moment they [the] enemy may annoy us. I could not do my duty if you were here. Otherwise I would send for you to come here and spend a few days. But it cannot be. I would not have you here for any consideration in the event of a fight. Absence, with me, cannot conquer my

---

42. A breech-loading rifle manufactured by the Sharps Rifle Manufacturing Company. The shorter barrel and rapid loading made this a popular cavalry weapon.

love for you, but it only grows stronger. No one likes to stay long here, there is too much danger for weak nerves.

Kiss Willie for me & tell him I congratulate him on his recovery. I expect to find him a big boy when I return. Kiss Mary and tell her to hurry through the measles before I come to see her.

Remember me kindly to Mr. and Mrs. Campbell, and believe me ever and truly

Your true & devoted husband
Jno W. Geary

Have you heard anything of Brother Edward?

*   *   *

Encampment 28th Regt. P.V.   Point of Rocks, Md.
December 24th 1861

My Dear Mary

Your very kind letter of yesterday was duly received. I think Mary will get along very well with measles. You must not take trouble so hard, I think you should not murmur so much at the dispensations of Divine Providence when we reflect how often and how much worse it might be. I do not say this in any but the very kindest spirit, nay, indeed, I say it in the profoundest depths of love. That instead of constantly grieving over life's ills, we should rather rejoice that they are no worse.

Permit me, therefore, with my most complimentary military bow, to tender to you the compliments of the season. Eddie and Willie are sitting at my elbow and join me most heartily in the same. Willie is reading the account of the affair at Drainsville Va. and takes an intensified interest in every military movement.[43] Eddie is reading the "confession of Jeff Davis." Every thing is quiet in camp. The men are preparing for a grand Theatrical display to morrow, consequently every thing is activity and preparation for the festal Holy-day. I will send you a programme, from which you can make your own estimate of the amount of *fun* they expect to receive and impart. I wish every thing suited [so] I [could] have you here to witness

43. The need for forage brought on the engagement at Dranesville, Virginia, on December 20, 1861. Confederate Brigadier General J.E.B. Stuart led 150 cavalry and 4 infantry regiments on the expedition for supplies, but ran into forces ordered to seize goods from loyal Confederate civilians. Southerners had 194 casualties; northerners had 68.

the performance, but that cannot be.[44] There may be an appeal to arms before it is closed.

To day is unusually wet and cold, the trees are covered to the minutest branches with a thick coating of ice, and as the sun fitfully breaks through the clouds, the mountains around us glitter as though coated with molten silver. The prospect is extremely grand and picturesque, and has to be witnessed to be fully realized. It has one good effect, for not a Southerner has had the nerve to show himself to-day.

Col De Korponay has gone home, I think he will resign, *cause* he drinks too much whiskey. I would not be surprised if he does not return. This is between us, and will not be spoken of.[45] I have no news, for future movements, but cannot tell how soon a movement will be made. I would like to be with you a little while on Christmas day, and enjoy some of Mr. Campbell's good cheer.

By the way, it is rumored here that Mr. Campbell has taken the Girard House.[46] How is this? Is it so?

Give my compliments of the season to our host and hostess and all other friends of the Hotel.

Accept for yourself my dear Mary the renewed assurances of my love for you. Kiss the babies for me. God bless you.

You loving & devoted husband
Jno W. Geary

*   *   *

Encampment 28th Regt. P. V.   Point of Rocks, Md.
Jany 1st 1861 [1862].

My Beloved Wife

Your very kind letter of the 29th instant is received and I hasten to write you a few lines in reply. I am glad to learn that Mary is a singer, but you

44. The colonel used such performances to increase the spirit of the men and ingratiate himself to superior officers. A member of the 28th Pennsylvania noted about a theatrical performance in camp: "Old *Colonel Geary* appears to be quite fond of anything of that Style[.] *General Abercromby* was there[;] the Colonel introduced him to the audience & told us that the time would be short untill he would lead us on to Virginias soil." Bob [Robert M. Ervin] to "sister," January 28, 1862, Ervin Letters, Jay Luvaas Collection, MHI.

45. De Korponay returned to the army, remaining until sometime after Antietam. His official resignation was dated March 26, 1863, but from September 1862 he no longer served in the field because of a kidney problem.

46. Girard House was a hotel in Philadelphia owned in 1860 by Presbury, Sykes & Company.

ought to be very careful of her voice for some time after having measles, the throat and lungs are so tender that a permanent hoarseness might ensue. My own voice has been rendered hoarse for life from measles.

Brother Edward was with me in Frederick on Sunday last. The boys were also there. He went to Washington City on Monday and after attending to some business there will visit you at St. Lawrence, Phila., I suppose very shortly. Have his *bill while there charged to me.*

Rumors of wars as well as wars surround us on all sides but the end is not yet. The rebels are greatly cast down by the settlement of the "Trent affair."[47]

I send you a check for $50. I may telegraph you to meet me at Frederick for a few days, if you can leave the children with safety. I do not think it would be prudent to bring them with you under the circumstances. Write me by return mail whether you can come.

My health and that of E[dward] & W[illie] is good. Edward goes to Harper's Ferry this morning to relieve another officer there for a few days.

A Happy New Year to you, Mary, and may you ever be happy and be beloved as I do love you.

May God's choicest blessing be showered upon you and the little ones at home, and His protecting care be with us in the field, and restore all once more in peace and happiness is the prayer of your loving and devoted husband

Jno. W. Geary

P.S. Charge Mary E. Logan with $50.00. I sent her another check for that amt.

*   *   *

Frederick,   Jany 3rd 1862

My Dear Mary

I arrived here yesterday, and am now engaged upon the duties of the Examining board of which I am a member. The duty of ascertaining the

47. Hopes for British recognition of the Confederacy grew as Union Captain Charles Wilkes of the USS *San Jacinto* on November 8, 1861, stopped the British steamship *Trent* in the Bahama Channel to remove Confederate diplomats John Slidell and James Mason. Wilkes let the steamer sail to England but sent the diplomats to Fort Warren in Boston. The British protested and appeared headed for war as they sent troops to Canada and beefed up their Western Atlantic squadron. The administration announced on December 27 that the diplomats would be released and reparations made, but it saved face in two ways. First, no apology, which the British demanded, was extended. Second, the United States admitted that Wilkes acted without instructions, but claimed he erred only in not taking the *Trent* to a port for a judgment before a prize court. London accepted this compromise, and the crisis ended.

qualifications of men, and thereupon deciding their qualifications and fitness for holding official position in the Army is to say the least of it, an unpleasant duty. However, as it has got to be done, and somebody must do the work, I have made up my mind to grin and bear it, just as I do the picketing of the Potomac River.

My health is very good. I left the boys well. I hope to hear from you on the subject I wrote to you about in my last letter, viz: your spending a few days with me here.

Ever your loving & faithful husband
Jno. W. Geary

* * *

{*On January 5, Geary wrote Mary to look into buying the house in which she was born in Cumberland County. He directed her to purchase it with her own funds, meaning that he would supply the money but deed the title in her name. It would be another year, however, before the Gearys purchased the house.*}

* * *

Encampment 28th Regt. Pa. Vols.   Point of Rocks Md.
Jany 10th, 1862

My Dear Wife,

I have just arrived here from up the river, where everything for the present seems quiet, but we cannot tell how long it may be so. I cannot tell how long it will be until the next fight comes off, or where it will be.

Your two letters are received, and I hasten to give you an account of my return and welfare. I am well, and Willie has a bad cold but nothing serious. Edward went with his Section[,] 2 guns, to Hancock [Maryland], to report to [Brigadier] Gen [Frederick West] Lander. He is there now and well.[48]

If everything remains quiet I will *telegraph* you when to come. If you waited for the promised notice you would not have been dis-appointed before.

I will write you more fully by to[-]morrow's mail. Kiss the babies. Ever and truly your true and loving husband

Jno W. Geary

48. On January 5, Lander had defended Hancock, Maryland, against a Confederate attack.

* * *

Point of Rocks Md.   Feby 15th 1862

Dear Mary,

I hasten to drop you a line this morning to inform you of my continued welfare.

My health and that of Willie is good. Eddie is at Sandy Hook in charge of Dr. Logan. He is on duty occasionally and has a cough but is convalescing.

This day is cold and the snow is falling in torrents. The probability is that we shall have a deep snow.

Lieut Hindman of Co. N of my Regt. died yesterday. His remains will be sent home to-day. This is the first death among the officers. He is of the "Pardee Rifles No. 2" from Hazleton.

Cannon are booming below, at Edwards Ferry. Yesterday I was drilling my Regt. in firing blank cartridges. A Company of rebel cavalry appeared as spectators on the other side of the river. I immediately turned the cannon upon them [and] put shells into them. The discharge scattered the enemy in all directions, to the great merriment of the whole regiment. The curiosity of the cavalry was gratified.

I hope to hear from you frequently.

My love to Mrs. Church, Comfort, John & Lizzie and all other friends in the family & out of it.

Kiss Mary & Willie for me. If I can get time I will, procure my likeness tomorrow.

Ever & truly
your loving husband
Jno. W. Geary

* * *

Encampment 28th Regt. P.V.   Point of Rocks Md.
Feb. 24th 1862

My Beloved Wife

I sit down as usual to write you a hasty note. The festivities yesterday were the firing of one hundred guns in honor of the day and of the recent great victories achieved by the army of the West.[49] I visited Frederick, yesterday, by order of Genl Banks and acted as one of his staff officers during a magnificent review of the troops which took place there. The display of military consisting of Artillery, Cavalry, & Infantry was very fine. There were several fine Brass Bands present and the usual lateral accompanyments of dirty ragamuffins, boys & niggers keeping even pace therewith.

The "Farewell Address" of Genl Washington was read to the troops. Sword & flag presentations, cheering speeches and so forth usual on such occasions. There was also a fair display of Union ladies present. The rebellious portion of them not deigning to be present on the interesting occasion.

In all probability there will soon be a move forward in our division.

Enclosed I make you a remittance. You will never be out of money as long as you keep it.

Kisses to babies. Love to friends.

I am ever truly & affectionately

Your devoted husband
J. W. Geary

49. A combined naval and infantry force under Ulysses S. Grant had captured Confederate Forts Henry (February 6, 1862) and Donelson (February 13–16) in Tennessee. The festivities were also held in honor of George Washington's birthday, February 22, a national holiday.

Into Enemy Territory
March–December 1862

{Pressured by Lincoln to put the army into motion, George B. McClellan finally advanced portions of it in late February 1862. For Geary, this meant crossing the Potomac onto enemy soil. The effort began inauspiciously on February 24 with six men drowning as a storm upset skiffs ferrying troops across the river. Geary's command spent the remainder of the year patrolling northern Virginia.

Problems plagued the Union war effort. The commanders of the army underwent numerous changes. Lincoln demoted McClellan from general-in-chief to supervise only the Army of the Potomac, which went by sea to land on the peninsula and march on Richmond. Dissatisfied with both McClellan's advance and the defenses around Washington, the President in late June brought in Major General John Pope from the west to lead a new Army of Virginia formed from the three corps under Nathaniel Banks, Irvin McDowell, and John Frémont. After Robert E. Lee defeated Pope at Second Manassas on August 29–30, McClellan once again pulled the army together. But when Little Mac was slow to move after the battle of Antietam, Lincoln finally cashiered the general, replacing him with Ambrose E. Burnside.

Geary, meanwhile, made the most of performances that ranged from awful to adequate. He did little to distinguish himself during Jackson's Valley Campaign in late May when an imagined threat caused him to burn wagons and commissary

*stores while retreating hastily from Thoroughfare Gap. He did better when super-
vised at Cedar Mountain on August 9, suffering a wound that kept him out of
Second Manassas, Antietam (September 17), and Fredericksburg (December 13).
Still, his star was on the rise as he won promotion to brigadier on April 25, then
took charge of the 2nd Division, Twelfth Corps, in October. The year ended with
both armies hugging the Rappahannock River near Fredericksburg, which became the
northeastern frontier of the Confederacy.}*

*   *   *

Lovettsville Va   March 5th 1862

My Dear Wife

I have a few moments of leisure and I occupy them in a hasty note to
you. I am well and the health of my command was never better. Eddie is
with his *Gun* on the Short Mountain within three miles of me. He is also
well. I am here in command of an advance Brigade with my entire Regiment, 4 troops cavalry and 4 ps. cannon. We are within a few miles of
superior forces, but trusting in God and continual vigilance I do not fear
them.

Give my love to friends.

Kiss the babies.

Know me ever your loving
and faithful husband
Jno. W. Geary

*   *   *

Leesburg Va   March 9th 1862

My Dear Wife

This far famed place was taken by my command on Saturday.

The three strong-holds of Secession—Forts "Beauregard," "Johnson" and
"Evans," are ours. Will this do you for one day's work.

On my way here I took the towns of Hillsboro, Wheatfield, and Waterford.[1]

---

1. Hillsborough, Wheatland, and Waterford—like Leesburg—all fell without a fight. On March 5,
General Johnston ordered a general withdrawal of Confederate troops east of the Blue Ridge to the

I am well, also the boys.
My command is enthusiastic.
Kiss babies. Love to friends.

Ever your loving husband
Jno. W. Geary

*   *   *

Leesburg Va   March 12th 1862

My Dear Mary

I have received very kind letters from you since I arrived here.
The people of this place have very kindly extended their hospitalities to me and my command, and I really feel quite at home amongst them.
I am very well. Willie arrived here this evening. He is in good health. Eddie has gone to Charlestown from here with a Section of Battery.
The papers will doubtlessly give you the news.

Ever your faithful husband
Jno W. Geary

*   *   *

Upperville   Fauquier Co. Va   March 15th 1862

My Dear Wife

Last night I received your letter of the 7th inst. I arrived here yesterday and am now but a few miles from the far famed "Manassas Gap." We took a rebel officer and a number of privates prisoners here. Some of the people are very saucy in this region, but you know they cannot make much off me, on that subject.
We are all well. If I can find a good opportunity I will send you some money soon.
It is a cold rainey day and I will remain here until Monday. Genl Banks column is divided from *mine* by the Blue [Ridge] Mountains and Shenandoah River.

Rappahannock River line. The appearance of Geary's 28th Pennsylvania at Harpers Ferry on February 24 helped convince the already concerned Johnston that the Union threatened his left and that he must pull back. Federal troops marched into the vacuum left by the Confederates.

I have driven the rebels entirely from Loudoun Co.[2]
Love to all. God bless you.

Your loving husband
J. W. Geary

*   *   *

Plains   Fauquier Co Va   Mar 31st 1862

My Dear Wife

This place was reached by my command on Saturday afternoon, after a
tortuous march from Upperville, to Aldie, thence Snickerville, thence back to
Aldie, thence to Middleburg, where we encountered the enemy and made him
turn his back on the first charge, thence to this point on the Manassas R.
Road. Sometimes we have been entirely cut off from the rest of the army, and
we are now occupying a midway position between the main branches of the
army and the nearest U.S. troops we know of are about 27 miles east and west
of us. There you see we are left to sustain ourselves. This we have under God's
protection been enabled thus far to do. I may be in this neighborhood for
several days. We are in sight of Warrenton, and are the first U.S. troops in
this important portion of the state of Virginia.

My health and that of the boys is good. My command is in high spirits
and are ready for any emergency. May God favor the right and soon restore
our beloved country to her former happy condition & honor.

I hope Mary has recovered from her attack of fever. I hope Willie is also
well and that he loves to go to school and learns. Kiss them both for me.
Remember me most kindly to all our dear friends. Believe me my beloved
wife that absence does not conquer love, but only increases it for you.

My heart feels deeply your bereaved condition and especially so when we
are for days that we cannot communicate with each other, but we must rely
upon God for support in the day of trial and trouble. He will sustain us,
and bring us safely through the fiery furnace of tribulation and affliction.
God bless you my dear one, know me ever faithful and loving.

J.W. Geary

---

2. An exaggeration. The rebels had driven themselves, courtesy of the order of General Johnston.

*   *   *

Warrenton Junction Va   April 5th 1862

My Dear Wife

I arrived here yesterday and encamped beside the waters of the Occoquan Creek. There were here when I arrived about 18,000 soldiers. [Major] Genl [Irvin] McDowell's Corps de Arme 53,000 strong is beginning to arrive and will be here to-morrow. There will then be 73,000 men and 125 Cannon at this place, ready for the advance. I leave my encampment in the morning at 5½ a.m. for Warrenton, where it is probable I will encounter the enemy. Thence I will proceed across the country to rejoin Gen Banks at Woodstock.

I never was more agile and robust. The boys are well and are with me. My command is in high spirits.

In a few days there will be one of the most awful battles on record and he who lives over it will have seen one of the most sublime events of the age.

May God preserve us from disaster and save our lives.

God bless you Mary and the loved little ones of the family. If I live I will write again from Woodstock. Give my love to all our dear friends.

Ever your loving husband
Jno. W. Geary

*   *   *

Camp at White Plains, Va.   April 12th 1862

My Beloved Wife,

The storm having subsided, I left Camp Storm, and arrived here yester-day. The roads were more of the navigable order than for travelling. You will doubtlessly think strange of my being here the second time, but it will suffice to say that I am en-route to Woodstock, to support Genl Bank's movements in that direction, and I expect to cross the Shenandoah at Snickersville.

Eddie & Willie are well. My health is very robust. An outdoor life seems to be the one for my constitution, and the greatest exposure does not seem to injure me.

The weather is fine and all is beautiful in nature, except the mud under my feet, which averages about 6 inches.

MHow pleased would I be to spend an hour or two just now with [you] and the loved ones at home, and listen to the innocent prattle of our little cherubs.

Give them all kisses each, and a thousand for your own dear self.

Ever your true &
faithful husband
Jno W. Geary

P.S. I expect to move to Middleburg to-day. I write this to send with a messenger who will probably lose himself & it.

*   *   *

Camp "Pardee" Near Rectortown, Va.   April 16th 1862.

My Dear Wife,

This place is about 9 miles west of the White Plains. The town is a small place of about 250 inhabitants, it has several stores, one or two churches, two hotels, and two mills. The people are all secessionists and it affords me no pleasure to state that in addition, they are the meanest and most ignorant people we have yet met. Our Camp, however, is probably the most beautiful and picturesque one we have had during the war. On the West we have mountains rising one above another for 15 miles, until they terminate in the lofty peaks of the Blue Ridge. Manassas Gap is in full view. Goose Creek meanders its tortuous course close by us on the North and its channel is indicated by the greenness of its banks, every here and there as it breaks through the mountain. On the South & East we have beautiful undulating country, well adapted for cultivation or pasturage.

The enemy are watching us and we are watching them. On Monday evening we had a slight collision with them, and as usual we drove them flying.[3]

We are rebuilding the Bridges on the Manassas R.R. and if the enemy do not interfere in large numbers we will be done with it this week.[4]

---

3. This minor brush with cavalry resulted in the loss of two of Geary's men.

4. Southern soldiers destroyed these structures during their retreat. Geary's men rebuilt a 120-foot span over Goose Creek, and repaired two bridges over Piedmont and four more between Piedmont and Markham, Virginia. This work made good use of the Pennsylvanian's background as a civil engineer.

This country is rife with lying reports about the Western engagements, and the conduct of the Rebels reminds me much of the boy who whistled through the grave yard to keep his courage up.[5]

There is one thing, however, I do not like. The general discipline of our army is not as high as it should be, and it is one of the greatest drawbacks with which we have to contend.[6]

My health and that of the boys is good. The whole of my command is in good health and spirits. Give my love to all our dear friends. Kiss our babies. Tell Willie I will write him the next time. The boys send you their kindest love. God bless you.

> Believe me ever your
> faithful and loving husband
> *J.W.G.*

* * *

Camp "Pardee",   Rectortown, Va.   May 3rd 1862.

My Dear Wife

Your letters up to the 27th ult. have all been received, and I assure you I heartily thank you for your many kind missles. I too have written you many notes. I might almost say their number is legion but I think the detention in my mails to you occurs at Washington City. It is my opinion, that all the mails are so detained. The spring has thus far been remarkably damp and cold, and everything in the way of vegetation is very late. The Peach trees are now in bloom and the buds are generally bursting forth. Consequently we are in the most interesting season of the year. It would indeed be very pleasant to pay you a visit but it cannot be so now, and I must desist even in the thought.

5. At the battle of Shiloh, or Pittsburg Landing, in Tennessee, Confederates surprised Union forces under Major General Ulysses S. Grant on Sunday, April 6, and pushed the Northerners to the banks of the Tennessee River. Reinforced by Major General Don Carlos Buell the next day, Grant launched a successful counterattack. Some Southerners interpreted the battle as a victory, although it cost them General Albert Sidney Johnston. When Geary received a dispatch concerning this victory, "he sent a notice of it to Each Captain to be read to their Companies[;] there was some loud cheering the Boys are all as happy as [a] sailor." Bob [Robert M. Ervin] to "Parents—Brothers & Sisters," April 12, 1862, Ervin Papers, MHI.

6. Geary's concern for discipline sometimes struck other officers as extreme. When the Twelfth Corps transferred to the Tennessee theater of war, the general became known as the most notorious disciplinarian in William Tecumseh Sherman's army. He tried to enforce his ideas on other commands, which irritated those fellow officers and caused one to write: "Gen. G has such a reputation for severity that every poor soldier does not like to approach him." Quoted in Joseph T. Glatthaar, *The March to the Sea and Beyond: Sherman's Troops in the Savannah and Carolinas Campaign* (New York, 1985), 25.

I have not yet received my official papers and am consequently still acting as Col. of my Regt. and will of course continue to do so until they arrive.[7] Then I will form my staff. As to George I cannot say what can be done yet. There are many applicants and I think charity begins at home first, and I will take care of my own household, that is I think I will appoint Edward my Aid De Camp.[8] Of course this must not be told at present.

I do not think you have been extravagant, but on the contrary, *economical.*

You have my sanction to go to Phila and I will send you a check by next mail to enable you to buy such things as you may stand in need of yourself or for the children.

Kiss our dear ones. Love to all.

God bless my dear wife.

Believe me ever your faithful and loving husband
Jno. W. Geary

*   *   *

Camp Pardee   Rectortown Va.   May 5th 1862

My Dear Wife,

I have to write you once more from this place, that we are all well, although I must confess I am heartily tired of building Rail Road & telegraph lines, and guarding the same. The danger and responsibility are about the same as if we were advancing, and I think we have performed our whole duty on Picket while on the Potomac without having another siege of it here. Be it as it may, however, I will not grumble for probably I have prospered beyond my deserts. The crisis of the war is evidently approaching and ere long one or two decisive actions must decide it. I for one hope that the benign influences of peace may soon spread her wings over our once happy country. It is after tattoo, and the continued hum of camp is being hushed to sleep. The sentinels are pacing their lonely rounds, with ever and anon "who goes there," with an occasional discharge of a rifle at possibly a phantom. We never lay down with a certainty we shall not be roused to combat before the dawn again beams upon us.

Eddy & Willie are well, and send love to you.

7. Promotion to Brigadier General came on April 25, 1862.
8. Edward Geary remained with Knap's Battery instead of becoming an aide to his father.

Yesterday the 28th presented me with a splendid equipment for my new position, consisting of sword, sash, belt, hat, saddle, cloth holsters, epaulettes and all the fixtures of a Brigadier.[9]
This is the handsomest present I ever received.
Love & kisses for all.
God bless you Mary is my prayer

Ever & faithfully yours
Jno. W. Geary

*   *   *

Camp "Pardee"   Rectortown Va   May 7th, 1862.

My Dear Wife,

Lt. Lee goes to Washington via. the Manassas Rail Road[10] from this place and I hasten to avail myself of the opportunity to drop you a line, to inform you of my continued good health and that of the boys. They are both growing and improving finely and fill their respective places well.

Yesterday I received orders from the Sec'y of War through Maj. Genl. McDowell to report to Gen McDowell. This I suppose transfers me and my command to the Department of the Rappahannock from the Department of the Shenandoah under Genl Banks. I have a liking for Genl B. and in that respect I regret the change, but this must be "inter nos."[11]

Remember me in love to all dear friends. Kiss our babies and believe me as ever truly and faithfully

Your loving husband
Jno. W. Geary

9. The promotion created changes in officers throughout the 28th Pennsylvania. Gabriel De Korponay, whose drinking habits annoyed Geary, became colonel; Major Tyndale, lieutenant colonel; and Ario Pardee Jr., major.

10. Poor health forced Benjamin F. Lee to seek assignment in Washington. He never recovered enough to rejoin the unit in the field.

11. Banks returned the sentiments, congratulating Geary on the promotion and regretting "only that your brigade is not to join us again." He continued, "Our connection has been long, and to me most pleasant, and I shall be glad at all times to acknowledge the efficiency, alacrity and unsurpassed energy and ability with which you and your command have discharged *all* your duties." See Samuel P. Bates, *History of Pennsylvania Volunteers*, 5 vols. (Philadelphia, 1867), 1:424–25.

* * *

{While detached to McDowell's command, Geary made a nuisance of himself by overestimating the enemy threat and complaining of a shortage of troops. When Confederate cavalry surprised a small party of his men at Linden on May 15, he went around his commanding officer and directly petitioned the Secretary of War for reinforcements. McDowell believed, correctly, that Geary exaggerated matters, and instructed him to build block houses to protect his men.[12]*}*

* * *

Camp "Pardee"   May 16th 1862

My Dear Wife

I have not heard from you for several days owing to the absence of regular mails. I have not received any reinforcements yet, and with about 1800 men I am guarding 52 miles of the Manassas Rail Road, Every mile of which is menaced with enemies. Unless I receive the reinforcements I have called for we must have hard times here. I have no troops to do any thing with, nor have I any rallying point behind, we must take what we get, and there is no help for us. I place my trust in the God of Battles and feel that he is all powerful to deliver us, if it is His Divine will, as He has done heretofore.

We are all well & all join in devoted love to you & others of the household. I will write you frequently, and keep you advised.

Yesterday one of my Pickets 14 miles from here consisting of 17 men were surrounded by a large body of rebel cavalry. One was killed, 14 taken prisoners, and two escaped. This is very unpleasant, and I am unable to prevent it.

I will write no more lest I say too much. God bless you my dear Mary & the children is the prayer of

Your devoted husband
J. W. G.

12. *O.R.*, 12, pt. 1, 499–500.

*   *   *

{*On May 17, Geary was ordered to return to Banks's command, only to face the confusion caused by Stonewall Jackson's valley campaign, which temporarily cleared Union forces from most of the Shenandoah Valley. The Confederate general defeated Banks both at Front Royal (May 23) and at First Winchester (May 25), then eluded capture and turned on his pursuers, winning battles at Cross Keys (June 8) and Port Republic (June 9). Geary guarded the Manassas Gap Railroad and in late May positioned his command at Thoroughfare Gap. In a speech to the soldiers, he characterized the place as the "Thermopolae of the War," where the men should "fight until they made the welkin ring with their glory." When a contraband ran into camp claiming that a Confederate force of 20,000 was within a few miles, Geary lost interest in his Thermopolae, burned commissary stores and other goods of the 104th New York, and then—according to a disgusted Major Ario Pardee Jr.—"the Gen'l & command 'skidaddled' as though 40,000 devils were after them." Pardee concluded: "From what has been said I think you will come to this conclusion that next to Jackson, Geary has contributed more to disturb the country than any other man."*[13]

    Pardee's assessment proved more apt than he might have thought. Geary contributed to a general panic that convinced Secretary of War Edwin Stanton and Lincoln that the Confederates had advanced to the eastern side of the Blue Ridge and threatened Washington with an army of 20,000. According to a historian of Jackson's campaign, the only Southerners in the area were one company of Ashby's Cavalry, which burned the Manassas Gap bridges—as Geary deserted them. Yet the alarms sounded by the Pennsylvanian caused Lincoln to write McClellan on the Peninsula: "I think the time is near when you must either attack Richmond or give up the job and come to the defence of Washington." The President could not send more troops to the Richmond theater when faced with this emergency.[14]}

13. Gertrude K. Johnston, ed., *Dear Pa, And So It Goes* (Harrisburg, 1971), 192.

14. Robert G. Tanner, *Stonewall in the Valley: Thomas J. "Stonewall" Jackson's Shenandoah Valley Campaign, Spring 1862* (New York, 1976), 238, 240–41. For Lincoln's letter and a similar assessment of Geary's hysteria, see William Alan, "Jackson's Valley Campaign," *Southern Historical Society Papers* 43 (September 1920), 237.

*   *   *

Head Quarters   Ashby's Gap, Blue Mountain
Near Shenandoah River   June 1st 1862

My Dear Wife,

During the last week there has been much activity amongst us. After Banks defeat, finding myself nearly surrounded by forces numbering more than twenty to one of my command I deemed it prudent to fall to Manassas Junction. After having rested there one day, I set out with my command via Aldie, Middleburg, Upperville, and Paris, to this place, and having driven the enemy across the river, I have encamped here, and while my Pickets are on one side of the river, those of the enemy are on the other. Genls McDowell & [Brigadier General James] Shields are in Manassas Gap with a large force south of my position. A great battle is evidently impending, and I think it will result in the capture of Jackson's Army.

The boys and myself are well. They send much love to you.

Give my kind regards to our Phila friends.

My Dear One, may God in His Infinite Mercy bless and protect you, and may He defend & preserve us all amid the trying circumstances which surround us.

Receive the warmest assurance of my devoted love.

Ever your faithful &
Devoted husband
J.W.G.

*   *   *

Camp "Carter"   Rectortown,   June 9th 1862

My Dear Mary

Your very kind letters[,] four in number[,] reached me yesterday, some of them at least ten days old but were not the less welcome on that account. You see I am again at the Old place, and my command again is extended for 52 miles along this road. This is indeed an outrage upon myself and men considering the immense am[oun]t of similar duties already performed by us.

You need not expect any thing good or glorious from me, if attacked I cannot defend myself against 500 men at any one point, and defeat must surely follow. If I could I would resign and go home, but that will not do, for it would only gratify a few inveterate political enemies and do myself harm. Come what may, happen what will, I am determined to stand it out: every thing must have an end. They are jealous and fearful of me.

The boys are well and send much love to you.

Kiss my baby and Master Willie, and give love to Mrs. Church, Comfort and all other friends.

I have not formed my staff yet. I have delayed doing so, in consequence of my not having a command suitable to my rank, and in fact nothing more than when I was a Col. commanding.

Things cannot remain in this condition much longer and I will keep you duly advised of any thing that may occur.

I mention these matters to you *confidentially*, not to be spoken of to the public.

I leave today for Manassas and will return tonight. I will travel by R.R.

Your loving husband
Jno W. Geary

P.S. Charge the acct of Hetty W. Moore as follows:

1st—With 150$ paid on note of W. W. Logan[15]
2nd—With 30$ check on Pittsburg Bank

Charge Mary Brown with 20$ check to Hetty on Pittsburg Bank.

* * *

Camp Near Rectortown Va   June 19th 1862

My Dear Wife

I am still at this place doing guard duty from which service although exceedingly dangerous, I can not hope to gain any renown, and if attacked only reverse. My forces are scattered for 53 miles and as a matter of course cannot resist any large body with success. I will not trouble you with my grievances, but I really believe there is *treason* lurking in high places, which will soon develope itself in more places than one.

---

15. William W. Logan, brother of Hetty Moore and Mary Brown.

Fig. 2. "The Union Generals," featuring John W. Geary (top panel, center) among key brigadier generals for the Union. Geary, who was made brigadier general on April 25, 1862, kept himself in the public eye by cultivating newspaper correspondents. (Massachusetts Commandery, Military Order of the Loyal Legion Collection, U.S. Army Military History Institute, Carlisle Barracks)

My health is good, also that of the boys. My command is healthy and in good spirits, but in good spirits chafed by the late transactions of the Government toward them.

I hope you are progressing well with your business, and that you have had, and are still having a pleasant time. Enjoy yourself where enjoyment can be found.

Should you want any information on the subject connected with your mission write to me at once. Circumstances may arise which may make this necessary, and I will immediately reply to you.[16]

The 15th, 16th & 17th days of this month have been very cold here. Was there frost in the north at that time. The season has been very backward here, and in general not as pleasant as in Pa.

Corn and other spring crops are very backward. The fruit crop will however be abundant.

Give my respects to all friends, and know me ever & truly your loving husband

J.W.G.

∗ ∗ ∗

Winchester, Va.   June 28th 1862

My Dear Wife

Your kind letters from New Alexa[ndria]. were received. I have destroyed them, and consequently I cannot recall the dates. I destroy nearly all the letters I receive now-a-days for fear they might fall into other hands. The Manassas Rail-Road having been abandoned, and my command transferred again to Maj Genl Banks Department, I accordingly rallied it at Snicker's Gap, crossed the river and arrived here yesterday. To-day I am engaged in fitting up the men, and tomorrow I hope to reach the Genl Head Quarters at Middletown, about 15 miles south of this place.[17]

Then I expect either to be transferred to a Brigade, have one transferred to me, or resign and go home.

16. Mary had gone to Westmoreland County to settle the rent for the farm. She visited Pittsburgh, Greensburg, New Alexandria, and Salem Township, stopping at Eliza Logan's home to visit Geary's former mother-in-law and her daughters Hetty and Mary.

17. Major Ario Pardee Jr. believed Geary chose a course that added twenty-five miles to the quickest route for connecting with Banks. "You can scarcely imagine the revulsion of feeling that has taken place with regard to Geary," Pardee noted, adding, "As far as I am personally concerned I have no faith in him" (Johnston, *Dear Pa*, 194–95).

You are getting along well with your collections. Have a little perseverance and you will most fully realize your Expectations.[18]

My health is good. Also that of the boys.

Everlasting love to you, my dear wife.

Your true husband,
Jno W Geary

*   *   *

Camp "Hammar"   Middletown Va   June 30th 1862

My Very Dear Wife

I arrived here yesterday with my command and reported to Maj Genl Banks. We were very pleasantly received by the Genl, Staff & Corps, and indeed I must say after four eventful months absence it seems like getting home again to return to our old Division & friends. Genl Banks promises speedy and large reinforcements to my Brigade and it is rumored that I am again to lead the advance Guard in onward movements.

The weather is fine and my health is good. The boys are also well, and are growing finely.

I regret to state that my friend Capt. Warden of Co. B., now Major Warden, is lying extremely ill and is not expected to recover. He is from Westmoreland Co.

Remember me affectionately to all our friends.

I hope you have had a pleasant time in Pittsburg.

This place is 14 miles South of Winchester. Tomorrow we will advance to the front of our lines near Strasburg or Front Royal.

We have not any definite information as to the whereabouts of Jackson's forces.

Rest assured of my warm and undying love and believe me ever your true & affectionate husband

Jno W. Geary

18. Mary hoped not only to collect the rents owed on the Westmoreland property but also to find potential buyers for the farm. The Geary family needed to raise money to purchase a home.

*   *   *

Camp at Buck's Ford, Shenandoah River   July 4th 1862

My Dear Wife

It is several days since I have had the pleasure of a letter from you. Although I am aware of the safety of yourself and family, still I cannot help feeling some uneasiness and anxiety, when your accustomed letters do not arrive daily, about your welfare and happiness. The weather here is very cool and there has been much rain lately that all the streams are swollen banks full. Any movement, therefore, either of ourselves or of the enemy, is retarded.

My health is very good. The boys are also well. The health of the command is generally good. We will move southward very soon under a consolidated command of Maj. Genl [John] Pope.[19] We will certainly have some fighting, and if circumstances should go against us, God's will be done.

Of one thing rest assured that whether I survive or perish, I will continue my affection and devotion to you in life and if we have consciousness hereafter I shall never forget you, and my spirit as a Guardian angel shall watch over you continually. To God I commit you and all concerned with us. His kindly care will be over us I am certain. He has never deserted us under any circumstances through which we have passed already, and I feel equally assured he will be with us in the trials to which we may yet have to pass.

I will direct this letter to New Alexandria, and will be guided in my next direction by the probabilities of your remaining where you are.

Please remember me in kindness to our friends about you.

Believe me your affectionate
& faithful husband
Jno W Geary

19. Pope assumed command of the Army of Virginia on June 27, 1862.

*   *   *

Buck's Ford, Va.   July 4th 1862.

My Dear Mary

I have already written you one letter to-day, and the arrival of your esteemed favor of the 25th and 29th ult. makes it necessary to write again.

I have examined the accounts of Hoopes and Keys. They are both cunning and would cheat if they could, but it is on such a *small scale* it is not worth while to say any thing about it.[20] I guess the accounts in the main are correct, and may be passed.

You might have an article drawn up and signed for the rent in the cases of Malin & McCowen.[21] The rent of the farm should not be less than *one hundred dollars*, per annum. This must be paid, or if refused they can give it up, and you can rent it to somebody else for what you can get for it. The case of Sheffler[22] was right, and I am glad it is paid.

I think you are a first rate agent and collector. You can do so much better than I can that I think it is a good school for you, and it may hereafter be of service to you. I have no fault to find "comme il faut."

The sad news from Richmond is just received.[23] I have no further news than we expect to move forward in a day or two.

Remember me with high respect to Judge & Mrs. McCandless and family.

Believe me ever
your loving husband
Jno. W. Geary

20. The 1860 manuscript census shows a Thomas C. Hoopes, age thirty, and William Keyes, age thirty-two, living near Geary's farm in Salem Township, Westmoreland County.

21. "McCowen" probably referred to Samuel McKowen, a tenant farmer who lived near Geary in Westmoreland County. No "Malin" could be found in the 1860 census.

22. In 1860, a laborer named Daniel Sheffler lived in the household of Robert Brown, the Greensburg doctor married to Mary E. Logan.

23. Robert E. Lee had pushed McClellan's army from near Richmond to Harrison's Landing on the James River in a series of battles known as the Seven Days' Campaign (June 25–July 1). Confederates had sustained a total of 20,141 casualties during the week of fighting; the Federals had 15,849 casualties. On July 5, Ario Pardee noted that the news caused the Fourth of July to be observed "in a quiet and unostentatious manner"; however, the troops took heart when they learned that the Southerners had suffered more casualties. See Johnston, *Dear Pa,* 197.

* * *

Camp near Washington,   Rappahannock Co. Virginia
July 17th, 1862

My Dear Wife

We have arrived at this place, having left Warrenton day before yesterday, crossed the Rappahannock River, through a portion of Culpepper [Culpeper] Co. to this place which is a county seat. The scenery is mountainous and unusually variegated with hill and valley. The herbage is exceedingly green, and the pasturage fine. The wheat is much injured by the fly and jointworm. This county has about 900 voters—500 of whom are in the rebel army. Some skirmishing has taken place in our front, and it is said Edward has seen some of them. I have not heard from him for two or three days, he is well or I should have heard. Willie is well, and is with me.

It is said that considerable of the enemy's forces are in front of us.[24] I do not feel very sanguine of our success, from reasons connected with head quarters. The administration seems to have no *vim* in it.

Give my love to our dear friends at home. Kiss our babies and know me ever truly and affectionately your devoted and faithful husband

Jno W Geary

* * *

{Geary's brigade broke camp on July 6 to report to Brigadier General Alpheus S. Williams at Front Royal, as the 2nd Brigade of the 1st Division, Second Corps. The designation was changed in August by Banks to the 1st Brigade, 2nd Division, and increased to 2,500 soldiers with the addition of four Ohio regiments. Most of the campaigning of the 28th Pennsylvania had taken place at little expense. A commissary for the regiment noted to his mother that the papers had been full of "General Geary's fighting regiment" but added: "Well! In all their skirmishes, retreats, advances and year's service they have lost one man killed and a few pris-

---

24. About this reconnaissance Ario Pardee Jr. wrote: "We ascertained that there was no enemy between here and [Newbury]. Gen. G. saw 8 rebels, so he says. I did not see them. In next week's paper there will no doubt be an account of 'A Dash into the enemy's lines. The 28th in the field. Flight of the enemy. Geary at work, etc., etc.'" (Johnston, *Dear Pa*, 202).

oners. In this war especially the Soldiers' risks are not so great as the outside public imagines."[25]

This changed abruptly. At Cedar Mountain against Stonewall Jackson's men on August 9, Geary suffered wounds in his left foot and arm, which earned him a special mention in Pope's report while keeping him from command until late September. The letters resume with Geary on his way back to the army. He had returned to a different war: Lincoln on September 22 issued his Preliminary Emancipation Proclamation, adding freedom to Union war aims.}

* * *

Hagerstown   September 22 [18]62

My Dearest Mary

Seldom or ever have I left home so depressed as I did today. My short sojourn with you and our dear friends has so attached me to you all that I could scarcely take up courage to snap assunder the cords which bound me and which your tender care & carresses had woven around me. It is often difficult to tell why we are so spellbound and how it affects us, but I assure [you] it required all my strength and energy to break my chains. Once in the cars I was soon surrounded by gentlemen and I had enough to think of to drive dull care away but not to forget the dear ones at home.

I started from Harrisburg, and my whole career through the valley to this place was a continuous ovation of cheers upon cheers and introductions of hundreds of persons. You must not be jealous but all the women and children had to have a shake of the General's hand. They all vied with each other in doing me honor and kindness. I could not move my arm but two or three would spring to help me with my handkerchief. The utmost indignation was constantly expressed at the surrender of Harper's Ferry by Col Miles and the constant expression was being made, "Oh! if *he* had been there, a different story would have been told."[26] Compliment upon compliment was showered upon me until I was ashamed. I reached here in safety and am stopping with Mr. Marshall, cashier of the Bank, he is an Union

25. James Gillette to Mother, August 4, 1862, Gillette Papers, Civil War Times Illustrated Collection, MHI.

26. On September 15, during the Maryland Campaign of 1862, Union Colonel Dixon S. Miles surrendered the garrison of Harpers Ferry to Stonewall Jackson. Miles died the next day from a wound to the leg caused by artillery fire.

man. My relatives are tinctured and I have not called to see them.[27] *Nuff sed.*

The town is full of troops, a great many wounded.

I have not yet heard where my Brigade is, but it is supposed to be somewhere between here and Harpers Ferry.

Give my love to Mrs. Church and Comfort. Kiss the children and believe me ever and truly

Your loving husband
Jno W Geary

* * *

Hagerstown Md.   Sept. 23rd 1862

My Dearest Mary

I have had to remain over here to-day in consequence of the non-arrival of horse. The great battle field [of Antietam] is about 12 miles from here and the road to that place is thronged with visitors from all parts of our State.

Last night the rebels made an attempt to recross the river at Williamsport, but were soon repelled by our Cavalry. There is something going on down the river. I cannot find out what it is, but I judge from the movements of the troops and artillery toward the southward. I have not yet learned the whereabouts of my Brigade, nor any thing concerning it or the battery. As soon as my horse arrives I will start for Sharpsburg and will from thence take up the trail of my command and follow it until I find it. After I leave here my letters will be very uncertain, in consequence of irregular and uncertain mails.

I have visited to-day at Han Dixon Romains and find them to be rank secessionists, a stench of course in my nostrils. I also visited the widow Price who is a sister of Mrs. Romain. She is an out and out Union woman, thus showing how families are divided. The Union feeling seems to predominate here among the mediocrity and common people, but the Bontons are Secesh to the backbone, *"squirts generally."*

The weather is very propitious to my arm and I find it still improving slowly. Every thing is going on well. I feel very lonely without you and dear little Mary, but you all live in my memory and love.

27. Relatives of Geary's mother, Margaret White, born in Washington County, Maryland.

I saw old "Nelly" to[-]day. She says she was the first person that ever nursed me, and she used to call me her dear little "Johnty." She was very affectionate and I loved her $5 worth. She is about Eighty years of age. Give my love to all the family. Ever your loving and faithful husband

J. W. G.

*   *   *

Hagerstown   Sept. 25th /62

My Dearest Mary

I had the pleasure to receive your welcome and kind letter yesterday morning, and I assure you it afforded me no little pleasure to learn the welfare of my loved ones at home. John Guistwhite[28] arrived last night safely with the horse and I will leave to-day for the battle field near Sharpsburg, and probably thence to Harper's Ferry as I learn that my brigade is either at or near that place. The rebel pickets are still within 6 miles of this place on the opposite side of the river at Williamsport, and at places along the river from Hancock to Sharpsburg, or rather I should say opposite to it. The President's [Preliminary Emancipation] proclimation is the most important public document ever issued by an officer of our Government, and although I believe it, in itself, to be correct, I tremble for the consequences. Of course it will meet the opposition of the *delectable*. And I fear our country is on the verge of anarchy and despotism. God save us individually and, our country from the treason which surrounds us on every hand. But still there is much sound and devoted patriotism amongst our people and in the army, perhaps enough with God's blessing to save us from the wrath which seems suspended over us by only a single hair. Dear Old Pennsylvania I think still claims patriots sufficiently devoted to save the country. Her tens of thousands are still in the field with stout hands and hearts ready to brave any danger. Many of her bravest and best sleep upon every battle field—and truly it may be said of them as the members of the "Old Guard" used to speak of their Comrades. When the name of the dead were called, some of the rank and file would step forth, and say "died upon the field of honor." I cannot close this subject without quoting the last verse of Judge Miles famous war hymn written in 1775.

28. John H. Guistwite also served as a sergeant in Company I, 28th Pennsylvania. He may have been related to Adeline Guistwite, who was listed in the 1860 census for Westmoreland County as a servant of the Geary family.

"Life for my country and the cause of freedom
Is but a trifle for a worm to part with;
And if preserved in so great a contest,
Life is redoubled."

I will probably leave here about one P.M. I have just met an old college friend, the Revd Mr Baird of Woodbury, New Jersey.[29] He will accompany me and will be a pleasant and intelligent companion.

Can't say when you will receive the next letter from me. My arm is in about the same condition. Most devoted love to you and all the family.

Lovingly & faithfully,
J. W. G

*   *   *

Loudoun Hights, Va. Near Harper's Ferry   Sept 30th 1862

My Dearest Mary

You will see, my dear One, that I am once more in the front of strife. My Command is upon these hights, and should we be attacked by the enemy, I am nearest him, and of course will have to engage him first, and perhaps stand the brunt of the action, well this has always been my luck, and it is mean compliment either to be considered the right kind of stuff for that place.

All is going on well, and we are busy fortifying to the utmost, determined to make the most vigorous resistence should we be attacked; but what the rebels are about we cannot exactly tell. Things will be developed in a few days. My Old Veteran Brigade received me with great enthusiasm, and I find myself in command of a Division. God grant I may guide them to victory and success, under the direction of the God of Battles. He who directs the storm, can preserve and defend.

Edward is very well, the battery and the 28th Regt. did excellent service, and are highly distinguished.[30] I never saw Edward look better. He

---

29. Geary attended Jefferson College at Cannonsburg, Pennsylvania, but never finished because of the death of his father.

30. For once, Geary did not overstate matters. At Antietam, the 28th Pennsylvania chased a brigade of North Carolinians from the East Woods, swept through the Corn Field, and pushed into the West Woods by the Dunker Church before losing momentum. Acting as commander of the Twelfth Corps, Alpheus S. Williams on October 16 cited the regiment—led by Hector Tyndale—as a star in the otherwise lackluster 2nd Division. See *O.R.,* 19, pt. 2, 435–36.

sends kindest love to you, Willie, and all the children. I hope, hereafter, at least while I may remain at this post, to keep you daily advised of my welfare.

The citizens of Harper's Ferry all of whom know me, inform me, that the surrender of Miles, of this place, was a piece of the most infamous *treachery*, unpardonable to the last degree. The soldiers who were surrendered by him are loud and long in their imprecations of the man. Never has such disgrace fallen upon our ill-fated country before, God grant we not be destined to look upon its like again. The weather is dark and lowering and seems to indicate an approaching Equinox.

My Dear Mary, I miss your kind attentions very much. Your caresses have endeared you, if possible, more than ever to me. I cannot forget your devoted *love* & my heart yearns towards you over many mile. Give my kind love to Mrs. Church and Comfort, Willie and Mary, kissing the latter.

My prayers to my Heavenly Father are for your protection and happiness and for the restoration of our bleeding country, and my speedy restoration to your kind embraces.

Ever faithfully & loving
your husband
J. W. Geary

P.S. My arm does not improve as I could wish. It is very painful & sore.

*   *   *

Head Quarters 2nd Division, 12th Corps.
Loudoun Heights, Va.   October 2nd 1862

My Dearest Mary

Tis now nearly 9 o'clock at night, and at the close of a busy day I cannot sleep without first a few lines to my dear ones at home. This morning clad in full uniform, I ordered out the entire division, for review by President Lincoln, who, accompanied by Generals Sumner & Franklin[31] reviewed my command precisely at 8 o'c[loc]k. It was accompanied with the firing of a Salute of 21 guns and all the honors. Every thing went off satisfactory.

---

31. Major General Edwin V. "Bull" Sumner commanded the Second Corps, and Major General William B. Franklin commanded the Sixth Corps. Lincoln visited the camp for four days to check on the army's condition and see if he could prod McClellan into an offensive.

Abraham looks quite care-worn and not nearly so well as he did when I last saw him.

I am unable to say when we shall move from here, or to what position I shall be assigned. This Division consists of three Brigades but in consequence of the recent battles they are much reduced below their original strength.

My general health is good, but my arm does not get along as rapidly as I could desire, it is however daily improving. I am on horse back nearly half the time, and performed part of the review this morning in that manner. I have as much as I can do, and my mind is occupied all the time, consequently time does not hang so heavily with me as with you. Some nice peaches were sent to me to-day. I thought of our dear little Mary. How gladly would I have shared with her and the Willie's and to have caressed you all once more, but the distance is too great and disappointment was the result. I could scarcely eat the fruit.

Eddie is well, and I expect him and the whole of Knaps battery to join me from Sandy Hook in a day or two. Willie Geary will explain the geography of our position to you.

Give my love to Mrs. Church and Sister Comfort. Kiss the boys and Mary. Write me very soon. Give me the news. I have the honor to remain your loving and devoted husband,

Jno W Geary

*   *   *

Head Quarters, 2nd Div. 12th Army Corps.   Loudoun Heights
Oct 8th /62

My Dearest Mary

I have written to you almost every day since I have been here, and am astonished that you have not heard from me, but I presume the mails will yet do their duty, and deliver them up to your custody.

Your two kind letters of 2nd and 4th instant are just received, together with the enclosure from Thos. C. Hoops, relative to the farm [in Salem Township, Westmoreland County].

I am very happy to hear from you all, but extremely regret that you have been pained by not hearing from me, which I assure you is not my fault.

I will not decide that Mr. Hoops shall have the farm until after a final settlement for the last two years has been made, and all arrearages have been paid. Then I will decide who shall have the farm.

I have just finished the Inspection of 20 Regiments which occupied my time for the last 5 days and which has been very laborious. I have already performed more labor since my return with one hand than any other Brigadier Genl in the service.

I work day and night and if I am not promoted it shall not be because I did not deserve to be.

I miss your kind attentions very much and sometimes I wish I had not left home so soon. But "'tis as it is," and cannot now be helped, and can only [be] endured.

My arm is still very weak, and I am not now suffering under the infliction of a boil as large as the one was on the side of my arm.

The enemy are close in front of us and I capture some of his men daily. We have an immense army here, I cannot tell how many. That of the enemy is supposed to be 150,000[32] and Geary's Division still occupies the proud front of our lines. Some pretend to say the enemy contemplate a retreat. Others that they mean to fight. Be this as it may time alone can tell.

Remember me affectionately to all our friends, tell Willie Geary I expect to have a letter from him at least once a week. I hope Willie H. and he will learn much at their new school.

Kiss papa's pet baby and tell her papa is away upon the mountain's top, among the clouds.

Accept my continued and most devoted love and believe me ever and truly your faithful husband,

Jno W. Geary

* * *

Hd Qrs 2nd Div. 12th Army Corps. Loudon Hights Va.
Oct. 9th 1862

My Dearest Mary

Another day has past & gone, and I need not sigh, "Oh! for a lodge in some vast wilderness," for here I have that forlorn fellow's wish to perfec-

---

32. The Army of Northern Virginia had nowhere near this amount, and only a few times during the entire war did it approach even half of Geary's estimate here.

tion, with all the concomitants "fixins" etc. (i.e.) Rattlesnakes and Katy-dids by the millions.

The tattoo beats upon a hundred drums for the infantry. The thrilling bugle informs the cavalry and artillery that it is time to retire to the rocky couch. The light and smoke of the enemy's fires are in full view. Bang goes a cannon at some poor devoted picket, while I am sitting unconcernedly dropping you a few hasty lines. Such is the moment here as it flies, and while the soldiers are rapidly answering *here* to the roll calls I cannot but think of the many noble-souled heroes who will never answer the call until the last trump shall raise the quick and the dead.

Please look in the package of commissions I left with you. I think you will find one for John B. Nicholson, Quarter Master of the 28th Regt. Please forward it to [m]e by mail at this place without delay.

Enclosed please find a correspondence so nearly like our own was, or might have been, that I cannot help submitting it to you.

Give my love to our friends at "sweet home." Reiterate my instructions for the boys to write to me.

Kiss dear "Mary."

Believe me ever true and loving,

Jno. W. Geary

*   *   *

Oct. 11th 1862

My Dearest Mary

I observe by to-day's papers that the rebels are again in Pa.[33] This is certainly not the result of good management somewhere. The everlasting old game of getting in our rear will never it seems be learned by our Generals. I do feel ashamed to think it is so, but I cannot help it.

All I have to say is, look out for yourself and little ones if there be danger. There is no use of waiting for other people.

---

33. Ordered by Robert E. Lee to burn a railroad bridge over Conococheague Creek just north of Chambersburg, Pennsylvania, cavalry officer J.E.B. Stuart took 1,800 men on the raid between October 10 and October 12, 1862. Lee also wanted information on the intentions of the enemy, hostages to exchange for Southerners held by the North, and horses. The Confederates won the surrender of Chambersburg but could not destroy the bridge, which was made of iron. Stuart's force, however, captured roughly 1,200 horses and eluded capture by Union cavalry.

I have not heard from [name omitted] yet. No changes here. Love & kisses to all.

> Ever your loving husband
> *Jno W Geary*

* * *

Loudoun Hights Va   Oct. 15th 1862

My Dearest Mary

It is now 10 o'clock and the busy turn of the day has gradually quieted down into perfect silence. The camp fires are sinking into the deep surrounding gloom of a very dark night, and the last few of my waking moments of the day are devoted to you. How good & how pleasant it would be to dwell together in perfect unity forever, with nought but love, sacred love, for our ambrosial food. But this horrible unnatural war has been forced upon our beloved country and the little of happiness that Satan saw blooming in the world must be by him desolated and destroyed[,] and loved and loving ones are torn apart for fear that peace and good will should longer reign upon the earth.

The intriguer, the liar, and slanderer, all join to produce hell upon earth generally, and fair finds they are of his Satanic majesty to produce his desires. The destruction of mankind and most of all the happiness which may fall to the lot of poor mortal man.

Eddie is in Command of Knap's Battery, and to-day I moved it from Sandy Hook into Loudon Co. near to my quarters. He has been threatened with chills but I trust with care he will escape them. He told me that he had received a letter to-day from Comfort and that you are all well.

There is nothing new here, the enemy seems to be in great force near us, but there is as yet no prospect of a movement.

I have had several letters from friends in the army now at the city of Washington but none from you. I suppose when they come I will get them all in a bundle.

Give my love to all kind friends. Kiss Little Pet, and the boys, and believe me your ever faithful & loving husband

> *Jno. W. Geary*

My arm is still greatly afflicted with boils. No less than four are in volcanic operation just now. I am becoming accustomed to them. My arm seems nevertheless to improve. Otherwise, my health is good.

* * *

Loudon Heights Va.   Oct 24th 1862

My Dearest Mary

I find I was mistaken in my letter of yesterday when I supposed that I had received all your back letters, for to-day I had the honor to receive your 6 paged letter of the 10th inst. together with that of the 22nd, making 9 accounted for yesterday and two to-day—11 in all.

I have been handsomely complimented by Genl McClellan for the success of my late expedition and for gallantry and military skill displayed in it. Orders to the above effect have been issued.[34]

Your kind expressions of love and deep regret for my absence [are] deeply appreciated and I assure you are fully reciprocated.

I am so much engaged, I have hardly time to write you a decent letter, and I pray you excuse me unfortunate and hasty scrawls.

Every thing around me bears the note and preparations of war and things would seem to indicate an impending movement, but as to how, when, or where, I cannot tell.

Accept every assurance of love that language can express, my dear Mary, for yourself. Love to the boys and pet. Also to Mrs. Church and Comfort.

Your devoted husband,
Jno. W. Geary

* * *

"Between the Hills" Va   Oct. 28th 1862.

My Dearest Mary

To-day I moved the greater portion of my Division to this valley situated immediately east of Loudon Heights and between it & the Short Mountain.

34. Major General Ambrose E. Burnside ordered the trip to Lovettsville. The only enemy found was a small body of White's Cavalry Battalion under Captain R. B. Grubb. A skirmish at the Glenmore farm one-and-a-half miles north of Wheatland resulted in one of Geary's men killed and two wounded, while the Confederates lost two dead and twelve wounded. See *O.R.*, 19, pt. 2, 99–100. A written compliment from McClellan could not be found.

It is a beautiful place, easy of access and about the same distance from Harper's Ferry that the top of the mountain is. It is very warm and well sheltered from the storms by the surrounding mountains. You see I am still "advance guard."

My Command consists of 17 regiments of infantry, three Batteries of 6 guns each and one of 5 guns, making in all 23 Cannon.[35] To this will probably be added a regiment of cavalry "*probably.*"

The foregoing will explain to you more fully than words why I was so anxious to resume my command, and if I am not yet a Major Genl I have a Major Genl's command, and have three Brigadiers under me.

This is not as bad as to linger about home and lose a chance which may only come once in a lifetime.

The excitement of the active and busy scenes around me makes time perhaps fly more rapidly with me, than it does with you. But the spheres allotted to us has a propriety to our sexes, and is I have no doubt, as God has, in his infinite goodness, directed it should be.

If you fail in obtaining some money from Hoopes I will send you a check when you need it for what you may require.

Edward is well and sends his love to you.

I have just received two letters dated Oct. 23rd & 26th respectively. I thank you for them. Rest assured, my Mary, I never will find fault with you for loving me too much. No, no, not I, for I love you myself with a burning and undying love, and why should I not wish it to be returned, even if it should be a besetting sin, but a sin of that kind is no sin for the scripture [says] to us "love one another," and I think you and I obey the command.

Give my love to Mrs. Church, Comfort and the boys. Kiss "Pet" and believe me ever faithfully & truly yours

Jno. W. Geary

* * *

Bolivar Heights Va   Nov 2nd 1862.

My Dearest Mary

Your kind letter of the 29th ult. from York was received to-day. I am pleased to hear of the pleasure & gratification you have enjoyed among your

35. The strength of the 2nd Division was reported at just under 9,000 men on November 1, 1862.

friends there. I trust you will be truly happy in the enjoyment of your friend *"Dosia's"* society, and while on this subject do not forget to remember me to her most respectfully, and also to any other friends you may meet there.

You must not think me vain when I tell you I have been trying *something new*. Now, if you were to guess from morning until night you could not tell what it was. And, indeed, the baby would cry her eyes out before she could tell.

Well, it is neither more nor less than that, I made a *Balloon ascension* on Saturday in Professor Lowe's splendid balloon "Intrepid," for the purpose of ascertaining the precise position occupied by the enemy.[36] I experienced no sensations of *giddiness*, and upon the whole if it had not been quite so windy, my aerial voyage would have been rather a pleasant one, as it was I could not complain of it. Having satisfied myself, and obtained the information I desired, I descended in safety to *Terrafirma*.

Having experienced storms at sea & on land, Battles and Earthquakes, and having descended in a diving bell, the *foregoing feat* was necessary to complete the catalogue of transactions of which many men who have performed or seen any one of them so greatly boast. St. Paul says *try all things*, and me thinks I hear you exclaim that having completed the catalogue I might now cease. I must confess my curiosity on the aerial question is fully satisfied, but still would not fear to make a voyage.

The enemy's pickets are close to ours, and I have a daily view of those demons of Satan. Whether they will attack my position or not will doubtlessly be determined with the present week. Some skirmishing has occurred to our forces upon the east bank of the Shenandoah somewhere near Snickersville. The results of which have not yet transpired. The entire week is pregnant with important events, and in all probability a bloody battle will soon be fought.

This is Sunday evening and I am fatigued with the labors of the day. I would not have known it to be the Lord's day if my calender did not so inform me.

May God in His Infinite Mercy preserve you in health. May He permit us to enjoy life and the full fruition of the love which so ardently exists between us.

Rest assured my beloved one of my unabated and ardent love for you &

36. Thaddeus S.B.C. Lowe became chief of army aeronautics in August 1861, with the pay of colonel. Before resigning on May 8, 1863, he had fashioned a balloon corps of seven airships used to spot enemy positions and direct artillery fire.

believe me ever faithful and true. Give my love to all our kind relatives. Kiss "Pet" and the boys, and accept half a dozen kisses from your loving & ardent husband

Jno. W. Geary

*   *   *

Bolivar Va   November 3rd 1862

My Dearest Mary

Your esteemed and kind favor of the first inst. is received, for which please accept my kindest thanks.

Your fond and pleasant allusion to our anniversary wedding day[37] brings back the memories of the past. The ceremonies that made you mine, the gay and festive company, the trip to Washington and the enjoyments there, with a thousand other recollections all rise before me as so many gleams of sunshine amid the stormy path of my life, and render it for your sake still worthy of preservation. May it be the pleasure of Divine Providence to prolong our lives for the enjoyment of the pleasures of life and of usefulness in our day and generation. I trust my beloved Mary no act of mine will ever make you regret the day you became mine, but that as life wears away, and "we totter down together," our mutual love may strengthen until it assimilates to that beautiful type which knows no change in time, and after we cross the bitter waters, enjoy the full fruition of love and happiness throughout an endless eternity.

Some fighting has been going on in the direction of Snickers Gap, which I believe has been a success to our arms.[38] I have taken the same place two or three times, but *now* since it has been taken by the *Great Little Man* [McClellan], I suppose it will be considered a great *strategic feat*, and will of course be gloried greatly, even so. Amen.

The enemy is still hovering around this place in great numbers, and you must not be surprised if I have a fight with them myself in which, I hope, it being the will of the God of Battles, that I will be victorious and drive back the insolent foe with well merited punishment.

I direct my letters, as you indicated, to New Cumberland. I hope they

37. The couple married on November 2, 1858, in Philadelphia.
38. A minor skirmish by roughly 300 cavalry and infantry attached to the Fifth Corps, which was to scout enemy positions. Federal troops experienced the worst of the encounter.

reach you punctually. Your letters are learning the road to Harper's Ferry and don't go playing phantastic tricks around the land.

The *box* has not yet been received. It is long looked-for and its contents will doubtlessly be good when they arrive. *Under all the circumstances* I think you had better not send any more.

When you go home give "Pet" a good apple for me. She will relish it perhaps as well as she did the peaches. Kiss her a dozen & tell her "Papa loves her."

Kiss the boys also. Give my love to the family and believe me ever and truly thine.

Jno W. Geary

*　*　*

Head Quarters　Bolivar　Nov 7th 1862

My Dearest Mary

This has been a very cold and snowey day. The snow is about 3 inches deep.

It is indeed cold for campaiging, but the presumption is, it will not last long, and when the weather moderates we may have several weeks of very pleasant weather.

I am well and have my quarters in a house. Our dining room is in a tent. Mess consists of four persons. Today Hon J. K. Moorhead,[39] M.C. from Pittsburg dined with me. He is a clever gentleman and hereafter maybe of some use to me. He is re-elected to Congress.

There will soon be some radical changes in military and Cabinet circles. And I would not be surprised if [Major] Genl [Joseph] Hooker takes command of the army in the field, but of this latter you must not make mention until it is consummated.[40]

39. A president of the Monongahela Navigation Canal and the Atlantic & Ohio Telegraph Company (later Western Union), James Kennedy Moorhead served as a Republican in Congress from March 4, 1859, to March 3, 1869. Geary, a Democrat, courted both sides of the political fence during the war, keeping the way open for his eventual switch to the Republican Party in the 1866 gubernatorial campaign.

40. Changes did come, but the expected appointment of Hooker was premature. Lincoln removed McClellan from command of the Army of the Potomac on November 7, 1862, and chose Major General Ambrose E. Burnside as the successor. Hooker and Geary knew each other from California; the former was stationed there after the Mexican War when the latter served as mayor of San Francisco. Later in the Civil War, Hooker became something of a promoter for Geary as the two forged a new relationship when transferred to the West.

Eddie is well and is now Quarter Master and Commissary for three Batteries under my command.

I would love very much to be home during this cold weather and enjoy the comfort of home and *so forth* but this cannot be for the present at least.

Give my love to Mrs. Church & Comfort. Tell Willie Geary his letters are like angels' visits, few and far between. Tell Willie Henderson I would be pleased to know [how] many walnuts he has collected. Tell "Pet" I want to know how many kisses she has in store for me when I come home again. I send her a few nice ones.

I am my dearest Mary ever truly and affectionately

Your faithful husband
Jno. W. Geary

∗   ∗   ∗

Bolivar Va   Nov 10th 1862

My Dearest Mary

God, in infinite mercy, has permitted me once more to return from an extended pursuit with the enemy, also another collision during a reconnaissance of 14 miles into Jefferson Co.[41] Let us thank Him who giveth victory. For it is God only who can.

Your kind and sweet letters of the 6th and 7th are received. Thank you for all. I am not deserving of so much love.

I send you a check for $100. This will square that which I borrowed. Makes Hoopes pay what he owes. He can deposit with Thos. J. Barclay in Greensburg and send you a check for the amount.

I think better not to go to Harrisburg for the present. I have ulterior designs—not yet matured, which may indicate another location for a home.[42]

My health is good, but I am much fatigued. Eddie is well and sends love.

---

41. This reconnaissance came in advance of the Federal march on Fredericksburg. With 2,500 men and six sections of batteries, Geary on November 8 patrolled the area of Halltown, Charlestown, and Berryville, routing the 12th Virginia Cavalry. The reconnaissance revealed that not more than 3,000 or 4,000 Confederates were on the eastern side of Front Royal. See *O.R.,* 19, pt. 2, 160–62.

42. Geary may have contemplated running for Congress—a possibility he toyed with again in 1864. That would have made Washington, D.C., a potential location for a home.

Remember me in your prayers to Almighty God, and may His blessing rest upon you and our dear little ones.

Tell Willie G. I will write to him in a few days. I wish him to be a good boy and try to become learned. Tell Willie H. I hope he is a good boy and that he must try to beat Willie Geary learning *if he can*.

Tell Pet I hope her "new broom" "sweeps clean," and that her kisses are very sweet. Remember me in love to all at home.

And receive my continually renewed assurances of love and fidelity.

> Ever yours in love
> *J. W. Geary*

* * *

Bolivar Va.   Nov 11th 1862

My Dearest Mary

I have not had the pleasure of a letter from you to-day. I suppose I must lay the blame on the mails, as they are generally the most delinquent.

These are times of changes. You see our commanders are changed almost with the breeze. For my own part I am quite quiescent and easy. I think [Major General Ambrose E.] Burnside a first rate man & I think there is no doubt he will be much more active than his predecessor. If so, it is a Godsend to the country. "Nuff sed."

My arm still improves. It is still very weak, but it is becoming quite supple. I hope it will soon gain strength as my necessities require two good arms.

I have nothing to communicate which has not already appeared in the newspapers.

I send you the new N.Y. Herald with marked paragraphs.[43]

Eddie and I are both well. He joins me in love to all the family.

> Ever your loving husband
> *Jno W Geary*

43. Geary used contacts with correspondents to publicize his actions. A staff officer within the Army of the Potomac wrote on November 30, 1862, about an expedition to Shepherdstown that resulted in the capture of guerrillas and the killing of their leader, Redmond Burke: "I see the correspondent at Harper's Ferry of the *New York Herald* puts it down to the credit of General Geary who had nothing whatever to do with it or with us in any way." See Worthington Chauncey Ford, ed., *War Letters, 1862–1865, of John Chipman Gray and John Codman Ropes* (Cambridge, Mass., 1927), 31.

* * *

Hd Qrs 2nd Division, 12 Corps   Bolivar   Dec 8th 1862

My Dearest Mary

Yesterday I returned from a lengthy and most important recognaissance, in which 4 skirmishes occurred, 4 of the enemy were killed, 24 wounded, and 127 were made prisoners. I took the towns for thirty-five miles south of this place—viz: Charlestown, Rippon, Berryville, Millwood, Newtown, Winchester, Bunk[er] Hill, and Smithfield. For further particulars, I beg to refer you to the newspapers which will undoubtedly make mention of the same.[44]

I have been very much exposed lately, but my health is very good. Eddie was in the late campaign and performed his duty in a heroic manner. He did the job, up for Ashbey's [Ashby's] cavalry. He is a good, brave boy.

Your loving epistles up to the 1st inst. have been duly received. I thank you my jewell, for the many kind expressions they contain. True love, you know, is based on a sound personal estimation, and may be either real or imaginary. It is the ripe fruit of admiration for the excellent qualities of another, and when once thoroughly established, lasts forever, amid the storms and sunshine, rejoicings and sorrows, it is ever the same and is never diminished or augmented. Such I trust is my love for you, my dear Mary. Such may it ever be without shade or shadow of turning.

I duly appreciate your oft expressions of devoted love. You cannot express those emotions too frequently. They are ever pleasant and grateful, like the balmy breezes from the aromatic shrubbery of Arabia, like the ambrosial food upon the lips of the gods.

Dr. Logan, sorely afflicted with the disease which I once mentioned to you was compelled for his own health or life to resign. His resignation is accepted and he is now at home.[45]

Tell Willie Geary that letter of his is not forthcoming yet. I feel anxious concerning his writing and spelling. I am pleased to hear that Willie H. & he are both rapidly improving in their studies. How is our "*Swate*" little

44. With 3,200 infantry and twelve guns, Geary roamed sixty-five miles during a reconnaissance to Winchester, December 2–6. He met only a smattering of resistance from two regiments of Confederate cavalry, but gained information concerning Confederate troop movements. He bragged that he had captured Winchester, even if only for an hour. A Richmond newspaper observed the advance of the "notorious Geary" and noted that Confederates reoccupied the town as soon as the Union withdrew. See *O.R.*, 21:31–35; and *Richmond Daily Dispatch*, December 9, 1862.

45. Samuel Logan's resignation was dated October 3, 1862. He practiced medicine in Greensburg, Westmoreland County, after the war.

jewell, Miss "Pet." I hope she will not forget me while I am away. I know the big pet will not.

Love to all friends.

Ever & truly your affectionate husband
J. W. Geary

*   *   *

Camp at Fairfax Court House   6 o'clock A.M. Dec 14th 1862

My Beloved Mary

I have made a successful march with my Division to this place. Thus far I have had no opportunity of communicating to you my whereabouts and welfare and I am not sure that this will go through. I am well, and all my time is fully occupied with my command. Today I expect to reach the Occaquan [Occoquan]. I cannot tell you what our destination is at present, and will write you wherever it possible to send you a note. Eddie is with [me] and is well.

Let your prayers be lifted up for our safety. Accept my life-long love for yourself. Love to all the family. Kiss the children. Ever the same

Your loving husband
Jno. W. Geary

*   *   *

Hd Quarters 2nd Div, 12 Corps Camp,   Near Fairfax Station
Dec 22nd 1862

My Dearest Mary

A mail will leave here to-day for Washington, and I hasten to avail myself of it, to write you a brief note. The weather is very cold but as it continues to be dry we are comfortable. My health is good and Eddie is well.

The Country here is the meanest part of Creation, consisting of pine swamps, barren lands, and low people. Indeed, it is almost in the primitive conditions, and does not seem to have improved a whit since the days when Tom Moore, the poet, visited it.[46] In a letter to a friend he thus describes it.

46. Thomas Moore (1779–1852), Irish poet, toured the United States during the spring and summer of 1804.

"Dear George! though every bone is aching,
　　　After the shaking
I've had this week, over ruts and ridges,
　　　And bridges,
Made of a few uneasy planks,
　　　In open ranks,
Like old women's teeth, all loosely thrown
Over rivers of mud, whose name alone
Would make the knees of stoutest man knock,
　　　Rappahannock
Occoquan—the heavens may harbor us!
Who ever heard of names so barbarous?"

To which Tom might have added, the "Neabsco," "Quantico," & "Mat-tawoman,"[47] on account of their [e]uphoniousness. As to the bridges, they remind one of Mahomet's precarious bridge at the entrance of Paradise, placed there doubtless to enhance the pleasures of safe arrival. I think a Virginia bridge would have answered his purpose there very well.

The people are so ignorant that they may be with truth stiled *natural* "*Know-nothings*"[48] and the depravity of the youthful portion of the community is monstrous, gross ignorance is rampant. And in my opinion the remark of Abbe Raynal[49] is here fully verified, viz: "When the youth of the country are seen depraved, the nation is on the decline."

The deplorable condition of our country at this moment, in every respect awakens our liveliest sensibilities, and the future looks sometimes like a dark abyss. In all this I think I have the consolation that I have endeavored to act well on my part. I hope that my course will meet the appropriation of my God and my fellow citizens.

I have just read of a calamitous fire at Lock Haven. I suppose all is burnt that is interested in your affairs. Thus showing conclusively that after they had determined to cheat you out of your just dues, they cannot keep it themselves, and the vengeance of God lights upon them. Nevermind, my dear, God will always provide a way for those [who] trust in Him, even as He provided the ram in the hedge when Abraham, the faithful, was about to sacrifice Issaac, his son, *his only son*. Faith in God is the sheer anchor of

47. Tributaries of the Potomac River between Mount Vernon and Dumfries, just south of Alexandria.

48. A play on the American Party, nicknamed "Know-Nothings" because the portion that came from secret organizations was instructed to respond to all inquiries: "I know nothing." Formed after the collapse of the Whig Party in 1852, the American Party embraced temperance and antiforeigner sentiments.

49. Guillaume-Thomas-François de Raynal (1713–1796), French writer and historian.

our lives, it is the pillar of cloud by day and of fire by night to guide our feet through the bloody seas which surround us, and when God is for us, who can prevail against us?

Kiss the babies. Kind regards to friends. Ever purely and devotedly your loving and affectionate husband

Jno W Geary

Remember me kindly to Capt. Lee[50] and tell him to write to me soon, letting me know the signs of the times.

*   *   *

Camp near Fairfax   Decr 23rd, 1862.

My Dearest Mary

I hasten to drop you a hasty line, merely to inform that I am well.

The troubles at Washington are casting a greater gloom over the country than the affairs of the army.[51] I hope soon to see our nation in the hands of such men as will appreciate its true honor and good.

God grant our national troubles may soon be over and that peace will reign in war's stead, when all may enjoy its benign influence.

I do not yet know where your abode is, but you are I suppose in New Cumberland. If so, remember me kindly to Capt. Lee & Mr. and Mrs. Feeman and other friends.

Believe me, Mary, your devoted and loving husband. Eddie joins me in love to you and all the household.

Ever truly thine
Jno W Geary

50. Benjamin F. Lee had resigned effective October 10, 1862, because of poor health.

51. The Union defeat at Fredericksburg created a cabinet crisis in Washington. Rumors were rampant that the President himself might resign in favor of Vice President Hannibal Hamlin and that Radical Republicans planned a coup to reorganize the cabinet. This last was partially true, as some pressured Lincoln to force out Secretary of State William Henry Seward, who had offered to resign. At a cabinet meeting on December 19, Lincoln adroitly defused these problems, but the turmoil added to the gloom throughout the North, much to the satisfaction of Confederates.

*   *   *

Camp Five near Fairfax Station,   Dec. 24th, 1862

My dear little "Pet" [daughter Mary]:

On this Christmas eve I have no doubt you have been enjoying yourself, perhaps with the toys of the season, eaten your nuts and cakes, hung up your stockings in the chimney corner for old Krisk[r]inkle, when he comes along with his tiny horses, "dunder and blixen" and his little wagon to fill in *lots and gobs* of sweet things, sugar, candy, sugar plums, and if you please, sugar every thing.

Well, when I was a little boy, a good many years ago, I was very fond of such things myself. And when I look back, they were indeed the happiest days of my life.

Enjoy them my little "Pet"—They come but once.

The boys, I mean the two Willies, are getting too old for the enjoyment you can have. When ignorance is bliss 'tis folly to be wise.

I wish you a Merry Christmas and many of them.

I must close. There is a lot of soldiers at my door giving me a seranade and I must give it some attention.

Your affectionate Papa.

*   *   *

Hd. Qrs. 2nd Div. 12th Corps. Camp, Near Fairfax Station
December 25th 1862

My Dearest Mary

No cheering letter from your loved hand has reached me yet, to tell me of the welfare of my loved ones at home. Well, I suppose we will have to blame the mails again. They are always making a fuss and detaining things, even Gen Burnside seems to have cause to find fault with them. Upon their action in carrying his dispatches may have hung the fate of the battle of Fredericksburg, and upon that battle may have depended the fate of our nation. Who knows? Were it not for treason in our own army this wicked rebellion would have been, doubtlessly, long ago crushed. You doubtlessly recollect Moore's opinion on rebellion as expressed in Lalla Rookh.[52]

52. Thomas Moore published *Lalla Rookh, an Oriental Romance* in the United States in 1817. The title

"Rebellion! foul, dishonoring word,
   Whose wrongful blight, so oft has stained
The holiest cause that tongue or sword
   Of mortal ever lost or gain'd."

Such is the opinion all good men should entertain of the present Rebellion, but, alas! I think northern sympathizers are rapidly on the increase, in numbers, as well as in spirit and madness. Well I will not attempt a reformation on this subject, for being unable to effect anything, it would only be extreme folly. I will, therefore, henceforth, be content to float with the current, unless prevented from doing so by conscientious motives.

'Tis Christmas Day! and when I reflect how much pain is taken by almost every one to beautify and adorn the "Christmas tree," I think how much more fortunate we are here, where nature has bedecked and adorned her tens of thousands of "evergreen pines," with a profusion of superabundance, but alack-a-day, we have but little to eat, no roasted turkey with cole-slaw and all the *et ceteras* of a Christmas dinner. What-ho! Here comes a bundle. Well I'll stop and see what is in it. Undo the towell—out comes a good round turkey, celery, &c., &c. Ho! Cook! Come and *cook* this, and hasten our Christmas dinner. Cook comes, and I am in extacies about *le dinnaire*. At all events it will not be too late for *ze suppaire*.

This place is the most forsaken country I ever saw, it has, in addition to its natural want of fertility, been eaten over several times by alternate packs of federal and rebel soldiers, until even a blade of grass seems too lazy to grow. We are still in the field, without tents, and many other of the comforts of life which may be relished even by a soldier. I cannot tell whether we will remain here, go back to Harper's Ferry, or whatever.

We must await the development of coming events, for we cannot devise what the *strategic skill* of the wiseacres of Washington, may conjure up, and of course *we* must hold *ourselves* in readiness to march at the twinkle of a *black-cats-eye*. Well, I am nearly through. Don't forget the babies. Kiss them all. Write me soon. Ever your loving husband

Jno. W. Geary

---

featured the name of the main character, a daughter of the Arabian emperor. The romantic work rivaled that of Sir Walter Scott in popularity.

* * *

Hd. Quarters 2nd Div 12 Corps Camp near Fairfax   Dec 26th 1862

My Dear Sons Willie G. & Willie H.,

Yesterday (Christmas) I issued an order allowing the men of my command a recreation from all military duties, except such as could not be dispensed with. They all enjoyed themselves much, I assure you. On Christmas morning the men had erected two triumphal arches of evergreens before my tent. They were beautifully arranged with pine-vine, Holly, Cedar, Bamboo, Mistletoe boughs, Sumac, etc. The Holly is beautiful & Green covered with berries. The whole thing was the most beautifully wreathed affair I ever saw. I wish you could have been here to have seen it. Every thing is quiet in the army since the battle at Fredericksburg, and the probabilities are something will be up before long.

I would have liked to be with you all on Christmas day at home, and I am sure we all would have enjoyed it much. At least I would.

I wish you would write to me how you enjoyed your Christmas? How you are improving at school? & How you like your studies? How is little "Pet" (Mary) and how did she enjoy her Christmas? Does she remember me?

I would like to be home a while and have a romp with you all, but it seems to be the longer I am in the army the more my cares and responsibilities increase. Perhaps this may arise from the more extended range of my command.

If we go into winter quarters, I will obtain leave and visit you for a few days.

I received your mother's letter of the 22nd inst. last evening. I was pleased to learn you were all well, and that you were good boys. If you are not good, I wish you to be so.

Kiss little "Mary" for me. Give my love to all the household. The time is now up for my writing & I must close.

Give much love to your mother.

Your affectionate

Father.

Edward is better.

* * *

Hd. Quarters 2nd Div 12th Corps. Camp near Fairfax Va
Dec 31st 1862

My Dearest Mary

Today I had the pleasure, after my return, to receive your kind and loving favors of the 19th, 20th, 21st, and 26th inst. Accept my thanks for many kind expressions of love and fidelity. Rest assured my Dear Pet they are all fully reciprocated with Compound interest.

Eddie will be the bearer of this, and he can tell you of the wars and of our recent fight with Hampton's Legion, how Stewart [Stuart] and Lee refused to fight me, and run away, &tc. &tc.[53]

I thank you much for your graphic description of the family fireside and would love to hear much more of it.

Remember me kindly to Mrs. C[hurch]. & Comfort. Also to Capt. Lee and all the rest of the family and friends.

Eddie has jaundice and I send him to get cured. I hope you will succeed.

Love to the boys. Kiss "Pet," and accept the warm and devoted love to yourself.

Jno. W. Geary

53. This was part of a raid by 1,800 Confederates under Brigadier General J.E.B. Stuart on Dumfries and Fairfax Station, December 27–29. The 2nd South Carolina of Hampton's Brigade was nearly trapped by Geary's Division on December 28. Confederate Colonel M. C. Butler extricated this force, losing two wounded. Both W.H.F. Lee and Fitzhugh Lee led portions of the Confederate forces. See *O.R.*, 21:731–35.

To Gettysburg and Back
January–September 1863

{After the disaster at Fredericksburg, Burnside offered to resign, but Lincoln convinced the general to remain. The soldiers settled into winter camp, where morale suffered not only from defeat but also from supply problems. Pressure from civilians and Congress forced an offensive that came to be called the "Mud March," January 19–24, when it bogged down in the quagmire caused by storms. This last embarrassment finally caused Lincoln to replace Burnside with Joseph Hooker.

In the first nine months of the year, army positions seesawed as Lee capitalized on the battle of Chancellorsville, May 1–3, by conducting a raid into Pennsylvania. The battle of Gettysburg resulted in both armies returning to positions along the Rappahannock River. Mary Geary nearly had experienced the war firsthand, for the Confederate army stopped just short of New Cumberland.}

* * *

Hd. Qrs. 2nd Division, 12th Corps Camp near Fairfax Station
January 8th 1863

My Dearest Mary

Your letter of the 1st inst. is the last I have had the honor to receive from you. The everlasting mails I presume are at the phantastic tricks again, I suppose, and according to the old adage, I suppose "what cannot be cured must be endured." Edward is at home with you and I suppose his leave will run around with lightening-speed. You know leaves of that kind always do. I almost envy him, his happiness, for I certainly could enjoy a trip homeward about as well as our contrabands[1] enjoy their government pap without labour, when the burden of their song is—

> "Old Uncle Sam is the landlord,
> We eat and drink our fill
> But the wisdom of the measure is,
> There's nothing for the bill."

I would be exceedingly happy to spend a few days home, and *if I can, I will.*

You of course have all the news from the west, long before it reaches the wild scenes around the confines of Virginia.[2] I wish the war was over, and that we could enjoy life together once more.

I send you a little scrap for your book. Give abundance of love to all the household.

I am ever faithfully Thine
Jno W Geary

*   *   *

Camp near Fairfax Station, Va.   Jany 9th 1863

My Dearest Mary

I have just had the pleasure to receive your kind and loving favor of the 4th inst.

I am happy to hear of Edward's safe arrival home, & of the pleasure and benefit his visit has afforded. I trust he will soon be entirely restored to health. He need not leave home until the expiration of his furlough, if he is a day or so over time, I will make it all right by an extension.

It affords me pleasure to know the "Pet" & he are on such good terms. Poor little, dear, if she proves to be a good girl when grown up, her

---

1. Slaves who had fled the South. Benjamin Butler coined the expression in 1861 when he refused to return slaves because they were "contraband of war."

2. Forces under Union Major General William S. Rosecrans and Confederate General Braxton Bragg fought the battle of Murfreesboro, Tennessee, December 31, 1862, and January 2, 1863. The battle ended in a tactical draw, but Bragg retreated.

numerous brothers may be of use and protection to her, while she will be a solace and comfort to them. The Psalmist says, "Behold how good and how pleasant it is for brethren to dwell together in unity, &c." I hope we may live to see it verified in our case by the well doing of our little stock of progeny.

Every thing is in statu quo here. Nothing new. The enemy are still before us. He may give us a fight at any time, if the dry weather continues, and if he does, we will give him the best shot in the locker. As I said in my last letter, I would like to pay you a visit, even of a few days if I possibly can. [Major] Genl [Henry W.] Slocum [commander of the Twelfth Corps] is absent and when he returns I may ask *leave,* provided the exigencies of the service will permit.

The weather is clear and cold, and may be turned pleasant for winter, but we will undoubtedly have plenty of mud to pay up for all this.

I had a letter from Capt. Lee this evening, in which he informs me of his *resignation*[;] taking everything into consideration I think he has done wisely.[3] I trust he will soon recover his health and usefulness.

Remember me in greatest kindness to all our household friends. Kiss our babies for me.

Tell the boys I wish them to write to me frequently.

You need not fear of your letters tiring me, my dear wife, they are the sunny spots of life, and when they arrive, all other business is set aside and the contents as eagerly devoured as if I had never had one before. You know you have my love in its heighth, depth, length, and breadth not as a mere theory, but as a vital, living reality.

Ever lovingly and truly thine
Jno. W. Geary

✳   ✳   ✳

Hd. Qrs. 2nd Div., 12th Corps Camp near Fairfax
January 12th 1863

My Dearest Mary

Yours of the 6th inst. was rec[eive]d last evening. I thank you for your frequent, kind, and loving favors. They are a sunny spot in the dreary

---

3. Although illness forced him home in October, Benjamin F. Lee's resignation was not official until January 19, 1863.

monotony of a winter camp life, and of course I like to have an often repetition and would be miserable indeed if they did not at least make their appearance three or four times a week.

My health continues good, and in all respects I am about as comfortable as persons can be in camp.

The recent rains are making the roads exceedingly muddy and if it continues a few more days will render them impossible as the bottom soon falls out.

From every thing that I can learn the enemy are contemplating a *raid* in great force north of the Rappahannock.[4] But as usual *our distinguished* leaders are giving their attention to any and every thing else. Thus it has always been, and thus it will always be, until their treachery and want of zeal is either exposed and *satiated* by the destruction of our country.

I hope you are all enjoying yourselves as well as you can.

Give my love to all friends. I hope Eddy is recovering. Why don't he drop me a line? Willie owes me a letter I think, and [I] would like him to pay his debts. At all events write anyhow.

Kiss Mary & Wm. H. Believe me most truly

Your affectionate husband
Jno. W. Geary

*   *   *

Camp near Fairfax Station   Jany 16th 1863

My Dearest Mary

Your letter and one from Edward are received & I am happy to learn the welfare of all concerned.

I am aware of the many vexatious trials you must have, but persevere, every thing must have an end, and I suppose that will too.

I sent Edward an extension for *ten days*, if he is not recovered by that time, I will have it further extended. There is no use of his coming here sick.

We are still under orders to be in readiness to march and have three day's

---

4. Geary interpreted these designs from minor movements of the Confederates as both sides probed for each other's army in small skirmishes conducted primarily by cavalry. Union Brigadier General William W. Averell sent one scouting party on January 8–10 to Catlett's station, where they brushed with J.E.B. Stuart's cavalry. Another small affair occurred at Fairfax Station near Geary on January 9.

cooked rations on hand. Every thing is ready, but nobody knows whither we go or for what purpose. The only thing is to be ready.

This of course is a confining business, to be in constant expectancy. Certainty is preferable.

Every paragraph we read now-a-days, seems to be a disaster to our cause and arms. Still we must not be disheartened. He that quails before the darkening cloud is unworthy to be a soldier. We will go forward under a firm and relying trust that God will bless the arms of my command with victory as always heretofore. To His glorious name be the praise[,] for the past, whatever I have done, has been performed in a full reliance upon the "God of Battles," who has always sustained me in the storm of battle. I have never been deceived in my reliance and faith upon Him. I feel a joyful confidence that so long as I implore His aid, I will be ever victorious, even upon the field of battle. May he guide and direct me with infinite wisdom in all future operations is the humble but devoted prayer of the writer.

I hope soon to learn the result of the house matter if every thing can be arranged properly. You can purchase it for yourself and with your own funds, and no one need be informed *how* obtained or from *whom*.

Give my love to Ed. & the Ws. Kiss little Pet, and tell her she must not forget her papa.

Remember me kindly to Mrs. Julian Church and Mr. & Mrs. Keller, Frank [Captain Lee], Mrs. Church & Comfort. Also to Mr. & Mrs. Feeman. If you want the house you must act with promptitude, or you will lose it.

Ever your faithful
and loving husband,
Jno. W. Geary

*   *   *

Hd. Qrs. 2nd Division, 12th Corps
Camp near Fairfax Station, Va. January 17th 1863

My Dearest Mary

Tomorrow morning we leave this place under orders from Gen Burnside, and we will probably take the road once more to Dumfries, at which place I expect to pick up my first Brigade and a Battery of Artillery left there for the protection of that place. What our further destination will be, time

Fig. 3.　John W. Geary as brigadier general. (Massachusetts Commandery, Military Order of the Loyal Legion Collection, U.S. Army Military History Institute, Carlisle Barracks)

alone can tell. The general opinion is we are again on the eve of stirring events. Enclosed herewith you will please find a likeness of Brig Gen [Alpheus S.] Williams, comdg. 1st Division & one of Brig. Gen. Geary, comdg. 2nd Division, 12th Corps., U.S. Army. Methinks I hear you say they are a pretty hard pair of *soldados*. Well, I'll send them anyhow, and, if you think proper, you can give them a place in your album.

The weather is very cold, and it will be peculiarly hard for the men who will have to bivouac, without tents. Such is the tyranny, however, of necessity, and of public opinion, that it must be if it costs the life of every soldier in the army. I will continue to write to you from every point from which a letter can be forwarded.

Affectionate love to all our dear friends and children. Kiss the little ones for me.

Come what may my dear Mary, I will ever continue to love you, and be faithful to our marital vows.

May God be merciful unto us all and spare us from the surrounding dangers of life.

God bless you
Jno. W. Geary

* * *

Hd. Qrs. Dumfries
Jany 23rd 1863

My Dearest Mary

Our daily intercourse as far as written matter is concerned has been cut off, and suspended for several days, during which time we have been winding our weary way from Fairfax Station to this place and Stafford Court House. The *mud* has no bottom—10 horses cannot move a cannon. I wish some of the "winter campaigners" from the north were here and I their commander for about a week. I would make them think that there is no *fun* in it.[5]

The First Division of our Corps is at Stafford C.H. The 2nd & 3rd Brigades of my Division are at the Chopawamsic River, 5 miles south of this place. The Artillery Brigade is also there. The first Brigade is at this place.

---

5. Geary refers to the political pressure in the North. Lincoln needed victories to boost Northern morale as the public clamored for an offensive by the army.

I have made my head q[uarte]rs here for a few days for the purpose of recovering from the carbuncles on my back. I have one very bad one just now but I think it will be better very soon.

I will write again from this place before I go to Chopawamsic. Had it not been for the heavy and continued rains which have made it impossible to move, some movement would have been made ere this, but now it is impossible.

There are many things I would like to say about the "situation" but dare not.

Love to Eddie, the Willies and Mary, and all other friends. I am dearest one ever faithfully and truly

Your loving husband
Jno W Geary

* * *

Dumfries, Va.   Jany 28th 1863

My Dearest Mary

From this ancient and far-famed City I have the honor of again address-ing you. This city consists of about 50 houses and has about 200 inhabit-ants. On the one side the soil consists of arid sands and on the other it would remind you of the "Slough of Despond" spoken of in Bunyan's Pil-grim's Progress.[6] But this place "is not as it used to was." It was first settled by the Scotch as will be indicated by its name. It is situated on the Quantico River, near its entrance to the Potomac. The place on[ce] num-bered about 8000 inhabitants, it had 60 stores, several churches, a Theatre, a Custom House, and was a Port of Entry, but alas *ichabod* is written upon its walls, and its glory has forever departed. The grave yard, now covered with a dense pine forest, shows at least 2000 graves, the last resting place of those who have performed their *part* and have retired from the world's stage.

The country all around seems to have been once thoroughly cultivated, but the *noble* first families have dwindled away and the country has almost returned to a forest more dense than was the primeval one with which it was first clothed. What a wonderful commentary upon the *immortal beauties of slavery*.

6. The allegory *Pilgrim's Progress* (1678), by John Bunyan, was one of the more popular books in early America.

The curse of God seems to follow its every trace, and yet we have so many who would hug the viper to their own bosoms, aware of the destruction it portends. There is scarcely a man in this county (Prince William) who can read and write. Another of the results of the peculiar and beautiful system.

I wrote you two or three days ago concerning the purchase of the house, and sent you a draft for $1600. Have you received the said epistle and draft. Let me know at once.

I also received a letter from Edward at the same time I received the last one from you. I do not wish to hurry him to the camp, but he *must be particular* to send a medical certificate of his illness weekly to his immediate comdg officer.

I will write my next letter to Willie Geary. I am pleased to hear that he takes a pride in his studies, and that he is progressing rapidly. I hope he will make it a point to excel every one in his class. He has intellect sufficient to do it, and if he only will, he can.

There is scarcely a probability that the army will move for several days, simply because it is impossible on account of the mud, which averages from two to three feet, or to the hub of a wagon. Oceans of it upon oceans.

It has been snowing very rapidly all day, but it melts about as fast as it falls. Consequently, it has accumulated but little, and the *mud* is only increased.

I wish I could drop in & see how you all do. God bless you all. My love to all.

Ever your affectionate husband
Jno. W. Geary

* * *

Dumfries   Jany 30th 1863

My Dearest Mary

I drop you a hasty line from here, and if the weather be good I expect to advance tomorrow morning as far as Stafford Ct House. The roads are near impossible as it is possible to conceive of anything to be, but nevertheless I will try them, and if I try, my motto is success. So you may expect my next to be dated from that place.

The snow and mud are about 16 inches deep on an average. Consequently the whole earth is on the move.

The changes at the head of our army indicate anything except good, and the possibilities are that we will have to go back to McClellan at last.[7] That would certainly be gratifying to our soldiers at least.

Things look blue generally, but perhaps the cup is nearly full and brighter days are about to dawn, although I must confess I cannot see it.

Give my love to the boys.

Kiss "Mary."

Regards to friends & believe me

Your true & affectionate husband
Jno W Geary

*   *   *

Stafford Ct House   Feby 1st 1863

My Dearest Mary

I have arrived here safely. All well. The mail is just leaving and I have stopped it to write this note.

Love and Kisses to all.

Have you received the draft for $1,600.

Ever your affectionate husband
Jno W Geary
Brig Genl.

*   *   *

Camp at Stafford C.H.   Feby 2nd 1863

My Dearest Mary

This is one of the hardest countrys in the known world. Its immense poverty, the poorness of its soil, the meanness of its inhabitants, and the scarcity of provisions are such as to eminently entitle it to soubriquet of "Hardscrabble," or as some of our polite Pennanites would say "Pinch Gut." The officers here are generally at the starvation point, but I trust the next few days will bring with them visible improvements in the way of edibles. This place contains about a dozen houses of *small calibre*, and is

7. Lincoln removed Burnside from command of the Army of the Potomac on January 25.

about 7 miles from the Aquia landing, from which place we draw all our supplies of subsistence and forage. We are about 10 or 11 miles from Falmouth where the most of our Army are encamped.

The health of the troops is generally good, considering the inclemency of the weather. The appointment of Gen Hooker is more popular than I at first apprehended it would be,[8] and should he succeed he will knock the wind out of some peoples sails that I could name. This is a possibility, for Hooker will fight *"to whip"* when he makes a start, and you may look out either for a great victory, or for a corresponding defeat when he strikes.

There will be nothing done for some days yet and consequently Eddie need not hurry sooner than he can fully recover, for this is no place for a sick man.

I have not yet heard from you concerning my letter containing the $1,600 draft, and relating to the purchase of the house. I suppose of course you have written if it is rec[eive]d and I must lay the delay upon the mails.

Sometime ago I promised to write to Willie Geary but up to the present moment I have not found time to do so. I have so many things on my mind that I have but little time for correspondence.

Kiss little Mary. Give my love to the boys, Mrs. Church and Comfort, and without delay give me all the news about the house, the draft, &c. &c.

Ever truly, devotedly, and lovingly yours,
Jno. W. Geary

* * *

{*Geary's letters ignore the action at Chancellorsville, May 1–3, in which Lee's Confederates won a battle over a larger Union force. The 2nd Division protected ground in advance of the Chancellor House near Fairview, where the men constructed earthworks and felled trees to form abatis. The hottest fighting for the division came on the final two days. The men held on the night of May 2 as Stonewall Jackson's men routed the Eleventh Corps on the Union right, and on May 3 put up stern resistance to Confederate attempts to join two sections of separated lines before being ordered to pull back. The division suffered 1,209 casualties in the fighting. The general exposed himself repeatedly to fire, although he turned command over temporarily when the concussion of a shot robbed him of his voice.*[9]}

8. Concentrating first on improving the morale of the army, Hooker resolved supply problems and instituted corps badges to promote unit cohesion. He achieved results quickly, as Geary's comment attests.

9. James Gillette to parents, May 3, 1863, James Gillette Papers, Louisiana State University.

* * *

Hd. Qrs 2nd Div 12th C.   Acquia[10] Landing, Va.
May 27th 1863

My Dearest Mary

I have the honor to acknowledge the receipt of your favor of the 23rd
inst. I am happy to learn you are so near finishing up the repairs. I think
you will confess, I told you truth as to how much trouble the repairing an
old house was.

Enclosed you will find a check for five hundred dollars on the Western
Bank of Philadelphia. You had better have it cashed at the Bank.

Wishing you a pleasant and successful journey, I am ever your loving
and faithful husband

Jno. W. Geary

P.S. A Genl's wife must not forget that her husband is not *rich*.[11]

* * *

{*A month after the victory at Chancellorsville, Lee marched 70,000 Confederates
north to secure supplies and forage, move the Federals out of northern Virginia, and
possibly influence the growing peace movement in the Union. The Southerners slipped
around Hooker's right and into the Shenandoah Valley. For the Gearys, the advance of the rebels presented a dilemma. For two years the general built a reputation
as a severe warrior who destroyed the property of secessionists. Now the tables had
turned. Mary in January bought a home for $1,600 in New Cumberland, within
the path of the Confederate march. Geary counseled her that the best protection
would be to remain at home rather than leave. The advice proved sound as Lee's
advance stopped in Carlisle, just short of New Cumberland.*}

---

10. The currently accepted spelling is Aquia.

11. In the 1860 census for Westmoreland County, over which Geary presided as an assistant marshal, the
general had listed his personal assets at $16,000. Real estate, however, accounted for most of the assets
($15,000), which meant the general had access to little cash without selling portions of his holdings.

* * *

Hd. Qrs 2nd Div: 12th A. C.   Acquia Landing, Va.
June 13th 1863

My Dearest Mary

Your favors up to the 10th inst. are received, and I must certainly apologize for my apparent neglect of the last few days in not writing to you more frequently. The facts are, we have been under marching orders for some time, to move at a moment's notice, and the booming of cannon is constantly heard in our front, indicating that a general battle may at any time occur. Besides I have been almost constantly in the saddle, and when out of it, a multiplicity of other duties surround me, and you know I do not wish to neglect any thing connected with duty. I have very little doubt that we are on the eve of stirring events. Our army and that of Lee's are constantly manoevering and you no doubt observe the collisions that are occuring, as described in newspapers. Tonight I am informed that some of the troops from Fortress Monroe will pass the Chickahomonie river towards Richmond. Also that the troops from Suffolk will pass the Blackwater in the same direction. Thus you cannot fail to see that there is *work* on hand. Tomorrow morning two of my Brigades will move from this place Southwestward a few miles. I will know in a few days what part of the play my command is to perform.

This is no place for ladies— Officers who have their wives here are considered a nuisance, both them and their wives, and there is now an order requiring every body not connected with the army to leave, I am most heartily glad of it. However, when circumstances are such as will be proper I will invite you here, but not now. Mr. Logan left for home today, he saw a fight, was in close proximity to some cannon balls from the enemy, and I am of the opinion he has seen enough and finds that there is no fun in our affairs.[12] This is generally a curative to newcomers. I received Willie Hs excellent letter. Please assure him he is an excellent correspondent. Much more prompt than Willie G, from whom I am daily expecting to hear. I will answer Willie Hs letters soon.

Keep Willie Geary informed that he is largely my debtor in the way of a letter.

12. Probably W. W. Logan, the former brother-in-law.

Edward joins me in love to you and all the family. Kiss pet for me about a dozen times.

I hope you will soon return from the city with your furniture and have your house fixed up. You will not find a drier time to fix up the pump this year than now.

The rebs intend to pay you a visit if possible soon. We will give our attention to prevent it. If they attempt it, they will sorely rue the day they commenced it.

I have been interrupted at almost every other line, while writing, and I must now close.

Your memory is ever present with me. I do not, cannot, forget you. First in my love, you have my undivided affection. I am well and as ever your true, loving and faithful husband

J.W.G.

* * *

Hd. Qrs. 2nd Div. 12th A.C.   Leesburg, Va.   June 19th 1863

My Dearest Mary

You will no doubt be somewhat astonished to find me at this place once more. After leaving Fairfax we made this place in 2 days hard marching and arrived here late last night. The other parts of the army are moving in this direction.

I have not heard from any place for the last three days, and of course cannot tell how you are getting along in Pa. Whether your house is burnt or not, I think I would stay at home and brazen it out. Do not do anything to offend them if they come. Tell the rebels who you are and they will not dare to injure you, they know retaliation will be terrible. Eddie & I are well. With love I commit to the kind care of Our Heavenly Father.

Ever your loving husband
J.W.G.

*   *   *

Leesburg, Va.   June 20th 1863

My Dearest Mary

I cannot under present circumstances write you a long letter, for the reason that it may possibly fall into the hands of the enemy. There is no change here in affairs since I wrote you yesterday. We are strengthening our position.

This is a lovely portion of Virginia and seems like paradise, after being at Acquia Creek. I can give no knowledge of the position of the enemy.

Yesterday the solemn spectacle of a military execution took place in our Corps. Three men belonging to Gen William's Division convicted *as deserters* were *shot to death* in presence of our whole command. It was certainly a solemn scene, and one never to be forgotten. Justice to the living requires some punishment for such crime, "Verily, the way of the transgressor is hard."

Eddy is well, and performs his duty faithfully. He joins me in love to you and all the family.

I commit you and them to the care of our Almighty Father, who never fails to protect those who put their trust in him.

I received your letter of the 14th with note of 15th, which is the only news of any kind I have from any part of Pennsylvania.

> With renewed assurances of undying
> affection and faithfulness I
> am your True husband
> *Jno W Geary*

Love to Capt Lee, Mary, and all other friends.

*   *   *

Hd. Qrs. 2nd Div: 12th Army C.   Leesburg, Va.
June 2[1] 1863

My Dearest Mary

Your very highly esteemed favor of the 17th inst has been received today. I thank you much for the gallantry you have displayed by remaining at your post and home, and for making a proper distribution of the valuables. If you leave your home it will be ransacked and destroyed, and if you remain you will not be injured or the house destroyed. Besides, it seems so cowardly to run away. The rebels themselves will respect you more and if you tell them you do not fear brave men, that cowards alone would injure a defenceless woman; I will wager their love of being reputed *brave* would cause them to protect you and your house.

To-day a heavy battle is going on at Aldie about 10 miles south of this place, and has continued at least seven hours.[13] You may have some trouble with our own soldiers, a good plan to avert their impudence, would be to hang the U.S. Flag out boldly and conspicuously and let it float gracefully to the breeze. I think this would be effective.

I wish to compliment Willie G. for his patriotism and the services he is ever ready to render to his country. Tell him not to expose himself to much, to take care of [his] health, but if it comes to a fight, to show his fellow-soldiers that he is of the right stock, and not to exhibit the "white-feather," and he must show that he is of true Geary blood.[14]

Should that rebels burn your house, do not grieve about it, God will, I trust, give us a better one "Eternally in the heavens."

We know not the moment we shall engage the enemy, he is undoubtedly before us. We have a pontoon bridge across the Potomac at Edward's Ferry. Our right rests on Ball's Bluff, thus connecting us with Maryland above Washington. We have also a Pontoon Bridge over Goose Creek on our left. Our extreme right covers the old Battle Ground. I have just ascertained that the fighting before mentioned was between our cavalry and that of Stewart [Stuart]. The enemy were beaten and driven several miles with considerable loss.[15]

I hope to hear from you *every* day. Give me all the news of our affairs in Pennsylvania. Give me both sides of the question that is, what the rebs, and what the Federals are doing.

13. Union and Confederate troopers began sparring at Aldie on June 17 as both probed the other's positions. Skirmishing at times exploded into larger engagements. Battles continued in the Aldie-Middleburg area over the next few days, culminating on June 21 when Union Major General Alfred Pleasanton led five brigades of cavalry, supported by a brigade of infantry, in an attempt to cripple three brigades of Stuart's cavalry. The Union force drove the Confederates through Upperville and into Ashby's Gap, where Pleasanton broke off the engagement. See Edwin Coddington, *The Gettysburg Campaign: A Study in Command* (New York, 1968), 79.

14. This indicates that Geary's son Willie joined with local people who mustered into various emergency militia units in response to Lee's advance into Pennsylvania.

15. The Confederates lost 250 prisoners and one artillery piece.

Give my kind regards to Capt. Lee and love to Mary.

Remember [me] to all our friends. Kiss the boys and Mary G. for me.

Dearest One, your late letter if possible elevated you in my estimation, in which you showed signs of fearlessness I hardly thought you possessed. Accept my continued love and high appreciation for you and believe me ever your true husband

Jno. W. Geary

* * *

Hd. Qrs. 2nd Div: 12th A.C. Camp near Leesburg
June 23rd 1863

My Dearest Mary

The fight mentioned in my last letter was between our cavalry and one Division of Infantry, and Stewart's [Stuart's] cavalry and artillery. It was handsomely victorious,—driving Stuart from Aldie through Middleburg, Upperville and Paris into Ashby's Gap. The enemy left dead and wounded on the field, and lost several pieces of Cannon, a large number of horses, carbines, pistols, &c.

This is the most advanced post occupied by our army and we now find that in our haste to occupy it, it was a race between us and Longstreet who should get it first, in this we gained a handsome victory, for Leesburg is the most important point in our line at present, and is therefore the "post of honor."

The country is very beautiful here—there having been no soldiers of any consequence in the valley this spring, and I feel if the good of the service would permit, I would like to pass the summer here.

When our army was coming in, the people of Leesburg were taken completely by surprise. They were busy cooking and baking for their friends in the Rebel Army, who they were momentarily expecting. The *Drums' beat*, the children shouted, the young ladies danced and mammas waived their immaculate "Kerchiefs" when *lo and behold!* They perceived we were not their "kith and kin" and the shout was at once given, "They are the Yankees." The people were crest fallen, but they try to make the best of it by sharing with us some of the delicacies prepared for other *palates*. The *niggers* of course consider it a *good joke*. Edward and myself are well. He joins me in love to you and the children.

I hope to hear from you to-day. We had no mail yesterday, and we are much at a loss to know how the outside world is getting along.

My health is good but I am very busy superintending the fortifying [of] the place.

Give my love to the boys and do tell Willie Geary to be manly and not to adopt the vices of the men and boys around him.

Kiss Pet for me, and give my love to Mary Lee.

Ever your true husband
J.W.G.

*   *   *

Hd Qrs. 2nd Div: 12th Army Corps   Leesburg, Va.
June 24th 1863

My Dearest Mary

Your kind letter of Sunday last is received, and now since you see the soldiers so near you can begin to appreciate some of the horrors of war. I still adhere to the opinion that you had better remain in your house if you wish its preservation. If you leave, all you have will be destroyed and stolen; if you stay, every *good* soldier will respect you. These are trying times I must confess, but having been all my life nursed in the paths of danger, it is hard to tell what cannot be *braved*. Should we ever pass this perilous period in the history of our country we shall know how to appreciate the blessings and benign influences of peace, and perhaps not be so ready, as a people, to place ourselves again in jeopardy.

Be of good cheer, my dear wife, my [we] must [not] loose confidence in God, and although the cloud hangs darkly around us, still the "pillar of cloud by day, and of fire by night" will guide us to the promised land of peace as potently as it did the children of Israel through the dark wilderness of Arabia.

Heavy bodies of the enemy are before us and a general battle may soon occur.

Give kind regards to Capt. Lee and Mary. Love to all the children.

I think of you constantly, and sometimes I feel very revengeful, when the exposed condition of my family rises up before me. May God ever protect us & under all the surrounding troubles deliver us.

I am as ever your loving husband
Jno. W. Geary

P.S. If Willie "G" takes an active part in the defence of the valley, which I hope he will, try and get him in charge of some Genl officer as an aid (volunteer), orderly or messenger where he can ride, he can then use his horse. Capt. Lee can greatly assist you in this and I think Willie could be usefully employed and with advantage to himself. Tell him to be manly, brave, and true, to cast away boyishness, and whatever he does, to be sure he is right and do it with all his might.

*   *   *

Hd. Qrs. 2nd Div: 12th Army Corps   Frederick Md.

June 28th 1863

My Dearest Mary

We arrived here to-day with my command, in good health and spirits. We left Leesburg on Friday morning, and encamped at the mouth of the Monocacy Creek. On Saturday we went to Knoxville via Point of Rocks, from Knoxville here to-day. Eddy is here also. I suppose you are driven out by this time, and hardly know where to direct my letter. I think of you and home constantly, and your trials will nerve my arms to strike stronger and sterner blows than ever. May God grant that I may be instrumental in procuring a glorious victory, and driving the foe from our dear native state and from those we hold most dear. Ever thine in fidelity, love and truth,

Jno. W. Geary

*   *   *

{*At Gettysburg, the Twelfth Corps most often held the right of the Union army on Culp's Hill. On July 2, Williams's 1st Division and Geary's 2nd were shifted to protect against Confederate attacks toward the round tops. Poor staff-work on the part of high command resulted in Geary's wandering off on the Baltimore Pike and getting lost in the rear. Rather than find his way back or seek clarification of the orders, he compounded the error by placing his division in bivouac, which kept 2,500 soldiers out of the action.*[16] *By night, the division returned to the Union right.*

16. Coddington, *Gettysburg Campaign*, 433–34.

Geary mentioned none of this to Mary, concentrating on his performance in the defense of Culp's Hill on the third day. "The whole fight was under my control," he bragged on July 4, "no one to interfere." A noted historian of the battle, Edwin Coddington, called Geary's official report "romantic balderdash," and the account angered fellow general Alpheus S. Williams, who had directed the defense as temporary commander of the Twelfth Corps. But Geary's attentiveness to filing reports meant that his report, not Williams's, was on hand when Major General George G. Meade wrote the overall report of the battle. Williams complained to his daughter that Geary "gets all the credit of the operations on the right during the morning of July 3rd, and myself, who spent a sleepless night in planning the attack, and my old division commanded by Gen. {Thomas H.} Ruger, which drove the Rebs. from their double line of entrenchments, are not alluded to. Save me from my friends!"[17] For months Williams protested the slight to Meade, who finally issued a correction on February 14, 1864.}

*   *   *

Camp near Gettysburg   Hd Qrs 2nd Div 12th Corps
July 4th 1863

My Dearest Mary

With the devout thanks to Almighty God for His miraculous protection in passing the most terrible battle yet fought, I am enabled to announce to you that Edward & I are both unhurt, although in the heat of Combat.

Yesterday I had the honor to defeat Gen [Richard S.] Ewell's [Second] Corps (formerly Jackson's). They attacked my command at 3 oclock a.m. and we fought until ½ past 11. The result was I repulsed his command with a loss of about 1000 killed and 3000 wounded. We took also 500 prisoners, about 5000 stand of arms. My loss is 110 killed, 584 wounded. The whole fight was under my control, no one to interfere. *Thank God for so glorious a victory,* and that too, over the very troops who *broke my arm,* and whom we fought at Chancellorsville. Our prospects to drive out speedily the rebels is very good and I think in another week there will not be a rebel in the state. We have already killed, wounded, and captured about 12,000 or 15,000 of them, and extended much punishment to them.

Ewell's command consists of the following Divisions, viz: *Early's, Rhodes', & Johnston's.*[18]

17. Ibid., 470; Williams, *From the Cannon's Mouth,* 271–72.
18. Major Generals Jubal A. Early, R. E. Rodes, and Edward "Allegheny" Johnson.

Fig. 4. Brigadier General Alpheus S. Williams. Williams, who periodically led the Twelfth and Twentieth Corps, resented that Geary gained credit for action at Gettysburg that Williams had coordinated. (Massachusetts Commandery, Military Order of the Loyal Legion Collection, U.S. Army Military History Institute, Carlisle Barracks)

The country is already much devastated by the rebels, and of course it is not much improved by our presence. It is raining very hard today and there is but little fighting being done. We are burying our own and the enemy's dead.

Your letter of the 27th is received. I feel much for you, but hope you will not permit circumstances to overcome you.

Ever your devoted husband
Jno W Geary

*   *   *

Hd Qrs 2nd Div. 12 A.C.   Littlestown, Adams Co. Pa
July 5th 1863

My Dearest Mary

The enemy acknowledges his threshing by attempting to leave for Virginia. We left Gettysburg this afternoon and marched to this place where we are now in camp. We start again at 6 a.m. in pursuit of the fugitives.

My health is good, but I am much fatigued. Eddie is also here and is in similar condition with myself.

The enemy are being pursued with great vigor, and many of the stragglers are hourly captured.

I have seen so much death and suffering this month that I am perfectly sick of the times. My very clothes smell of death. The stench of the battle fields was horrible and beyond description.

Give my love to the boys. Kiss Mary a half dozen times. Accept for yourself my continued devotion and love.

Jno W Geary

*   *   *

Head Quarters 2nd Division, 12th A.C.   Frederick, Md.
July 8th 1863

My Dearest Mary

I have just received yours of the 1st inst. I am indeed thankful that you have not been molested at your home. Since then an immense amount of history has been made. Lee has been whipped, and routed, and we are now in hot pursuit. Tonight we expect to reach Crampton's Pass.[19] There may be some hard fighting yet.

Edward & I are well. God bless you and the children. May he preserve us in the impending conflict.

Ever yr loving husband
Jno W Geary

*   *   *

Pleasant Valley Md.   July 17th, 1863

My Dearest Mary

I arrived here to-day with my command and you will of course recognise in the place an old acquaintance from whence you received many documents almost two years ago. You will also remember it as the place where I first joined Gen Bank's command after entering the service. It is indeed a most beautiful place, cool, green, and delightful—mountains, lofty, rough, and craggy, on the East and West, while the majestic Potomac laves its southern terminus. On the West are the renowned Maryland Heights, with their lofty peaks surmounted with frowning batteries, bidding defiance to the "rest of mankind." The rocks of the Potomac river are full of the "debris" of the broken rebel bridges at Williamsport interspersed here and the[re] with a wagon, a *dead horse,* or a *dead man.*

Edward received his commission and is now mustered as First Lieutenant of the Battery. I think he is tolerably proud of his promotion, and justly so too.

We are now refitting the clothing and equipments of the command which will be completed tomorrow. We are under marching orders to have 3 days cooked Rations in haversacks & 3 days in wagons and there is consequently an extensive march before us. The result of the war seems no longer doubtful, and every thing in a military point of view seems more cheering than ever heretofore, the beginning of the end seems visible.[20] My orderly has just laid a letter upon my table. It bears your superscription and I stop to read it.

---

19. Crampton's Gap lies along the South Mountains near Sharpsburg, Maryland.

20. Gettysburg was not the only victory that cheered Northerners and made them feel as if a corner had been turned. On July 4, Ulysses S. Grant captured Vicksburg, Mississippi. With the nearly simultaneous fall of Port Hudson, the entire Mississippi River came under Federal control.

It is your 8 *pager* of the 12th instant for which please accept my thanks for the quantity of information it contains. I am well aware of the many difficulties you have had to overcome in the repairs of the house, and more particularly in the peculiar excitement of the times. You are a brave, good wife, and I wish you to accept my thanks and warmest praise for your noble bearing, under all the trials which have surrounded you. I hope it will please God to spare you during the approaching trials incident to female life, and to spare those of us who are exposed to the trials of battle for our country's cause.

Please give many kisses to our mutual pledge of love and to Willie H. Write to Willie G. frequently. Give him my love and tell him to be a good boy.

Eddie says he would have written to you, but he has been very busy making out the payrolls of his company. He sends love to all.

Trusting that Almighty God will preserve us from every danger & enable us fully to do every duty devolving upon us. I am your loving husband

Jno W Geary

*   *   *

Hd Qrs. 2nd Div 12th A.C.   Snickersville, Va.
July 21st 1863

My Dearest Mary

Once more upon the old track where some of my former labors were performed in my first Virginia campaign. We left Pleasant Valley Md, at the time indicated in my last letter from that place. After two days short march we have reached here. We find the country much desolated by the two years of war, and in many respects one can scarcely recognise it as the same, neither with regard to the inhabitants, or its physical condition.

To-day, in company with Genl Slocum [commander of the Twelfth Corps] I visited one of the highest peaks of the Blue Ridge. The atmosphere was clear and a very fine view of Loudon and the Virginia Vallies was afforded. The towns of Winchester, Martinsburg, Charlestown, Middletown & Millwood, with their surroundings were spread map like at my feet. The routes of many a difficult march, and the position of hard fought battles were before me. At Millwood lay a Division of the rebel troops, and while we were looking at them they broke up their camp and marched in the direction of Front Royal. At Winchester could be seen 3 well defined camps, and upon various road were their trains of wagons moving chiefly to the south. Enough was thus gained to know the whereabouts of the enemy & that he was still in our neighborhood, say 16 miles from us.

In the Loudoun Valley could be seen the different national legions— their broad camps and extensive wagon trains parked almost [one word undecipherable] the plain, all giving evidence that the conflicting hosts yet "lived and moved, and had a being."

I am [not] able to say that a battle is at all eminent but might occur at any time. The Blue Ridge & the Shenandoah river are the barriers between the armies & our corps occupies the right flank in nearest proximity to the enemy.

The climate here is very pleasant and elevated. Water is cool and refreshing. It is probable we will move to Upperville tomorrow. Every horse fit for service is now being taken from the Virginians. Also every thing that can be used in the way of cattle, sheep and hogs. In a word, we are partly "subsisting on the resources of the country," *a la* "*Blenker.*" Capt Lee can explain this.[21] The Virginians have never seen *war before* the present invasion.

Give my love to all our friends and relatives.

Kiss the babies.

I have not received a letter from [you] since we entered Virginia.

We have just detailed three commissioned officers and six privates from each men [regiment] to proceed home to receive, and conduct to the army the *conscripts* destined to fill up our ranks.

From present indications I will have to make some tours of reconnaissance, probably in the direction of Winchester.

I would be pleased if I could pay you a visit.

Be assured you are ever present in my mind. May God bless you and our little ones is the prayer of

Your true and loving husband
J. W. Geary

---

21. Brigadier General Louis Blenker led a division in the Mountain Department of Virginia under Major General John C. Frémont. While en route to Western Virginia in 1862, a snowfall and injury to Blenker caused by a fall from a horse slackened his control of the officers and resulted in many from the division raiding farms to keep from starving.

*   *   *

Warrenton Junction Va.   July 28th 1863

My Dearest Mary

I had the pleasure to receive today your kind letters of 19th, 20th, & 23rd inst. and thank you kindly for them and the many warm expressions of friendship they contain. It had been more than 7 or 8 days since I had either an opportunity to receive or send you a letter. Our campaign was entirely confined to the passes and fastnesses of the Blue Mountains, in the immediate presence of the enemy, surrounded by Guerillas, and all of our communications cut off; hence having no possibility of sending you a letter until to-day I have not written you for the period above indicated. As we are again restored to the pales of civilization, it will be my pleasure to resume my usual prompt correspondence. My narrative from Harper's Ferry to Snickersville, is two days travel. We lay at Snickersville one day. We had skirmishing with the enemy there, took some prisoners and killed a few of the rebs. We then marched to Paris via Upperville, and remained in Ashbey's [Ashby] Gap only for a few hours. The enemy was found to be pressing to Front Royal, and we were immediately ordered to Manassas Gap, near to that town, we reached there about 8 o'clock the next morning, having made a forced march of 30 miles under the expectancy of a general battle at that place. The fight was soon over for the enemy skedaddled. Several hundred of them were killed and wounded. We captured several hundred of the Pennsylvania cattle and horses, also a large number of their sheep & hogs. Thence we marched via Piedmont, Salem, White Plains to Thoroughfare Gap in the Bull Run range. Thence via Haymarket, Gainesville and Greenwich to Catlett's Station and this place. We have now both telegraphic and rail-road communication with Washington City and of course our communications will be much more regular for at least a few days in the future. This would be a pleasant place, if we had a good supply of water, which as a general thing is very poor east of Bull Run Mountains.

My health is very good, but I am sunburned so badly you would not recognize me.

Edward is here and is well. Give my love to all our friends. Kiss "Pet" and Willie H. for me. I hope you will try and have Willie G. write as often as you can.

It would have been the highest pleasure to me to have visited home while I was in Penn[sylvan]ia, but duty, that stern, unflinching duty, required of the soldier, prevented me from that pleasure. However unpleasant it was, I had to obey.

From the appearances of the war horizon I trust we can in the dim vista see faint glimmerings of *peace*. God grant it may be so. I long for home and my usual retirement. God bless you, my dear Mary, is the devout prayer of your faithful and devoted husband.

Jno. W. Geary

* * *

Hd Qrs. 2nd Div: 12th A.C.   "Camp in the Wilderness Near Ellis Ford, Rappahannock River"   Augt 3rd 1863

My Dearest Mary

This is the *hottest* weather I ever saw. To call it *warm* would only burlesque the whole thing. I came here yesterday from Kelly's Ford, 4 miles above, where the first Div: of our corps is. My position is only a few miles from the confluence of the Rappahannock and Rapidan rivers. On the opposite side we can see two regiments of Rebel Cavalry and one Batty of Art[iller]y. The greater part of Lee's army is supposed to be massed at Culpepper [Culpeper], and a great battle would occur at any time if we attempted to cross over. Should the enemy remain quiet, I do not think we will move much until we are re-inforced by conscripts and otherwise. This is a very poor country. The inhabitants are in a starving condition. The only things that do grow here to any extent are whortleberries, blackberries, and snakes.

My health is good. Eddie is with the Battery at Kelly's Ford 4 miles from here. He is well.

There is a considerable amount of sickness in the army at this time, mostly of a febrile character.

I hope you will write as often as you can, and not expect my letters as punctual as when on a thoroughfare of Rail-roads. I have to send this letter ten miles by a friend before it can be mailed.

Kiss the children for me. Give kind regards to all our friends and believe me as ever faithfully and truly your loving husband

Jno W Geary

Excuse this scrawl. It was written on my knee.

*   *   *

Camp near Ellis' Ford Va.   August 3rd 1863

My Dear Wife

Day after day passes away and still your letters do not reach me, owing to certain imperfections in our mail arrangements. I am almost devoured by the intensity of the heat, which still continues unabated, and we are laying perfectly still in hopes we can wear away the time of inaction under the umbrageous trees of the impoverished valley of the Rappahannock. To-day, notwithstanding the heat, I have been on horseback very much reconnoitreing our new position. And now [I] sit down to drop you a hasty line to inform you that you "still live" in the fond memory of your soldier-husband.

The people here are very tired of the war, and would make peace to-morrow if they could induce their leaders to do so. If the leaders of the rebellion were but half as tired as the people there would be peace in ten days. My own opinion, however, is, if no mishap occurs to our arms, that the rebellion will crumble to pieces within the next 90 days. *Deo. volente*[22] I hope it may be so.

I have no news to communicate. My health is good. Eddie is well, and joins me in love to you and all friends and the family.

I sincerely deplore your unpleasant condition, and hope you may be endowed, from on high, with fortitude to bear up under all your afflictions. Of this rest assured that my affection for you remains undiminished, that I am faithful and true. Hoping that God will bless us both, and preserve our lives to a good long old age, I remain your affectionate husband

Jno. W. Geary

*   *   *

Hd. Qrs. 2nd Division, 12th Army Corps Camp at Ellis's Ford, Va
August 7th 1863

My Dearest Mary

Amid a very heavy shower of rain I sit myself down to write you my brief, diurnal letter, informing you of my continued health, existence and

22. Latin for "God willing."

general well being. Edward is also well and is located about 5 miles west of this at Kelly's Ford.

The heat of the weather continues unabated, notwithstanding we have a heavy rain every afternoon.

I observe by yesterday's papers that Andrew G. Curtin is once more the candidate for Governor of Penn[sylvani]a. Poor Covode must have been greatly deceived when he withdrew his name for a *new man*, and then find Curtin nominated on first ballot. He had better go to school before he tries his hand again, but of this say nothing.[23] I do not wish to mix in yet. I am a soldier and a patriot, and therefore cannot be wrong.

I had a letter from Brother Edward a few days ago. I think he is a little touched with mob law—Copperheadism, or something else. Sometimes I think either I am crazy, or else a great many other people are. There seems so little patriotism among the people at home, the country appears scarcely worth preserving, but on this subject I will say nothing for the people will think I am a fool.[24]

A *nix wiser* or a "Know nothing" would be a good thing in a family now-a-days. 'Tis a hard thing to keep one's tongue under proper control between the teeth.

Please remember me in great kindness to our friends Mr. Musser and his excellent bride.[25] Tell them that my most earnest invocations are for their prosperity and happiness and that the choicest blessings of heaven may be theirs.

Remember me in love to Capt. Lee and Mary. I will be happy to have a letter from him, on politics, at his earliest convenience.

Give my love to the children. Most devotedly and affectionately and lovingly, your true husband

Jno. W. Geary

23. In 1863, ill health nearly forced Curtin to withdraw from the race. John Covode of Westmoreland County, a Radical Republican in the U.S. House of Representatives, was offered as a successor, but others within the party convinced Curtin to run for reelection. During the nominating convention, Covode had withdrawn, thinking that someone other than Curtin would receive the party's backing. Covode had resigned as a congressman but successfully ran for the same post in 1866, where he served until his death in 1871.

24. Democrats who, unlike Geary, did not support the administration were termed "Copperheads" for their supposedly venomous, snakelike attributes. During 1863, Pennsylvania was in political turmoil because of war-weariness and outrage over national conscription. State Supreme Court Judge George Woodward, the Democratic candidate for governor, believed that the draft was unconstitutional and was suspected of harboring peace sentiments. Curtin survived the election, but only by 15,000 votes out of the 500,000 cast.

25. An "M. Musser" was listed in the 1860 census as a clerk with the lumber establishment of Mary's brother, J. B. Church.

*   *   *

Camp at Ellis's Ford Va.   August 9th 1863

My Dearest Mary

This is Sunday, a calm and beautiful day. The blue either of heaven un-
tinged throughout the spacious firmament except here and there a pillar of a
midsummer cloud stands erect as it were upon the very horizon with its gilded
fringes and almost all the varied tints of the rainbow. Old sol pours down in
unremitted rays of light and heat upon our devoted heads, his entire strength,
and we poor soldiers are enduring all like well-tanned veterans. This is also the
ninth day of August, the anniversary of the battle of Cedar Mountain. The
cycle of one most eventful year has passed away since that awful day of carnage
and blood. How many who escaped that day have laid down their lives upon
other fields perhaps more sanguinary but certainly not contested with more
determined courage or unconquerable valor.

I am here still, the monument of God's mercy. He not only shielded me
then, notwithstanding my wounds, but He has stood by me where ten
thousand deaths were on every side of me, and with the hollow of his hand
He has shielded me from every danger. Edward also, ever in the fiercest of
the battle, has been preserved, not one of us injured. How thankful should
we all be to Almighty God for the many mercies He has vouchsafed to us
all in preserving our lives and preventing us from being maimed, in preserving our health and strength, and enabling us through His mercy still to
live, move, and have a being. Thanks, yes, ten thousand times ten thousand
thanks to Him for all this, but also for the many victories with which He
has seen proper to bless our standard. May our beloved country soon be
restored to all the benign influences of peace, and our little family circle
again restored to the domestic roof of our dear little home.

Time wears away apace, and since my departure from Phila with that
noble old veteran Regt. the "28th." Over two years have elapsed and the
men are now beginning to count the term of their enlistment by months,
no longer by years. Still the war is not over, so far as we can discern in the
continued notes of preparation among the rebels. They do not seem yet to
have reached that "last ditch" in which they are to lay down and die.

Europe, too, it seems is likely soon to be convulsed with war.[26] Central,

---

26. Tensions around the world at this time were growing, as a number of nations vied for position in
Europe and the western hemisphere. France had troops in Mexico to establish a puppet government under
the Emperor Maximilian. Italians had begun consolidating their various states into a nation. France and
Prussia would shortly be at war, in which Germany would emerge.

and South, as well as North America seem to have their share of it, and I am often called back in memory to the preaching of Mr. Milligan[27] and others, in predicting the very things that are now transpiring, and within the period designated, viz: between the years 1860 & 1866. Will the millenium follow? We now have wars and rumours of wars, but I suppose we need not fear, for the end shall not be yet. I believe in the mercy and power of God that all yet will be well. To Him we will give the Glory and the honor forever. I hope you will not consider this the voice of one crying in the Wilderness, but that of one who loves his God, his family, and his country.

I am glad to hear from Willie Geary, that he is getting along well and that his health is good. Tell him I watch over him with the tender solicitude of a father, that I hope he will imbibe no bad habits and always to remember his name must never be dishonored. Let him like "Rob Roy"[28] say "My name is *Geary*," my foot is on my native heath, and never to turn his back upon a foe. I regret Willie H.s illness but hope he is better. Tell him I am looking for a letter from him in answer to mine which contained the copy of Jackey Horner. I want his opinion on the song.

Tell "Pet" she has a right to kiss paper's picture as often as she pleases and I won't scold.

With my most ardent love for you, my dear Mary,

> I am truly & faithfully your husband
> *Jno W Geary*

*   *   *

> Camp at Ellis's Ford   Aug 22nd 1863

My Dearest Mary

A word or two this sultry morning will not be amiss. It is now over 4 weeks since we have had the honor to lead the van, or in other words, my "White Star" Division has occupied the most advanced position of the army, and our pickets are constantly in view of those of enemy. We are also on the left flank of the Infantry and are only flanked eastward by a portion of the cavalry. Deserters from the enemy frequently come into my hands and we obtain much information concerning the operation of Lee's Army,

27. The Rev. Alexander M. Milligan, a Presbyterian clergyman from Westmoreland County.

28. Novel by Sir Walter Scott. Rob Roy was the nickname of Robert MacGregor (1671–1734), a Scottish freebooter.

their whereabouts, and their intentions. It sometimes seems queer to me that during nine-tenths of the time I have been in the service, I have been face to face with the enemy & consequently have been in the front. Either the "powers that be" think *the thing* is safe in my hands, and place me in the rank of honor, which is only another name for *forlorn hope*, or they, thinking the chances may be against me, hope I may be *laid out*, and thus get rid of a troublesome character for the future.

But whatever may be the intention, my efforts have thus far been eminently successful. Indeed, I feel that through the kind and special providence of God I have often been spared when there seemed to be no hope. I pray God that thus it may continue to be and that he will again restore me to the bosom of my family and the benign influences of peace, when we can enjoy the society of the loved ones so long lost to our embraces and enjoyment.

Lee threatens our left almost daily with a raid.[29] He may come in such numbers as to give us trouble, but ultimately he will be beaten. The weather continues with almost unendurable heat, and neither army can move with any propriety or hope of success. Some of the conscripts are beginning to arrive, they are almost exclusively *substitutes* and are far inferior to the old patriotic vols. who came "without money and without price." One of the *old* is worth ten of the new. Some of them have deserted, and if caught, *they will be shot*. Father Abraham will not save them. I am glad to hear Willie Geary has got home again. I hope he will now, more than ever, devote himself to learning and prepare himself to act a prominent part in the stirring scenes of the future. Those letters from the Willies I hope will be forthcoming without delay.

I think it "most time" for Pet to write me a letter. She might now and then send me a few kisses. Kiss the little ones for me. Give my love to Mary and Captain Lee and all our friends.

Meanwhile I am your loving and faithful husband.

Jno. W. Geary

In my last I sent you $350

---

29. On August 20, Geary had reported to Major General Slocum that an informant at Aldie, Virginia, claimed that citizens there became jubilant because they expected an advance by Lee's army. No such movement came. See *O.R.*, 29, pt. 2, 77–78.

* * *

Camp near Ellis's ford   Augustus 29th 1863

My Dearest Mary

Your kind and loving letter of the 26th is just rec'd. I thank you much for it. I have been unwell for several days but feel better to-day. I have not been in bed, but have discharged all my duties as usual. I feel deeply for you in your present case, and rest assured you have all my most tender sympathies with you. And I trust you will have faith in God to enable you to safely pass through the peril of your situation. I sincerely pray it may be so. But you ought to console yourself that women in such condition generally entertain the same emotions and fears upon the subject, and yet see how many pass the ordeal unscathed, and how few in proportion fail. May you pass safely through the vale is the humble prayer of one who lives but for you, and the tender ties cementing our Union. If we cordially believe that He in whose hands are the issues of life, is our friend, we can trust Him in affliction, as well as praise Him in prosperity. The sweet consciousness of the favor and protection of that Being who disposes of events, with the assurance that all things will work together for good, is sufficient to support the mind under every vicissitude.

Give my love to the boys and tell them, I think they don't care anything about me. They never write. Tell Willie Geary I want him to write me some account of his travels during his late enlistment [during the Gettysburg emergency]. This he must do, for I am totally ignorant of his career. He must not waste time, altogether, and if there is no school in town, he must devote his time to study and refresh himself in such studies as he may be called upon to pursue. After studying a few hours, he will relish his amusements much better.

Kiss "Old Pet" a hundred times for me. Let me know her *prattle*, it is always pleasant to hear or read. I have just received a letter from Capt Lee. Give him my kindest regards and say to him that I will write to him soon. Give my love also to Mary Lee. Also to Mrs. Church, Comfort, and all the rest. And now, weary with the labors of the day and ready to sink to the *luxuries* of a "soldier's couch," I catch my last glimpse of the placid waters of the Rappahannock as the light of the moon glances upon them, and bid adieu to the world and thee.

Good night.

Jno W Geary

* * *

Hd Qrs 2nd Div. 12th A.C.   Ellis's Ford   September 8th 1863

I write you a hasty note this morning, my Dearest Mary, to inform you that I have almost fully regained my usual health. I have been very *critically* and *closely* engaged for the last two days examining deserters from the enemy, and persons in the neighborhood of my camp, upon whom I found large quantities of arms and Accountrements belonging to the U.S. Gov[ernmen]t. Many arrests have been made, and the work of examination devolves upon me. The meanest, lowest, vilest people on earth, purporting to be civilized, is to be found here, and if it were not for a *principle* it would be no great loss socially to lose the whole of them. The more the condition of the local affairs of Virginia are examined into, the more desperate and rotten we find its society.

There is considerable movement among the rebels this morning. Whether they intend to fall back, or to attack us or to make another invasion of Pennsylvania, we cannot tell—any one of which is probable and possible.

Accept my warmest love and believe me ever and truly

Your affectionate husband
Jno. W. Geary

* * *

Hd. Qrs. 2nd Div: 12th Army Corps.   Sept 11th 1863

I have just received your kind letter of the 8th instant. For which I hope my dearest Mary will accept my warmest thanks, I was much amused with Mary's talk about me slipping into bed and "breaking a slat," poor little innocent she may never forget that incident. I wish I could see you both and we would run the risk of breaking another slat or two.

I hope you will cheer up under all the difficulties about your situation. Do you remember the play of "Toodles"? If you do— It may be a boy, and that boy may be a "Major Genl" Maybe President or something else very great and good, and then Oh how proud the mother would be. So cheer up and have faith.

Every thing here bears the usual monotony of camp life. I am constantly watching with eager eyes every movement of the enemy. This morning there was quite a spirited cannonade some distance on our right, but I have been unable to tell what it was, probably a cavalry skirmish.

Edward is well and is encamped about one-fourth of a mile distant. He sends love to all the family.

My own health is improved. I have received no money up to this time. It will require more than five months to get square again with the world, and as to selling the property or any part thereof it "can't be did." As soon as the paymaster arrives I will send you a *draft*. I have but one month's pay due, and of course cannot send you much. Do not incur any fresh debts that can possibly be dispensed with and in a short time all will I hope be right again.

Yours of the 9th instant is just handed me by the Divisn Post Master. The copy of the bond I believe is all right, and I must thank you for your promptitude.

I would be pleased to know what Capt Lee says about our battle field at Gettysburg. He seems to think it was "awful." If it is awful to look upon now, what must it have been when the scene was enlivened by the actual contest, or after it was termined, when the dead lay piled in all directions. The wounded, Oh! heavens what a sight of misery—the broken arms and all the panoply of war crushed in one common ruin. When I recur to it, my heart sickens within, then *it was awful*.

Kiss my pet just 20 times. Tell her papa hopes the war will soon be over, but there may be some hard fighting yet. Tell Willie he must write to me the history of his late campaign. I also wish a letter from W.H.

Ever truly and affectionately
your faithful husband
Jno W Geary

P.S. Tell Frank if Stewart still wants the farm [in Westmoreland County] to sell it, if he can obtain a proper price.

* * *

Camp near Ellis' Ford   Sept 14th 1863

My Dearest Mary

Your letter dated "Aug 11th" was received last night. I suppose of course you meant Sept 11th. I was heartily delighted to hear from you, that you are all in the enjoyment of usual health and that every thing is moving along in the usual way.

We have had several heavy showers here today which I suppose to be the commencement of the equinoctial storm. Yesterday a reconnaissance was made by our cavalry in the direction of Culpeper C.H. A number of prisoners were taken, and there was considerable cannonading. I have not heard any further particulars, nor do I know how far they penetrated into the country beyond the Rappahannock River.[30]

Tell Pet she must get a nice little picture book and begin to learn to spell, and after a while I would like to hear that she can read, and then she will write me a letter. What nice times we can have then. She and I can talk by letter and have lots of fun. You did not mention Willie Geary in your last letter. What is he doing. Tell him he must not get into idle or lazy habits, but I hope that he will be industrious and try and learn something upon which he can be a man among men. Tell him I am anxiously awaiting that letter in which he is to give me an account of the campaign in Penn[sylvani]a. Is he going to school, or what is he doing.

If you have no use for the little mare—she might as well be sold. Willie should answer this. There is no use in keeping a horse when its labor does not pay.

Give my love to the boys and Mary and tell them I will expect them to be good and obedient.

Accept my kindest love and believe me ever

Your true hearted husband
Jno. W. Geary

*   *   *

"Raccoon Ford" Va.   Sept 19th 1863

My Dearest Mary

Yesterday I had the pleasure to receive a letter from Willie Geary for which tell him I thank him very heartily and that I will write to him very soon.

Since the rain of this "equinoctial storm" the weather has become quite cool. So much so that [it] is unpleasantly cold. The enemy seems quite

30. The skirmish at Culpeper was part of a massive reconnaissance by Union cavalry on September 13–17. The collision at Culpeper Court House involved the 1st Vermont Cavalry, which took about forty prisoners.

uneasy in our front. They are busy throwing up fortifications on almost every spot of available ground, and seem determined to dispute the passage of the river, by us, under any circumstances.

A battle may occur at any time, and I suppose I will again have to take the brunt, as in all probabilities the first attack, if they attack us at all, will be upon my Division.

I place implicit reliance upon the God of Battles for support, and I feel if it is His holy will He [will] grant us the victory.

Yesterday, two soldiers of this Division were executed for the crime of *Desertion*. They were shot to death by musketry, in presence of entire division drawn up in a hollow square of three sides. The men were killed by a firing party of 12 men each after which the entire Division marched past the place of execution, and then the deceased were buried without honors. Such is military life and discipline. There was also *one* man shot for the same crime in the first Division of this Corps. and 16 within the entire army. Thus you see the crime of desertion will no longer go unpunished, when so many expiate their crimes upon the same day. There are three others in this division who will probably meet the same fate.

The roads are in many places almost impassible since the late rains, and our old enemy is again in the field in full force—I mean the *MUD*.

Give my kindest love to all the children. Kiss pet six times, right hard on her mouth. Tell her I want her to send me some word in your next letter.

I commit you my dear Mary and our family to the care of our Heavenly Father, who I humbly hope will continue His kind and protecting hand over us all.

Ever and truly your loving husband
Jno. W. Geary

Eddy is well.

4

Transfer to the West
October 1863–March 1864

{During the fall of 1863, fighting sputtered in the eastern theater, and momentum in the western theater slipped from the Union as Confederate General Braxton Bragg defeated Union Major General William S. Rosecrans at the battle of Chickamauga, September 19–20. Bragg failed to capitalize on his triumph, but Rosecrans did even less, allowing the army to become penned in Chattanooga, Tennessee, by a Confederate siege. When Lincoln saw Rosecrans acting "confused and stunned like a duck hit on the head," he agreed with Secretary of War Edwin M. Stanton to transfer the Eleventh and Twelfth Corps to the western theater. Once the decision came in the early morning hours of September 24, Stanton coordinated the movement with presidents of the railroads, who assembled dozens of trains to transport the soldiers 1,233 miles through Union-held territory over the Appalachians and the Ohio River. The effort moved more than 20,000 soldiers and equipment—a considerable logistical achievement.

Geary and the 2nd Division were among the soldiers heading to Tennessee. The transfer at first made Geary uncomfortable as he noticed the contrast in discipline between the western and eastern soldiers. (He would acquire a reputation for being one of the strictest disciplinarians in Sherman's army.) Presently, his letters stopped mentioning differences between eastern and western troops as the men melded into a *new army.*[1] *He still overestimated enemy strength, wandered into skirmishes with insufficient caution, and led straightforward assaults that lacked tactical adroitness, but he also at times performed capably, without the panic over phantom troops or the suspicion of high command voiced in the Virginia theater.}*

* * *

Belle Air, Ohio   Oct 1st 1863

My Dearest Mary

You will perhaps be surprised to receive a letter from me dated here, but I am *here* with my whole command and expect to embark for Cincinnati in an hour or two. We took cars at Bealeton Station near Rappahannock, and came through Washington, thence via Relay House, Harper's Ferry by the Baltimore and Ohio Rail Road to this place. By tomorrow night we expect to be [at] Louisville and will take cars thence to Nashville, and thence by Rail to Chattanooga. The whole distance to be travelled will be about one thousand miles.

It is with the deepest regret that I have to make this trip without first see[ing] you and our little ones, and at least giving and receiving the parting kiss of love, but the stern orders from the War Department are such that all Officers from the highest to the lowest *must* be with their *commands*, and you know I will not violate an order.

God will watch over us with his usual care and will, if we trust in him, protect us from all harm. May His choicest blessings be upon you and the loved ones at home.

Preparations are being made to start, and I must close. I will write as frequently as the incidents of travel will permit.

Ever your loving husband
Jno. W. Geary

This place is 4 miles below Wheeling.
Give love to the children.

1. For how the eastern and western elements of Sherman's army merged, see Glatthaar, *March to the Sea and Beyond*, 30–33.

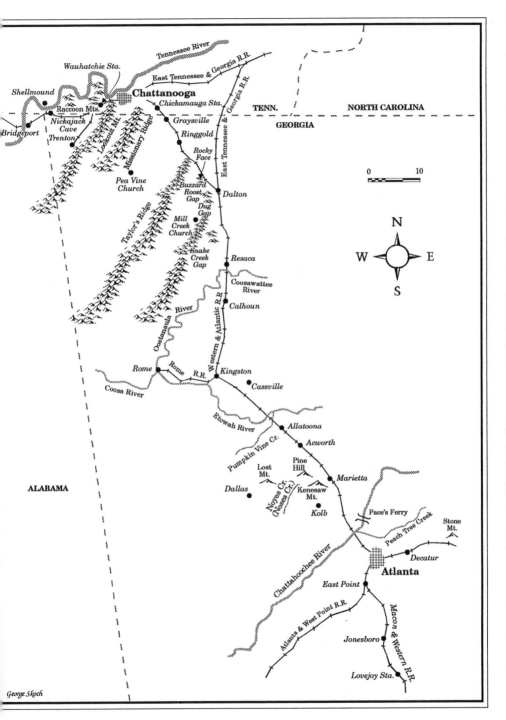

Map 2. Chattanooga and Atlanta Campaigns

*   *   *

Murfreesboro Tenn.   Oct 8th 1863

My Dearest Mary

When I was in Louisville I promised to write you from Nashville, but my stay there was exceedingly short, owing to the fact that there was a *raid* of the enemy on the Rail Road in our advance, and I was sent forward to meet their forces and check their advance. The 28th Penna and 66th Ohio Regts had a slight fight, repelling the enemy. Our advance was checked temporarily as the enemy had burned a bridge on the Rail Road about 3 miles East of this place, which is now being repaired.[2] I expect to leave this place to-morrow however and proceed as far south as Tullahoma, and may remain there until we are again fully equiped with transportation and other matters.

I cannot tell you how things are in our front, but rumor says all is right. I think however, they are somewhat *mixed.* I cannot tell you how I will like it in the West, but "as far as I have got" I dont like it very well. There is quite room for improvement. There seems to be considerable lack of brains among some of the commanding officers about whom we read so much.

The system of the Great Army of the Potomac is entirely wanting here. Edward has not yet arrived here. We are expecting the Battery to-day.

The weather has been and still is uncommonly cold for the season and the latitude. We expect it will soon moderate. This is indeed a most beautiful country and if our national difficulties ever become pacified, it would be a very desirable location for residences of families. It is a good country for office seekers as "many almighty mean men obtain position here," as the boy wrote to his father.

I will endeavor to keep you posted daily as to our whereabouts and our doings. Give my love to the children and all our relatives and friends. Tell Capt Lee to write me as often as he can. God bless you all is my devoted prayer.

Your loving husband
J.W.G.

2. Confederate Major General Joseph Wheeler disrupted Rosecrans's communications in a cavalry raid from September 27 to October 17, 1863. The Confederates demonstrated against Murfreesboro on October 5 but did not attack the garrison because the vanguard of the Twelfth Corps had just arrived. Wheeler's men burned the bridge over Stone's River, to which Geary refers. They also tore up railroad track and interrupted the transmission of Union messages.

* * *

Hd. Qrs. 2nd Div: 12th A.C.   Murfreesboro, Tenn.
October 10th 1863

My Dearest Mary

I have received no intelligence from you since our departure from Virginia, none in fact since I announced to you that a change was in contemplation. I know that you have written, but also am perfectly informed that you are well from several persons who are just through from Harrisburg.

I am now in command of this post, comprising this city, the adjacent Fortifications, and 38 miles of the Rail Road to Tullahoma. It is an important position, & one of infinite labor and responsibility.

I have hardly time to turn around and scarcely time to devote to write *even you a devoted letter*—from morning until night it is one continued jam.

There has been considerable fighting in the neighborhood—about one hundred of the enemy were killed and wounded yesterday,—312 prisoners are now in my possession, also, four pieces of cannon, captured from the enemy.[3]

Our Lines are all now in working order from this place to the front. Every thing seems more hopeful and cheerful than when I last wrote to you. There seems to be no indication that the enemy under Bragg intend to attack Rosecrans, but will content themselves with making raids with a view of cutting off the rail road communications between our base of supplies and the army in front at Chattanooga.

There is much loyal feeling among the people of this state, but many others have become as thoroughly identified with the rebellion as to make it very difficult for them to retrace their steps to loyalty.

I will have very fine opportunities afforded me in my new situation as "Commandante" of the Post, to ascertain the true condition of affairs here both as related to the loyalty of the people and the present and future prospects of the Country.

Tell Willie Geary I hope to hear from him, and to receive his promised

---

3. The casualties resulted from the Union cavalry chasing Wheeler's Confederates and those under Brigadier General Philip D. Roddey. Skirmishing erupted across much of southern Tennessee and northern Alabama during the first two weeks of October. On October 9, small battles were fought at a railroad tunnel near Cowan, at Elk River, and at Sugar Creek, all in Tennessee. Prisoners were channeled through Murfreesboro, where Geary commanded.

letter soon. Henderson might write me a letter by this time, and Pet might now and then send me some words and a few kisses.

I send you to-day, a number of the "Nashville Daily Journal," and will continue to send you such papers as I may from time to time be able to get my hands upon, hoping they may afford you some further information of our movements in the Army of the Cumberland than I can possibly do in my letters.

I will write you as often [as] I can and hope you will continue to do the same.

Please open the box I sent home last summer. It contains my overcoat (the cape of which is here). Send the overcoat per Adams & Co's Express to Murfreesboro, Tenn., taking receipt in *duplicate* at Harrisburg from the company, one of which you will keep and forward the other by mail to me.

You have it nicely boxed up and carefully endorsed. Keep the flags you will find in the box with the coat safely.

Give my love to our dear children and friends.

May Heavens choicest be upon us all.

Ever your faithful and loving husband

J.W.G.

*   *   *

Head-Quarters United States Forces.   Murfreesboro, Tenn.

October 12th 1863

My Dearest Mary

I again have the honor to address you a few hasty lines from this far-famed city. Murfreesboro is a beautiful inland town containing about two thousand white inhabitants and about one thousand blacks. Many of the whites were highly educated, and refined, holding their heads high among the uppertendons of southern aristocracy. And *of course* were strong in the Secession faith, which here as among the northern Copperheads is considered quite a mark of intelligence and of virtuous independence. Many of the aristocrats are absent, having long since entered the ranks of the rebel army, and, indeed, if one may be permitted to judge from the fact that a large majority of those who remain wear the sad habiliments of mourning, there scarce remains a doubt that many of them would be heroes, now fill traitors graves. Such, however, is the soldier's fate, where'er he goes. The

Fig. 5. The general and his staff at Murfreesboro, Tennessee. Geary commanded the post there in 1863, from which he wrote on October 8: "There seems to be considerable lack of brains among some of the commanding officers about whom we read so much." (U.S. Army Military History Institute, Carlisle Barracks)

ladies make a vain attempt at fine dressing, and I often think you would crack your sides laughing at the antique modes of their finery.

There are two colleges in the city, one for males, and the other for females. I have visited both institutions, the buildings are stately and imposing, so far as the exterior is concerned, but the interior is rough, the brick walls being only white-washed. Each of the institutions has a tolerably extensive library, but upon inspection I found the volumes were mostly presented by the citizens of the North, and the now much hated and abused "*Yankee*," or Eastern states. The other public buildings consist of a very fine Court House, five churches and one or two school houses. The private dwellings are far above the average rate for the western country. The store-rooms are very superb. One hotel and[,] a la mode the south, about 50 grogeries constitute the accommodations for *man* and for *baste*. Eight excellent turnpikes enter the city from every direction of the compass, besides many other roads, and the Nashville and Chattanooga R.R. Stone River washes the western side, and at a distance of from two to five miles North West, was the scene of the celebrated battle of "Stone river" between the forces of Rosecrans & Bragg, which resulted in the capture of this place. The country bears the marks of a fierce conflict, and the numerous graves in the vicinity betray the fatality of the day.[4] Immense fortifications have been erected here by our army and this place is the Grand depot of all the Quarter Master stores, commissary stores, and of every description of ordinance and ordinance stores. The land is exceedingly fertile, being well adapted to the growth of maize and cotton. Three acres will produce two bales of cotton—worth at present prices at least $700. Like Virginia, it is entirely denuded of rails, but unlike her barren fields, the country is covered with a most luxurious growth of weeds from 7 to 10 feet in hight, and so dense that a bird could not pass through them. I am informed that wheat also grows finely here.

As I remarked before in one of my letters, this is one of the best places in the world for the variety of its productions and for its unsurpassed abundance, but alas war crushed its fairness and beauty, and caused it almost literally to return to its primitive wildness. I did not intend to devote my whole letter to Murfreesboro, when I commenced to write, but if it will be interesting or instructive to you, I will feel myself more than compensated for the attempted description.

Hoping you and children are well and happy, I remain your truly devoted and faithful husband

J. W. Geary

Eddie is here and is well.

---

4. Fought on December 31, 1862, and January 2, 1863, the battle ended with more than 30 percent of both armies sustaining casualties. Rosecrans claimed victory because Bragg withdrew on January 3.

* * *

Head-Quarters United States Forces   Murfreesboro, Tenn.
October 13th 1863

My Dearest Mary

I have received no letter from you up to this time. I cannot exactly tell why it is so, for almost every one else has already had some news from their homes, and I know of no reason why I should be an exception. I will continue to hope for a letter soon.

I wrote you yesterday and contented myself with giving you a description of this place. One [of] the citizens of the town is a Mr. Reedy who is the father-in-law of Gen. Morgan of Brigand notoriety, and who is now an inmate of the Ohio Penitentiary.[5] The old man and his family are of the meanest secession school, and I hold him in durance vile.

This place is noted also as the birth place of Mrs. Ex President James K. Polk, and her father's house is still extant, owned by Mrs. Polk. Mrs. P. resides in the city of Nashville in a house not any better than yours. Except the grounds are quite extensive around it. Mr. Polk is buried near the [Nashville] house within the enclosure. She claims, I am informed, that she is an Union woman, and insists upon the retention of the *franking* privilege which was granted to her some years ago by Congress.[6]

The weather has set in exceedingly wet and the water in the Cumberland and Tennessee rivers will rise, and if navigable will enable us to receive supplies by water as well as by rail. It will also enable our gunboats to penetrate into the Country occupied by the enemy. Every thing is about as usual here, I have sent 500 cavalry in pursuit of some Guerrillas who were venturing into too close proximity to my lines for comfort to us or safety to themselves.

My health and Eddie's is good. He joins me in love to you and the family.

5. Brigadier General John Hunt Morgan, whose cavalry raids into Kentucky and Ohio won admiration in the Confederacy equal to J.E.B. Stuart in Virginia. Captured in July 1863 in Ohio, Morgan and six of his men escaped on November 27, 1863. Ready was a recent in-law to Morgan, who on December 12, 1862, was married a second time, to Martha (Mattie) Ready of Murfreesboro.

6. Sarah Childress Polk was born on September 4, 1803, in Murfreesboro, the daughter of Major Joel Childress—a planter, merchant, and tavernkeeper in the town. She became one of the area's noted belles, marrying James K. Polk on New Year's Day of 1824. She died on August 14, 1891. Polk had appointed Geary postmaster of San Francisco in 1849.

Distance must not make us lazy in writing or in loving, it should only lend enchantment to the view.

May God bless you and our dear children with every blessing and restore us all again to each other's loved society and to "sweet home."

Ever your loving husband
Jno. W. Geary

* * *

Head-Quarters United States Forces   Murfreesboro, Tenn.
Oct 18th 1863

My Dearest Mary

I have just returned from a long and arduous trip to and from Tullahoma distant 45 miles from this place, I have been in the saddle for 4 consecutive days, and in a continuous rain for 2 days without intermission. So you may judge with truth that I am very weary, and of course not very amiable.

My trip was for the purpose of making a tour of inspection on the Chattanooga Rail Road and placing guards at the bridges and other vulnerable places upon it, and for the purpose of erecting such works for defences along it as I might deem necessary for a stout defence, against raiders and Guerrillas.

My health is good, but I am not quite so robust as I was in Virginia.

I notice the advance of Lee's army, and the retirement of Meade's.[7]

We all wish that we were with our old and long tried friends the Army of the Potomac, to help them out of the threatened difficulties, but we are now too far away to stand between "Our loved homes and the war's desolation." It always seemed to me that when we fought in Northern Virginia, that we were defending our homes, and hence I could do it "with a will."

Edward is with me, he is well, and desires to be remembered in love to you and all the children. Remember me also to them and our dear friends.

7. This was the Bristoe Campaign, October 9–22. When Lee heard of the transfer of troops from Meade's army to the west, he launched an offensive to take advantage of the reduced numbers of the enemy and to prevent further reinforcing of Tennessee. Lee hoped to repeat the maneuvers of his Second Manassas campaign by slipping around the Federal right and threatening Washington. By October 14, A. P. Hill's Corps of Confederates struck the rearguard of the Army of the Potomac at Bristoe Station, but suffered for it. Meade had skillfully pulled his army back, maintaining a strong defensive position between the Army of Northern Virginia and Washington. Lee withdrew toward the Rappahannock on October 17; several days later, the two armies returned to positions held before the campaign.

None of your letters have reached me yet. Hereafter you had better direct them "via Louisville Ky." as follows

> Brig Gen John W Geary
> Comdg 2nd Division
> 12th Army Corps
> (Via Louisville Ky)
> Army of the Cumberland

Let the address be in a larger and plainer hand than yours, and seal your letters well. Paul-pry's[8] now-a-days are plenty.
With deepest affection and sympathy

> I am your true and faithful husband
> *Jno. W. Geary*

* * *

Head-Quarters United States Forces   Murfreesboro, Tenn.
October 19th 1863

My Dearest Mary

I again sit down to inform you of my continued welfare. I still sit in supreme command of this place. I am in good health, and Eddy also enjoys the same blessing. There has been no movement of the Army in our front for some time, but from indications which generally precede a forward movement, I judge something of the kind is in contemplation. There is now an order [issued October 16] that [Major] Gen [Ulysses S.] Grant is to command the armies of the Ohio, of the Cumberland, and of the Mississippi, to be known as the army of the middle Mississippi. This arrangement will embrace the army of Burnsides, that of Rosecrans, and that of Grant, and I think you will agree with me that it looks very like a combined movement from this direction with great power. Gen. Rosecrans is to be relieved by [Major] Gen. [George] Thomas who will command the Army of the Cumberland.

This has not yet transpired to the public, but it will, I suppose by the time this note reaches you. The Western army dont like us much. They seem to want to do all the fighting themselves, for my own part they may

---

8. A reference to *Paul Pry* (1825), written by English playwright John Poole. The hero of this comedy was overly inquisitive.

do it and welcome as far as I care. For I have satisfied my curiosity as far as large battles are concerned.

I confess I am quite home-sick, and if I could consistently do so, I would dissever my copartnership with *Uncle Samuel*, but I cannot do this yet and must therefore grin and bear a while longer.

I feel deeply your bereaved condition, and glad indeed would I be to be at home to afford you some alleviation by my presence, but God who is present every where will not desert you in the hour of trial, and He will fulfill his promises.

The Agony of the election is over in Pennsylvania and Ohio. The child is born and his name is "Andy," McClellan's letter to the contrary notwith-standing.[9] "All's well that ends well."

Give my love to Mary and the boys and other friends.

My prayers are for your happiness and comfort, now and hereafter. I remain truly your loving husband

Jno. W. Geary

* * *

Hd. Qrs. 2nd Div: 12th A.C.   "Bridgeport," Alabama
[Oct. 25, 1863]

My Dearest Mary

Doubtless ere this you have received my last letter from Murfreesboro, in which I announced to you my intention of advancing to this place. I took cars with my command on the day I wrote to you, and passing through Tullahoma, Dechard, Anderson, and Stevenson, on the Nashville and Chattanooga Rail Road, we came thence on the Memphis and Charleston R. Road to this place where it crosses the Tennessee river. The bridge was burnt by the rebels when Rosecrans advanced upon Chattanooga, and is now in process of reconstruction by our men. I am in advance of the 1st Division, it being on the Nashville rail road to guard it from raids of the rebel Cavalry.

Our further movements will of course develope themselves from day to day of all of which I will keep you duly informed. The country here is very

9. Andrew Gregg Curtin, the Republican incumbent and strong supporter of Lincoln, had won reelection as governor of Pennsylvania. McClellan, the former commander of the Army of the Potomac, supported the Democrats.

bold and mountainous, the hills on all sides rising in bold, broken, abrupt, and precipitous and lofty dimensions. The timber is much the same as that which covers of mountains in Pennsylvania, and is now beautifully variegated with autumnal tints of every hue. The Tennessee River washes our camp on the south and as far as we can see, it is a beautiful navigable stream both above and below this place. The navigation, however, is obstructed below here about 35 miles from here by the "muscle Shoals" which obstruct navigation about 30 miles. The Shoals as the name indicates are made up of innumerable muscle shells which massed in such inconceivable quantities as to cause the obstruction named. Game of all kinds abound in the woodlands around us, and the streams are well stocked with fish. The soil is not nearly so exuberant as that which I described around Murfreesboro, and I am safe in saying is much below the medium of Penn[syl-vani]a lands. We are twenty eight miles from Chattanooga, and are in full view of the Lookout Mountains, which throw their lofty heads above their fellows and seem in haughty pride to cast their scornful glances around. One peak in particular, the tallest of them is directly east from us, stands like a "Saul," "head & shoulders above them all." The sun came up behind it and reaching its top seemed to pause for a moment and gaze in admiration upon the warlike scene, and the peculiarly grand and picturesque scenery before him, and then to resume his everlasting course with joy. Here we find the 11th Corps and with them we propose to advance very soon. We find every thing very different in the Army of the Cumberland from that we have been accustomed [to] in the Army of the Potomac. Discipline, the pride of that glorious body[,] is unknown here, and I must use the language of Willies last letter to me to describe it: "Everybody commands but nobody obeys."

Edward is here and is well. He has been chosen captain of the Battery [F in Knap's Artillery] formerly commanded by Capt [Robert B.] Hampton and nothing remains but for Gov Curtin to issue the commission. In that event he will be re-transferred to the Army of the Potomac, and although I dislike the idea of separation from him, still I will not let anything stand in the way of his promotion, for he is a noble boy, and well he has earned it.

I am so much engaged and may not be able to write you everyday, but will either write to you or Capt Lee tomorrow if we do not advance. Give devoted love to the children and other friends. May God our Heavenly Father continue his inestimable blessings upon us all and preserve and protect us as in times past, and permit us yet to enjoy happiness in each

other's society and be of service to the world, then to enjoy everlasting
peace in the world to come.

Your loving husband
Jno W Geary

We have spent our first night in Alabama, "Way down in Alabama wid our
banjo on our Knee," *old song*

*   *   *

*{The White Star Division next fought at Wauhatchie, a station along the Nash-
ville and Chattanooga Railroad, as part of Joseph Hooker's attempt to open the
"cracker line" to bring supplies into the besieged city of Chattanooga. Union forces
brushed off token resistance at Bridgeport, Alabama. Hooker then split his command
into two groups on the march through Lookout Valley, placing Geary at Wauhatchie Station while marching two divisions three miles north to guard the road to
Kelly's Ferry. On September 28, four brigades of Hood's division exploited the poor
arrangement of Union soldiers and surprised Geary's men by coming from the north
and east. Picket fire began around 10 P.M.; the attack opened in earnest near
midnight. Geary forced his regiments into a "V" to repel assaults that endured for
more than three hours. Reinforcements under Carl Shurz arrived only after the
attack died. Hooker praised Geary effusively: "At one time they had enveloped him
on three sides, under circumstances that would have dismayed any officer except one
endowed with an iron will and the most exalted courage. Such is the character of
General Geary." Even the usually critical Ario Pardee Jr., now commanding the
147th Pennsylvania, admitted, "Gen. Geary will stand in a fair way for his two
stars (for major general). This was his best managed fight—by far, and he deserved credit for it."[10]
     Darkness helped the defense as Confederates, led by Brigadier General Micah
Jenkins, stumbled across the ground. The night that proved a Union ally, however,
also contributed to the loss of Geary's son, Edward, shot through the forehead after
sighting a field piece and yelling "Fire." Southern officers had ordered their sharp-
shooters to fire on the Union artillery men whose muzzle flashes offered the most
revealing targets in the blackness.}*

10. *O.R.*, 31, pt. 1, 94; Johnston, *Dear Pa*, 269.

*   *   *

Hd. Qrs. 2nd Div: 12th A.C. Camp near Wauhatchie
Nov. 2nd 1863

My Dearest Mary

This day five years ago was the day of our union, when our hearts were united in one, as well as our destinies. That happy day is still vivid in my memory, and the joys and sorrows we each have had since then, serve to remind us as of a beautiful fountain from which flows a chrystal stream, but in its course here and there the foul Soil muddys it and destroys its purity. Again it perculates through the sands of time and resumes its wonted beauty. The day is one which will never be forgotten by me, it is a source of unallayed happiness to recognise an annual return. May God grant us many happy returns of it, in which we will mutually share its enjoyment. Were it not for the almost impenetrable gloom which hangs around me since the death of my beloved son, I would enjoy it. Poor dear boy, he is gone, cut down in the bud of his usefulness, but I trust in this chastisement, I may learn to love my dear Savior Jesus Christ, with unallayed devotion, and that through our noble, sainted son's example, I may be brought near to Christ, even within his very fold. Oh my God, I feel this chastisement for the pride I took in him, his rapid development, and general character and ability. None knew him who did not love him. His praise was on every tongue. He had been commissioned Captain in Hampton's Battery about one week previous to his death, and had he survived the action at Wauhatchie, he would now be on his way to the Army of the Potomac. But Alas! We are not alone in grief. Capt. [A. C.] Atwell of the same Battery was mortally wounded, and died yesterday. He leaves a weeping bride and a devoted father. There were but two sections of the Battery present and the killed and wounded were 22 in number. The number of horses lost were 33 out [of] 48.

The Battle was fought on the same ground that Gen. [Andrew] Jackson once obtained a victory over the [Creek] indians [during the War of 1812]. And now it was for a portion of my command numbering at 1200 men to be attacked at midnight by that celebrated Hood's Division of Longstreets Corps numbering over 5,000 men. They came upon us in three heavy columns with great rapidity and with the most demoniacal yell. I instantly brought my men into line and received them as only long of [and] oft tried soldiers can do. At first they outflanked my line on the left and subjected

us to a cross fire from that side. I then turned my artillery upon them in
the rear of my line of infantry and drove them back with great loss in killed
and wounded. Their next attempt was to turn my right and for some time
we were again subjected to a murderous cross fire from that side. This was
the time the battery suffered so severely. With well directed artillery and
rifles, they were again driven and thoroughly defeated. My entire loss is 34
killed and 184 wounded. The enemy's loss is 152 killed—as near as can be
ascertained—763 wounded and considerably over 100 prisoners. I have
gained a great victory and there is none to share the laurels with me. But
oh! how dear it has cost me. My dear beloved boy is the sacrifice [and]
could I but recall him to life, the bubble of military fame might be absorbed by those who wish it. Since the Battle I have been largely reinforced, and I now occupy a line about one mile from the Battle ground of
Wauhatchie, holding the line of communication south of the Tennessee
River. The object of the movement upon which we have been engaged was
to open a line of communication by which our army at Chattanooga would
be fed. At the time we started the main army under Thomas (late Rosecrans) was very nearly starved out and if some plan could not be devised to
get subsistence to Chattanooga, the army must fall back, the consequences
of which no one could foresee, but that it would be exceedingly disastrous
is admitted by all. The task devolved upon us. The Army is now fully
supplied with subsistence and forage, and the men who so nobly perilled
their lives to save the Army, are every where cheered for valorous deeds.
And we are hailed as the saviours of the Army of the Cumberland.

On my way hither about 10 miles above Bridgeport, I encamped at
Shell-mound, a place which takes its name from a large mound on the bank
of the river composed entirely of muscle shells. Another curiosity which
attracted our attention at that place was "Nickajack Cave." Accompanied
by our dear son Eddie I visited it, and viewed one of the most prodigious
grottos known upon the Continent. Within it is a large stream and a beautiful lake of chrystal water. Upon the lake Eddy with a party of friends
penetrated on the lake some three miles and returned much delighted. It
was, indeed, one of the most extensive and beautiful places of the kind I
have ever visited, and would well justify an extended description did I feel
disposed to do so. Some other time perhaps I will, but I cannot now in my
sorrowing condition.

My present position is about 3½ miles from Chattanooga between the
Raccoon and Lookout Mountains, and I am with[in] the range of the enemy's shell, of which they are by no means sparing in showering upon us.

Eddies horse was also killed. Capt. [Moses] Veale [assistant commissary] Telegraphs me from Nashville of his safe arrival there with the *remains* and is probably now at Louisville.

I have the pleasure to acknowledge the receipt of 5 of your letters and one each from you and Willie to Eddy. Alas! he never more will be sensible of your kindness and love. He loved you very greatly—nay almost adored you. Poor Willie is left alone. I hope he will emulate his brother's many virtues and be like him. He has my deep devoted love, and my prayers for his happiness, usefulness, and development, and knowing how well he loved Eddie, I deeply sympathise with him. I wish you to give my love to the Willies and to Pet, and to our other friends. God bless you dear wife & children.

Jno W Geary

* * *

Head-Quarters 2nd Division, 12th Army Corps,
Wauhatchie, Tenn. November 6th 1863

My Dearest Mary

I embrace the opportunity of addressing you, afforded by the departure of the mail. My health is as good as I could reasonably expect it to be under all the circumstances which have surrounded me. An impenetrable gloom hangs over my mind in consequence of the death of my beloved Eddie. His rapid development in every particular, his high attainments and manly deportment, had filled to the brim the cup of paternal pride, and perhaps he was my idol; I feel now that I almost worshipped him, and dwelt more upon the creature than upon the Creator. My grief knows no bounds, but my sense of propriety dictates, that He, who rules the universe knows what is best for us all, that all is dictated by Infinite Wisdom, and I am consequently constrained to say, Our Father, "Thy will be done."

I pray God that this dispensation of His providence may not be lost upon me, or any of us, but that we may be like him, whom we lament, "be not ashamed of Jesus," and that we may acknowledge Him before men and the world, even as we hope He will acknowledge us in presence of the congregated universe when He comes to make up the Jewels of His kingdom. The depth of God's providence is like that of the Ocean—infathomable, and our punishments may be blessings in disguise. Thy will, Oh God, be done.

Fig. 6. Lieutenant Edward R. Geary. The general's son was killed at the battle of Wauhatchie, Tennessee, as he sighted artillery to repel a Confederate attack at night. (U.S. Army Military History Institute, Carlisle Barracks)

The weather here is quite warm and is almost a continued succession of sunshine and showers, indeed it is more like a genial northern spring than anything to which I can liken it.

The situation of the Armies is much the same as it has been since our arrival here. Each is endeavoring to starve out the other, with what success time alone can ultimately determine.

I have nothing new to give you except to say that our camp is between Lookout Mountain and Raccoon range. We are perched on a transverse range and are placing ourselves in a position of defence, which we think we can hold.

Give my kindest love to Willie Geary and Willie Henderson. I hope to hear from them often. Kiss our dear little "Pet," the mutual pledge of our love. Tell her Papa loves her very much. Give my love to Capt & Mary Lee, Mrs. Church & Comfort, and to all our friends and well-wishers. Not forgetting Mr. and Mrs. Longenecker.[11]

I pray that all will be well with you. *Trust in God and all will be well. His will be done.*

I am your true, devoted, and loving husband

In deepest affection
Jno. W. Geary

＊　＊　＊

Wauhatchie, Tenn.   Nov 8th 1863

My Dearest Mary

I take advantage of a few leisure moments to address you once more from this place.

My time has been much occupied in fortifying this position and in making it a fastness which cannot be taken by the enemy without at least a more than severe struggle.

My health since the late battle has not been very good, whether it is from the shock of Edward's death, or from the exposure I have suffered from the unavoidable bad weather, I cannot say. I hope soon to be well again.

The weather has been as mild as May for several days, and as far as I can learn I am unable to discover that it ever becomes very cold here.

I am almost sick of the country, however, and would be glad to be back in the cold snowey north, in the enjoyment of the beloved society of my family.

I have this moment received a telegram from Capt Veale, who took the body of Edward home, that he had delivered it to Dr. Logan[12] for interment. I hope Willie has gone to the funeral. I forgot to instruct the Dr. to telegraph him to do so. Write me all the particulars you can learn relative to the funeral.

I hope all will be done well and with proper care. I hope you have not

---

11. This may be a reference to David Longenecker, a justice of the peace who lived with his wife, Ann, in Geary's former township in Westmoreland County.

12. Samuel Logan, Geary's former assistant surgeon.

attempted to go to the funeral for fear you would be injured by the length of the journey, and the consequent excitement. If we live we will deck his grave with care, and we will make our pilgrimages to it, to weep over the loved, departed one together, and mingle our tears in a common tribute to his memory. "Whom the God's love, die young," is an old proverb and whether there be any thing in the idea or not, it often seems as if there was truth in the remark.

God's judgments are unfathomable, and as it is His will, "God's will be done."

The situation of the Army of the Cumberland has been, and still is, very precaric-us for want of subsistence and forage. The men being upon half rations, and many of the horses are without any thing.[13]

Absent in person, I am with you in spirit. May God bless you and my dear children, bless and preserve you in your approaching trials, and deliver you from its dangers.

Give my deepest love to the boys and "Pet."

Remember me to all others in kindness.

Write me as often as you can, and give me all the remarks in the papers relative to the death of Eddie.

> Ever your loving husband,
> *Jno W Geary*

∗   ∗   ∗

Head Qrs. 2nd Div 12th A.C. Wauhatchie, Tenn.   Nov 10th 1863

My Beloved Mary

It is several days since I have had the pleasure of a letter from you. I know it is not your fault but the uncertainty in the transmission of the mails in this far away and apparently God forsaken country. It would be impossible for me to imagine just another country where such gross ignorance prevails amongst the people, and consequently such gross wickedness and want of propriety of conduct. They have not even houses in the country fit for pig-pens in the north. The citizens are in a starving wretched condi-

---

13. Food and forage became scarce for Federal soldiers in Chattanooga. Before Hooker opened the cracker line, animals had begun to die of starvation. Ario Pardee Jr., of the 147th Pennsylvania, judged that "had the communications remained two days longer as they were before we came up, a retreat would have been inevitable and it must necessarily have proven a disastrous one" (Johnston, *Dear Pa,* 271).

tion. Their animals are dying daily for want of forage, and the want which they experience is in many [instances] transferred to us. The condition of the Rebel Army before us is also a sad one, and indeed, I am informed by deserters who come in daily, and of whom there are many, that the rebel army are in a destitute condition and on very short allowance both for men and animals. As *usual* my command faces the enemy and has the important position of holding the right flank of our army. There must be either a great dislike to myself and Div. or else an overweening confidence in our integrity and ability, else why are such important positions continually intrusted to my care. I leave you and a generous host of friends to decide for me.

The booming of [Confederate] cannon from Lookout Mtn commences with the rising of the sun and continueth until the going down thereof, almost without intermission, yet still we have been so mercifully preserved as not to have received a Single casualty. Occasionally our guns open fire upon the enemy for a few minutes simply for the purpose of shewing the enemy that our army still lives.

Time wears away, and days and nearly weeks have rolled away since the death of Eddy, my dear son, and my grief is only the more settled and poignant. Oh how I miss his smiling face, in the evening, when he came to pay me his accustomed daily visit, when as he would enter my tent, with his face radient with smiles, and his accustomed salutation, "Well, Father." Upon his person I found the *Testament* which you presented to him and which he held in such high estimation. It was his constant companion, upon its sweet promises and consolations he relied under all circumstances, and upon the merits of his chosen Redeemer I feel confidant his soul rests in the bosom of his God.

His trunk containing his little worldly possessions will probably reach here by to-morrow. I will carefully examine and repack it and send it home, with a view if I shall be permitted to return, to embalm each relic with my tears. That they like Preachers may call me to my vows to my God to serve Him only and to devote the remaining portion of my unworthy life to His Divine service.

I have seen the evidences of your love to Eddy, and I assure you it has exalted and enobled you in my eyes beyond price.

May Gods choicest blessing rest upon you and all the children is my devoted prayer.

Your true soldier, but I trust Christian husband
Jno W Geary

* * *

Wauhatchie, Tenn.   Nov 14th 1863

My Dearest Mary

Your kind letter of the 6th instant came to hand yesterday. It was written in usual cheerful stile, and I wished you could remain in blissful ignorance of the great loss we have sustained in the melancholy death of Eddy. But there is no use of uttering such a desire, as it would certainly be a matter of respo[n]sibility to prevent your sooner or later knowing the sad reality. My affairs are somewhat embarassed and I hope in the present uncertain state of things you will do me the kindness not to make any unnecessary expenditure for mourning. I intend if spared to have a suitable monument erected to his memory as soon as possible.[14] This will be more gratification than senseless expenditures for clothing by which to let the world know how much we loved him.

My heart is nearly broken, and I care not for the adulation that so splendid a victory as that of "*Wauhatchie*" brings me, when my noble boy is lost at what a fearful price is glory obtained, its path but leads to the grave.

I dwell too much upon the subject, but his wounds have preached more to my heart than all the clergymen in the world ever could and it has touched a chord which I trust will never cease to vibrate. I mean that it has brought me to a closer walk with God, upon whom I will rely in every emergency that can arise even to death itself. May God bless the germinating blossom in my heart and soul, and cause it to grow up and magnify exceedingly, like seed cast upon good ground, and that it may produce an hundred fold, rendering more pleasant the life that now is, and that which is to come truly happy.

Our position remains unchanged with reference to the enemy. I am strongly entrenching my command, and I think can defend myself against largely superior numbers. Maj Genl [William Tecumseh] Sherman's command numbering 30,000 men are expected here in 3 days.[15] What movements will take place I am unable to state.

14. Edward Ratchford Geary lies next to his mother, Margaret, in Delmont Presbyterian Cemetery, a block from Route 66 in Westmoreland County. The father made good on his promise to mark the site with a suitable stone, which stretches roughly to head high.

15. The Fifteenth Corps, listed on October 31, 1863, as having a strength of 33,762, had only 23,442 present for duty. On October 27, Major General John A. Logan assumed command of the corps as Sherman took on the responsibilities for the Army of the Tennessee.

I have also to acknowledge the receipt of a long letter from Captain Lee, for which I ask you to thank him, and say that I will reply to it soon. The deed I executed as directed, which I hope has reached you ere this.[16]

Give my kindest love to the Willies and Pet. Also to Mary Lee, and all the rest of our relatives. I hope Willie Geary will see the necessity of writing to me more frequently. He is now my oldest son, and I must rely much upon his nobleness and manhood to compensate me for the heavy dispensation we have received. God bless and care for each and every member of my beloved family.

Ever your loving husband
Jno. W. Geary

*　*　*

Wauhatchie, Tenn.　Nov 17th 1863

My Dearest Mary

I am just in receipt of your dear kind letter of the 2nd instant, in which you fully renew the vows of our marital day. Five years have indeed rolled away almost without my knowledge or consent. In our marriage all has been happy, not a single event has occurred to make me rue the day which made us one. You have, however, grown more lovely in my eyes as time and circumstances have developed your many kindnesses and virtues. Circumstances over which I had no control, have left us poor, and were it not for your sake and for the sake of those whom God has yet spared to my care, I would rather rejoice at it than regret it. I have seen much affliction and suffered much, but God has thus far been extremely merciful, he has spared my life and health, and drawn me I trust forever into a closer walk with Him. In my present position, I can fully realize the position and feelings of the Psalmist, when in the morning I rise from my lowly bed. He said as I can say, "*I laid me down and slept, & have awaked, for thou Oh God sustainedst me,*" &c.

The death of my dear Eddie makes me sad and gloomy, and nothing keeps me up but the deep responsibilities which surround me on every side. Time may wear much of this away, but never can I forget my darling boy. His memory will ever be a sweet spot on my mind, and upon which I will dwell ever with a melancholy pleasure.

---

16. Benjamin F. Lee had arranged the sale of Geary's farm in Westmoreland County for $4,500.

Troops are still convening at and near Chattanooga. And it is reasonable to suppose that some active work will ere long take place.

Genl. Sherman's Corps is just arriving—it numbers, I am informed, in all about 30,000, of which about 15,000 are with him. Considerable cannonading took place on our left flank to[-]day, but I have not heard the result.

Desertions from the enemy are very numerous, and from all that I can learn the Army of Gen. Bragg is in a very bad condition. The whole country seems to be in a state of Starvation.

The health of my command is very good, probably never better. Since I whipped Longstreet, he has left my front and gone to try his hand on Burnside [at Knoxville, Tennessee]. He was replaced by Gen Cheatham, who has resigned and Gen. Stevenson is now in his place.[17]

Give my love to the dear boys and beloved little Pet.

I pray God for your safety and trial—may it have a happy termination.

Ever your loving husband
Jno W Geary

*   *   *

Hd. Qrs. 2nd Div 12th A.C.   Wauhatchie, Tenn.   Nov. 23rd 1863

My Dearest Mary

It is several days since I heard from you last. The irregularity of the mail is so great that it is with great difficulty we can get any news of the exterior world at all. I have not even had a letter from Dr. or William Logan on the subject of the interment of our dear sainted Edward. I had a letter, however, to-day from my pastor and friend Dr. McFarren,[18] who seems most deeply afflicted by the circumstances and does not fail to call to memory the following circumstances, viz: that the marriage ceremony of myself was performed by him, that Margaret A.[19] had first made a profes-

---

17. Major General Benjamin F. Cheatham attended a conference that President Davis conducted with the general officers of the Army of Tennessee after the battle of Chickamauga to air complaints about General Braxton Bragg. When Davis retained Bragg, who heard the criticism at the meeting, Cheatham believed his position was compromised. On October 31 he asked to be relieved and reassigned. Secretary of War James A. Seddon convinced Cheatham to return to the army. Brigadier General John K. Jackson took temporary command of the division—not Major General Carter L. Stevenson, who also led a division within the army.

18. The Rev. Samuel M. McFarren, a Presbyterian clergyman who oversaw congregations at Congruity Presbyterian Church in Salem Township, and in New Alexandria, Westmoreland County.

19. Geary's first wife, Margaret A. Logan.

sion of religion and dedicated herself to the service of God in his church. That he had baptized Edward. That he had communed with him. That he had officiated at the funeral of Margaret A. and now performed the same sad office to our beloved son. What a number of singular circumstances to be performed by the same man. He tenders to me much consolation, & good advice, calculated to lead to profit if we can only apply it to our real necessities. He inculcates the idea, that rather than mourn him as lost to us, we should accustom ourselves to look upon him as only having gone before us to that blest abode, that house not made with hands, whose builder and maker is God eternal in the heavens, where we, firmly relying upon the merits of Jesus Christ, may hope to meet him, and whose chief joy will be to welcome us among the holy angels in heaven.

The scenes around us are anything but peaceful. My troops have been in line of battle for two days. The roar of artillery & the rattle of musketry do not cease from morning's dawn to the latest gleam of evening. We have just been reinforced by Gen Sherman's Corps from the Mississippi, numbering 20,000 men.

Today I am in command of two divisions, and if the fight comes off, my command will perform an important part of the transaction. I will try to keep you constantly advised [of] my movements.

I feel the deepest solicitude for you as your time approaches and I pray God's kind protection for you. Have me duly informed of the results as soon as they take place.

Remember [me] in love to the *boys* and *Pet*. Mrs. Logan,[20] if with you, Comfort and Mrs. Church, John & family, & Frank and Mary Lee.

Remember me to the Feeman family, John Lee's and others.

> With deepest devotion I am your loving and true husband
> *Jno. W. Geary*

P.S. I send the key of Eddy's trunk. The trunk will go by Adams Express line: it is enclosed in a box marked to you

*   *   *

{Grant was not content merely with opening supply lines; he also looked for ways to regain the initiative. He sent Hooker with three divisions (roughly 12,000 men) to sweep aside two brigades of Confederates guarding Lookout Mountain southwest of

20. Eliza Logan, grandmother to Eddie.

Chattanooga, and then launched the bulk of his force against the Confederates on Missionary Ridge east of the city. At dawn on November 24, Geary left Wauhatchie Station in command of 4,000 men to climb the steep, wooded slopes of Lookout Mountain. Federal soldiers secured the summit by early afternoon; Confederates withdrew that night. Geary's first extended letter after the battle bragged, "This feat will be celebrated until time shall be no more." But he accomplished the "feat" against a far inferior force. A newspaper correspondent who witnessed the event wrote about the "Battle above the Clouds" after the war: "I wish to say once and for all on this subject that no engagement of the war was so magnified in public as this so-called 'Battle above the Clouds.' In those days it scarcely rose to the dignity of a battle. It was nothing but a magnificent skirmish from beginning to end."[21]

On November 25, Geary's men marched to the Federal lines attacking Missionary Ridge. Arriving late in the day, the 2nd Division reached the top by roughly 6 P.M. For the next two days, the men chased Bragg's army, skirmishing with the rear guard of Breckinridge's Corps at Pea Vine Creek on November 26, and then with Cleburne's Division at Ringgold on November 27. While the White Star Division sustained 138 casualties on Lookout Mountain, Ringgold cost another 203. The general bragged about repelling the enemy at this last fight, but the Confederates clearly did their job of blunting the Federal chase and protecting the retreating army.}

*   *   *

ATLANTIC AND OHIO TELEGRAPH LINES

Dated at: RINGGOLD, GEORGIA   NOV 27 1863
To: MRS. JNO. W. GEARY, NEW CUMBERLAND PA.

I AM WELL.

JNO. W. GEARY

*   *   *

Hd. Qrs. 2nd Div: 12th Army Corps   Wauhatchie, Tenn.
Dec 4th 1863

My Dearest Mary

I received your kind letter of the 25th of November, on the battle field of Ringgold, Geo. from which place I sent you a few lines in pencil, not,

---

21. Benjamin P. Thomas, ed., *Three Years with Grant: As Recalled by War Correspondent Sylvanus Cadwallader* (New York, 1956), 146–47.

however, in reply to it, but simply for the purpose of keeping you informed
of my whereabouts and of my welfare. The battle of Wauhatchie was one of
the most important to the welfare of our nation that has occurred during
the war, and a failure on our part would have entailed upon it the direst
calamities. The situation of the Army of the Cumberland was as follows, at
the time of our arrival. The enemy had possession of the entire south bank
of the Tennessee River, of the Memphis and Charleston Rail Road, and of
all the roads upon which subsistence would be transported to Chattanooga
except one through the interior of Tennessee, which had become perfectly
impassible to waggons. To subsist the army, therefore, at Chattanooga was
impossible unless something could be done to dislodge the enemy from the
south side of the river. Longstreet was in command there, and the prestige
of his name alone was almost sufficient for its defence. Our army was living
on *one-fourth* rations. The whole amount on hand was, *one full ration*. Had
we not succeeded, in opening the navigation it is easy to see, that our army
must evacuate Chattanooga from necessity. The calamities which would
undoubtedly have followed, it is impossible to describe. It would have
involved the loss of all artillery and transportation, and for want of subsistence our Army would have had to scatter over the country to procure a
forced subsistence and in such a demoralized condition as to become an easy
prey to the enemy. Our army thus destroyed, would not under the best of
circumstances been able to take a stand short of Murfreesboro, or Nashville.
The rebels would have been encouraged,—Our people depressed,—and the
question arises, could we have raised another army, to regain what we
would have lost. The successful battle of Wauhatchie solved the question.
And has been pregnant with results, viz: The navigation opened. The army
fed and impending danger removed. But alas! A portion of the price paid
for these essential benefits, was the precious life of our own inestimable
Eddie, brave spirit, it rests in the bosom of his Saviour and his God. I am
bereaved and transformed. Like the tiger robbed of his whelps, I have been
like a destroying angel ever since, no height has been too bold, no valley
too deep, no fastness too stormy, that I did not solicit to be permitted to
storm. Permission was granted, and with the assistance of bold hearts and
willing hands, I have been the instrument of Almighty God, of carrying
terror and *terrible destruction* wherever it has pleased God to direct my foot-
steps. Under such impulses I stormed, what was considered the impassible
and inaccessible heights of Lookout Mountain, I captured it, turned the
right flank of Bragg's army and drove him from his position. This feat will
be celebrated until time shall be no more.

Next day came the battle of Missionary Ridge upon which Bragg concentrated his whole army declaring his position impregnable. From this
too, toiling up the steep ascent, we drove him like chaff before the wind.
We came near capturing both Bragg & [Major General John C.] Breckinridge. We took the son of the latter, a captain upon his father's staff.[22]

Next day came the Battle of Pea-vine Valley. The day following came
the battle of Ringgold. All glorious victories. I burnt the town of Ringgold
because the enemy fired upon us from the houses.[23] It contained about 5000
inhabitants and was a beautiful place. I have returned to this place to
recuperate my command after their arduous and terrible labors. I feel that I
have performed my duty. Whether the nation will recognise my services or
not I cannot say. I have won promotion over and over, and it has come not,
such may be the case again. I am indifferent upon that subject. But we
betide the rebels whenever I can get my hands on them.[24]

I suppose that your period has about expired and I daily hope to hear it
is successfully finished. May God sustain you through all your trials, my
darling, and bring you safely through. Put your trust in Him and He will
not desert you. Give my warmest love to the *Willies* and *Pet*. Also to all
kind friends. God bless you all

Your true and faithful husband
Jno. W. Geary

22. J. Cabell Breckinridge, a lieutenant, was captured by men of the 9th Iowa, which was in the 2nd
Brigade, 1st Division, of Sherman's Army of the Tennessee. Geary often used "we" in a vague way that made
it appear as if his troops participated in action when they did not.

23. There is a discrepancy here between what Geary told Mary and what appeared in his official report,
where he made no mention of destroying civilian property but highlighted military targets such as mills,
tanneries, and factories.

24. Geary's analysis of this chase demonstrates either his lack of understanding of military objectives or
his desire to put the best spin possible on a mediocre effort. At Ringgold, Confederate Major General
Patrick Cleburne's men fought stubbornly to protect the army, which they did by forcing Geary's men to
stand and fight. The Confederates successfully shielded the retreat and punished the pursuers. This lessened
Grant's already low estimation of Hooker, whose days in the army would be numbered.

*　*　*

Head-Quarters 2nd Division, 12th Army Corp
Wauhatchie, Tenn.　Decem 12th 1863

My Dearest Mary

I have the pleasure to acknowledge the receipt of your letters bearing date "Nov. 20th" with Willie Geary's enclosed of Nov 23rd and of Dec 2nd. Thus you will perceive that after a time and a manner your favors came to light. Please accept my kindest thanks for the frequent missiles you send me. They are more frequent than I can under the circumstances hereafter expect. I burn all your letters immediately after reading them, for one can scarcely tell whose hands they might fall into and be read without the appreciation which they receive from me. We have just had a pageant of exquisite military beauty. The 29th Regt Pa. Vols. has re-enlisted under the order authorising Veteran Regiments and in consequence they have received a furlough as a Regt to go to Penna. and recruit maximum numbers.[25]

The whole division was turned out to give them the parting ceremonies, which I assure you were very imposing. You will doubtless hear and read much of them during their trip, and I mention the matter in order that you may understand it, and know that they are a portion of the heroic troops of the "White Star" Division.

The rainey season is just setting in here, and rains as if Noah's flood was about to be re-enacted. The roads are muddy, the streams overflowing their banks, and our campaign seems to have a veto placed upon its further progress by the hand of nature. But we think we have marched enough, and fought enough to entitle us to a little rest. If man will not give it, nature will.

In your next tell me what is thought of the victories in the West, and of the wonderful part my command has had to perform in them. Are our efforts appreciated?

25. The War Department anticipated the large amount of three-year enlistments that would expire in the summer and fall of 1864 by attempting to entice as many men as possible to enlist during the winter, when combat activity typically declined. Generals could offer immediate, thirty-day furloughs to units in which most of the men reenlisted—a considerable attraction with Christmas a short time away. These units then were designated "Veteran Volunteers." About 136,000 veterans decided to remain in the field. For the implications of this for the Army of the Potomac, see *O.R.*, 29, pt. 2, 556–58. On the policy in general, see James W. Geary, *We Need Men: The Union Draft in the Civil War* (DeKalb, Ill., 1991), 112–13.

I pray God that you are happily relieved from your burdens and pains, and that your happiness is complete in the addition to our family of a perfect babe. Dear little unseen one, I love it though unknown as to sex, or even as to its existence. Do keep me advised as to the course of events. You know I am all anxious to know results, perhaps as much as you are to know them after a severe battle in which you know I have been engaged. I constantly pray God for your safety.

Longstreet and Bragg have both been driven from East Tennessee,[26] the supplies rebeldom were accustomed to receive from this granary of the West are now fully cut off, and there is a fine chance for starvation down in "Dixie." The chances for peace should, if we were fighting a reasonable people[,] be good, for they are certainly a whipped people, but are too proud to acknowledge it. Pride "the never failing vice of fools" can only prolong the war. I hope sincerely the days of peace are near, when we can beat our swords into pruning hooks, and return to the benign pursuits of peace, and the nurture of our families. My health is good, but as usual with me when transferred to a Southern climate I have some diarrhoeah. The health of my command is generally good, and all our wounded are doing well.

I am still deeply distressed for the loss of our noble, sainted boy. My heart grieves deeply, and I plunge into every duty to keep from thinking of it and letting it overpower me. My dear Eddie is gone, and cannot be restored to me. What a terrible thought, and I am only consoled by the reflection that as he cannot come to me, I hope to go to him, when we shall be re-united forever in heaven through the intercession of Christ our Savior.

When Willie and Mrs. Logan come to Cumberland, you will not be so lonesome. I have just had a letter from William Logan in which he fully describes the funeral of Eddie, and deeply laments the circumstances of you and Willie not being present at the funeral and lays all the blame upon the telegraph agents, where I am sure it belongs, and under the circumstances what cannot be cured, had better be endured with a good grace.

---

26. In early November, Bragg detached Longstreet with 17,000 men to attack Burnside in East Tennessee. Maneuvers ended with the Confederates besieging Burnside at Knoxville, but a weakly coordinated attack on November 29 against the Union's Fort Sanders stymied Longstreet, who withdrew from the area on December 4. He had suffered 813 casualties, as compared with Burnside's 13. Longstreet remained in Tennessee for the winter but was not a factor there; his men returned to the Army of Northern Virginia in March 1864.

Give my love to all friends. Kiss Pet and the boys for me. Remember me to Mr. & Mrs. Feeman.

God bless you my dearest one

Believe me your loving husband
Jno W Geary

*   *   *

Hd. Qrs. 2nd Div 12th A.C.   Wauhatchie Tenn.   Dec 19th 1863

My Dearest Mary

I have received your letters up to Dec 9th and have written to you as frequently as we have had departing mails, most of which I presume reach you after reasonable delay.

Accept my thanks for your constant and unfailing letters, they have come forward daily almost at a period when I supposed you would not be able to write. But it is probable that your troubles are over by this time and I hope you will soon be able to resume your correspondence with your wanted energy and promptitude. God grant I may be correct in my conclusions. I am very anxious to hear from you as a matter of course, and the tediousness and uncertainty of the mails are very perplexing.

I have not written to you for two days, because there was no mail leaving, and because I have been so closely engaged in preparing my report of the part taken by my Division in the recent great battles, which of course must be done as early as possible for the information of the Generals Commanding, the President & Congress.

Most of my command are re-enlisting as veterans, and in that matter much of my time is occupied. All this together with the regular routine business of the Division occupy my time very thoroughly. My health is good, there being no time for getting sick that I have been able to discover.

I am notwithstanding still very lonesome. No more the smiling face, and the pleasant voice of my dear Eddie gladdens my heart, and when I am not overwhelmed in oceans of business, I am truly sorrowful. It is true God has given me victory wherever I have directed my arms, and all have a word of praise, still I cannot enjoy or appreciate it as I once would have done for his sake who no more rejoices when I rejoice, and whose congratulations in the hour of victory can never more be given, but "Thy will oh God, be done."

I hope to hear from Willie soon. Tell him to practice the virtues of his deceased brother, and "remember his Creator in the days of his youth," so that when he comes to die, he will not have cause to regret that he ever lived.

Give him and Willie H. my kindest love. Kiss "Pet" and tell her to read all her little prattles with pleasure which mama pleases to record.

Trusting you in the hands of Him who has promised to sustain you in your sorrows, I subscribe myself your loving husband

J.W.G.

* * *

Wauhatchie Tenn.   December 20th 1863

My Dearest Mary

I have just recd Capt Lee's telegram announcing "Mrs. Geary has a *daughter*, mother & child doing well," which I assure you relieved me from a long period of deep anxiety concerning you. I drew a long breath, much freer and deeper than before, and of course feel happy in accepting God's gift. I congratulate you on your successful accouchment, and hope you will soon be recovered safe and sound. I would like to know what Mary thinks of the little stranger, is she pleased or jealous? Well, I suppose she will be writing for a name for her as well as for her *baby* and her *bird*, and in my opinion it may just as well be settled at once as not, so let the agony on that question be settled at once.

I had a *mother*. She was one of the best women that ever lived. I am her youngest son. She loved me most tenderly, and that love was warmly reciprocated. No recognition of her name has taken place, and I now feel disposed to do so by naming this child after so beloved and Christian a person. Also my former wife's name was the same as that of my mother, and she too can thus be remembered. We may therefore make the name "Margaret," "Margaret Anne," or "Margaret Angeline," any one of which will be satisfactory to me.[27] If she will only be as good a woman as either of those named, we will never [have] cause to regret her birth, or blush for her faults. May God's blessing rest upon her in infancy and in her maturer life is my most sincere prayer.

27. The couple chose "Margaret Anne."

Write me all the particulars about our domestic affairs and particularly about the all important one that has just transpired. We receive very few newspapers here and consequently we are in a sort of out of the way place or backwoods where the sun of intelligence has never yet beamed, and where it has been the pleasure of the Southern Aristocracy to obscure the mental vision of the people in every possible manner. Truly darkness prevails, like that which prevailed upon the face of the great deep at the Creation and will continue to do so until this "cruel war" is terminated in the peaceful restoration of the Union.

I suppose by this time Willie Geary has returned. If so, tell him I request him to write as frequently to me as he can, especially during your confinement. Let me know how Henderson Willie, likes the stranger. I expect he will have some original sayings about it.

Tell Mary since you have got another baby that she shall be my baby, and that she and I will be the great friends hereafter. I don't think she will want any baby now, since little Maggie's arrival, she will have enough to do to nurse and take care of her.

I am still overwhelmed with business, and I am glad of it, as it in some measure alleviates my grief for the loss of my dear Eddie. I never, never will forget the devoted love I bore to him, for truly it was equal to any love I have ever enjoyed. I commit you to the care of our Heavenly Father, hoping He will restore you to your wonted health. Give love to all the children. Kiss them and don't forget little Mag

In love yours
Jno W Geary

∗   ∗   ∗

Hd. Qrs. 2nd Div: 12th A.C.   Wauhatchie, Tenn.   Dec 25th 1863

My Dearest Mary

I have just returned from a tour of observation with Gen Hooker on Lookout Mountain, we passed over the route upon which my Division made its famous charge on that far-famed mountain. I am very much fatigued, and cannot write you a long epistle. The day has been very pleasant and I think pleasantly and profitably spent. My health is very good, and my mind has been much relieved since the receipt of your letter of the 16th and Capt Lee's subsequent telegram.

The 28th P.V. leaves here tomorrow for Penna on furlough of 30 days.
I enclose you my likeness. Kiss the babies. God bless you all.

Ever yours
Jno. W. Geary

* * *

Hd. Qrs. 2nd Div: 12th A.C.   Bridgeport Post, Ala.
Jany 10th 1864

My Dearest Mary

I feel quite lost for the want of your faithful correspondence, since your confinement. It is true that, I have heard from you two or three times by Capt Lee's letters, and although they are all good enough in their way, still they are not as Graphic as though they have emanated from your pen. You know the news I desire to hear in the particulars of circumstances on which he could not write. Well I thank God it is all over and hope you will soon be restored to your wonted health and circumstances, and I hope also for the successful *entray* into the world of our dear little "Maggie."

I am now *"Commandante"* of this post, and I wish I was out of it for it is one of the most corrupt places I have ever seen. It requires much firmness and unflinching integrity and ability to administer affairs here, and you know, where I have the honor to command, *all must obey*.

The weather set in extremely cold on the 1st instant, and the ground has been frozen several inches in depth ever since. The mountains are white with snow. The whole idea of "Sunny South" is exploded, and much of the poetic idea of Southern beauty is with us fully exploded. It is a humbug and a false-hood, and a lie which this war has fully exploded. Southern greatness was always a humbug in my opinion, and more so now than ever before.

My health is good, and if it were not for my inconsoleable loneliness since the death of our dear Eddie I would in other respects feel comfortable. But we must be content with our lot, whatever, that lot may be.

I hope you will be out of bed before this reaches you, and be in the enjoyment of your usual health. Give my love and kisses to the children, and believe me as ever truly your loving and devoted husband

Jno. W. Geary

*   *   *

"Burnett House"   Cincinnati Ohio   Feby 13th 1864

My Dearest Mary

I arrived here safely in precisely 30 hours after I bade you adieu, making a distance of 750 miles, or 27½ miles an hour. The trip of course was monotonous as all rail road trips are. I met with a gentleman or two of former acquaintance which aided in passing the time without ennui.

I expect to leave here to-morrow on the Louisville Mail Steam Boat, and expect to take cars at Louisville at 7 a.m. and proceed to Bridgeport without delay on Monday.

I have nothing new to communicate, but I thought if you feel as badly as I do about leaving home, you would be pleased to hear from me, of my welfare & whereabouts.

As I did not sleep any last night I will bid you *"anoche bueno,"* and retire to my couch without delay.

I am very well.

Ever and truly
Your loving and devoted husband
Jno. W. Geary

*   *   *

Hd. Qrs. 2nd Division 12th A.C.   Bridgeport, Ala.
Feby 18th 1864

My Dearest Mary

I arrived at this place yesterday in good health but much fatigued from my long journey.

From Cincinnati I took passage on a Steam Mail Packet to Louisville, the "General Lytle," one of the finest boats I ever saw. I travelled upon her 150 miles, had dinner, supper, lodging, and breakfast, all for the enormous sum of *three dollars*. This was the most pleasant portion of my journey. At 7 a.m. on Monday I took passage on the Rail road for Nashville, dined at "Cave City" near the Mouth of Mammoth Cave, Ky. and arrived at Nashville at 5 p.m. just one hour after the train had departed for Bridgeport.

Thus I was compelled to remain there 23 hours. During the day I called upon Maj Gen Grant, and had quite a prolonged interview with him. He will not suffer himself to be made a candidate for the presidency, and says he will not give one thought about the subject but will devote himself exclusively to the spring campaign, and thinks he can break up the rebellion within six months from the present time, also that he prefers being a Major Genl in the U.S. Army to the presidency.

I next called upon Maj Gen Rosseau, the Commandante of the City.[28]

Finding I had more time than I could well dispose of I determined to pay a visit to Mrs. Polk. She received me with great warmth and cordiality. At the Outer Gate I was met by an old negro who officiated at the White House when Mr. Polk was president,[29] who bade me "Welcome," as I "looked like a good *conservative* gentleman" "like his good old Master who was dead and gone." Mrs. Polk received me as I stated above with highest respect, and told me she always regarded me as one of Mr. Polk's best friends in Penna and even chided me for not having called to see her when passing through the city previously. She inquired particularly for my family. I told her that you were a daughter of one of Mr. Polk's staunchest friends in Pa.[30] She seemed much interested in everything I told her, and she presented me with a photograph of her residence and of herself for your special benefit. The picture of the house and grounds embraces the tomb of the Ex president. She made many expressions of extreme unconditional loyalty, of which I took notice as she had been represented as somewhat rebellious in the early part of the war. I left her with the receipt of many invitations to repeat the visit and to bring you to see her too.

The tomb of Mr. Polk has the following inscription:

(1st side.)   "The mortal remains
                                            of
                                James Knox Polk
                        are resting in the vault beneath.
                        He was born in Mechlenburg Co.
                                North Carolina

28. Major General Lovell Harrison Rousseau commanded the districts of Nashville and Tennessee from November 1863 through the end of the war.

29. Polk's longtime personal servant Elias was a wedding gift from Sarah Polk's father.

30. Mary's father, Robert R. Church, had no extraordinary political positions, but did have ties with the Democratic Party through his wife's family, relatives of William Bigler, Democratic governor of Pennsylvania in 1851 and a U.S. Senator from 1855 to 1861.

And emigrated with his father
Samuel Polk to Tennessee
in 1806
The beauty of virtue was illustrated
in his life,— The excellence of
Christianity was exemplified in his death."

(2nd side.) "His life was devoted to the public service. He was elected successively to the first places in the State and Federal Governments; a member of the General Assembly; a member of Congress, and chairman of the most important Congressional committees; Speaker of the House of Representatives; Gov. of Tennessee, and President of the United States.["]

(3rd side.) "By his public policy he defended, established and extended the boundaries of his country.

He planted the laws of the American Union on the shores of the Pacific. His influence and counsel tended to organize the National Treasury on the principles of the Constitution, and to apply the rules of freedom and navigation to Trade and Industry."

Among other things I told Mrs. Polk that I had ordered the house in which she was born to be photographed, and that you had a copy in your album. "Oh," she said, "tell her something better than all that. I was married in it too, and that more than 40 years ago." So I suppose she is upward of 60 years of age.

Time rolled around and after a hard night's travel in a crowded car I reached this place nearly frozen. The weather is very cold here. I found my staff all present except Capt [W. T.] Forbes [acting assistant inspector-general] now in N. York. I was very warmly received by the command and seranaded by the bands in the evening.

But Oh! There is a vacancy still. My dear Eddie is not here, and my very heart is indeed full of loneliness. The thought of home, and bosom-partners, and dear ones of the fireside, all cannot be forgotten and I must to my lonely little couch repair. God's choicest blessings on you all is the devoted prayer of your loving husband. Give my love to the boys, to Capt Lee and Mary. Kiss the two little Pets.

Ever and devotedly yours
Jno. W. Geary

*   *   *

Bridgeport Ala.   Feby 27th 1864

My Dearest Mary

I have the pleasure to acknowledge the receipt of your first letter and Willie's &c., after my departure. I am glad to learn that Willie is nearly well, and that the rest of the boys and girls are well. I have felt very lonely since I left home and hardly know how to exist away from the endearments of home and wife and children. Indeed I feel the loss of our dear Eddie more poignantly than before I left for home and the realization of his death is greater than ever.

My health is good, but I am exceedingly busy watching for the raids with which this place is almost constantly threatened by John Morgan and his ilk, for if they do come they will be received with the highest *military honors,* and with a warmth he has seldom or perhaps never felt.

Considerable Skirmishing has already taken place near Ringgold and South of that place. Longstreet is said to have left the neighborhood of Knoxville. Sherman is pushing on towards Mobile, and we cannot yet tell exactly what will be done or where the next blows will be struck.[31]

Every preparation is being made for a vigorous spring campaign, which if successful in proportion to its magnitude will grind out the rebellion in *toto.*

Give my love to the Willies. Kiss "Mary" and "Mag." Remember me in friendship to Capt Lee and all kind friends. I regret to hear that Mary Lee has had the measles so badly, but hope she is well. Give her my love.

I am as ever truly and lovingly
yr faithful husband
Jno W Geary

*   *   *

Hd. Qrs.   Bridgeport, Ala.   March 1st 1864

My Dearest Mary

We have had two very rainey days, yesterday and to-day, it may be the commencement of the spring rainey season which the inhabitants say is about to begin, if so, what a wet time we shall have!

---

31. These observations were premature. Sherman was with his army in Mississippi, attempting to decide what to do next. Grant and others had designs on the important port city of Mobile, Alabama, but a movement there would be delayed in favor of other strategy.

I received your letter of the 24th ult. to-day, and I am extremely grateful for the kind information you have given me about the family and about our pecuniary business. How thankful we should be to Him who rules all things for the remarkable degree of health which every member of our family enjoys, for their fine appearance and their nobleness of character and mind. I think our children are all far above *mediocre* in the latter respect, and will mature to infinitely better advantage than many who appear more precautious [precocious] and who are possessed of superior advantages. I do not flatter myself on this subject, but I mention it as a subject of thankfulness. I hope we will never grumble against Providence so long as we still enjoy so many blessings from His hands as we do.

Your kind and loving words are not lost upon me but are duly appreciated and remembered. I feel deeply and keenly the deprivation to which I am submitting for our country's cause, and if *honor* would permit I would soon be in the enjoyment of the loved ones at home. But I think I know your refined nature would not respect me so much if I yielded *duty to love*. That while you part with me tears still you would not respect me so highly if I yielded duty implicitly to love and domesticity. 'Tis hard that it must be so. 'Tis a bitter cup, but cannot be passed away, not even if we wish to maintain our own self-respect.

Coming events cast their shadows all around us in the South-west, and if we can judge aright from the movements of our Armies, some blow must soon be struck which if successful, (and I have no doubt it will be so) will break the backbone of Rebeldom.[32] God grant it may be so and that the benign influences of peace may soon and forever extend through out the land.

Give my love to all the boys and girls about the house.

Write me soon about the amount you have paid out and how the money holds. After which I will be able to send you a *draft*.

Ever your loving husband

J W G

---

32. Geary likely referred to the Red River Campaign (March–May 1864) conducted by Union Major General Nathaniel P. Banks. Accompanied by gunboats under Admiral David D. Porter, Banks headed upriver for Shreveport, Louisiana, a supply depot and important city for access to Texas. Lincoln hoped to gain cotton and pledges of loyalty from planters in the area, but the effort failed because of bungling on the part of Banks.

* * *

Hd. Qrs. 2nd Div 12th A.C.   Bridgeport, Ala.   March 4th 1864

My Dearest Mary

Your long, kind, loving and excellent letter of Feby 25th is received—please accept my warmest thanks for your many kind expressions of love and respect, and be assured that they are all fully warmly and enthusiastically reciprocated. I have just finished a long letter to Dr. McFarren of Westmoreland Co. in reply to one written by him to me on the death of Edward. His was replete with the consolations of religion and most devoted friendship. I intend to write to Revd Mr. Milligan in order to express the high sense of gratitude I owe to him for the excellent Obituary. These things require a good deal of time and attention, but are the essential parts of the etiquette of life.

We have had considerable rainey weather lately here and the Tennessee River is now nearly bankfull, and may soon overflow. It is still raining and we are at present having a severe storm of wind.

The Climate is very mild, the frogs are chirping in every pond. The birds are carrolling most delightfully from every tree and rendering the valley vocal. The buds are bursting forth on every tree and many of them will be in bloom in a fortnight. All nature seems to be inclined to be peaceful, and to multiply and replenish the earth, each after its kind, and man alone is making preparations for the destruction of his race. O horrid treason, accursed ambition, which would destroy the last hope of human liberty and blast the hopes of untold millions, for one short hour's gratification and success.

God grant the war may soon be over, human rights vindicated, and our country saved.

I have sent the children several papers lately. Let me know if they appreciate them.

Remember me in love and kisses. Give my respects to Capt Lee and my love to Mary.

Send me an account of the debts you have paid, and as soon as the Paymaster arrives I will send you some money.

With deepest devotion I am as ever your loving and

faithful husband
Jno. W. Geary

5

The Atlanta Campaign
March–September 1864

{*The campaigns in spring 1864 contained enormous potential for ending the war. Northerners hoped Grant would crush Lee in the East. If not immediately force the South to surrender, success on the battlefield would sustain morale and ensure Lincoln's election. Southerners knew their best hope for independence lay in a protracted conflict that eroded Northern will. Recently promoted to general-in-chief of the United States, Grant planned simultaneous advances in all the theaters of war to take advantage of Federal numbers and pin Robert E. Lee's army in Virginia. Overseeing operations in the Tennessee-Georgia theater, William Tecumseh Sherman prepared to leave Chattanooga and head for the rail center of Atlanta.*

The western campaign progressed differently from the cataclysmic struggle between Lee and Grant in Virginia. The march produced few big battles, but the months between April and September 1864, as Geary's letters indicate, featured continual reconnaissance, skirmishing, and small engagements in which people died as readily as in the more spectacular actions. All told, the 2nd Division sustained 2,527 casualties (331 dead) in the ten brushes with the enemy leading to the capture of Atlanta on September 1. Geary told Mary that the campaign "was indeed but one grand battle, one grand victory from beginning to its end."

The campaign boosted Geary's morale. In the relative inactivity before it began, he worried about the "moral malaria" within the army and felt so homesick that he briefly entertained resigning. Also, the lack of recognition via promotion to major general bothered him. A sense of duty, heightened by the knowledge that quitting would hurt his political aspirations, convinced him to stay. Activity pushed such thoughts aside, especially when it appeared that the coming battles might well end the conflict.}

* * *

Hd. Qrs. 2nd Div 12th A.C.   Bridgeport Ala   March 19th 1864

My Dearest Mary

Your very kind and excellent letter of the 8th inst is received. Please accept my thanks for your graphic description of the children's excitement and pleasure on the receipt of the *pictorials* patterns &c. Keep them always assured that they are never forgotten even in the strife of the battle-field. I will send Mary Lee some patterns next time, which I hope will be satisfactory. It is always very pleasant to learn of happiness at home within the family circle, and still more so to feel that any effort of ours has been contributive to it. There is no happiness comparable to the domesticity of a cherished home.

On Tuesday I was one of a special dinnery-party at Maj Genl Hooker's Hd. Qrs at Wauhatchie. The party consisted of Maj Gens. *Thomas, Howard, & Hooker,* Brig Gens *Whipple, Brannan,* Elliot, *Steinweir, Ward, & Geary* together with sundry Colonels & Captains.[1] The Dinner was a good one, for a Camp getting up. The party was pleasant and refreshing from the monotony of a soldier's life. I returned next morning, having first examined that dear spot where our beloved Eddie was transfered from Earth to the bosom of God whom he loved & served so well. The horrors of that fatal and terrible night can never be effaced from the tablets of my memory. And on the other hand no one who understands "Wauhatchie" and its important bearing upon the Army of the Cumberland in saving it from starvation and disgrace, will ever forget that glorious victory no less than the salvation of the Army of the Cumberland and perhaps the country.

I have just returned from an important reconnaissance in Georgia, in the direction of Trenton and South of that place, which is about 16 miles South

---

1. Oliver Otis Howard commanded the Eleventh Corps; Denison Whipple served as chief of staff for Thomas's Army of the Cumberland; John Milton Brannan, chief of artillery; Washington L. Elliott, chief of the cavalry corps; Baron Adolph Wilhelm August Friedrich von Steinwehr commanded a division in the Eleventh Corps; William T. Ward led the 1st Division in the Eleventh Corps.

East of this place. I was out two days, bivouacking on the ground at night. The country through which I travelled with 1000 men, without wagons, ambulances, or artillery was almost an unbroken forest for 14 miles. I dispersed some small bands of the enemy and captured 6 prisoners without any loss on my side, I gained much important information concerning the country, the position and condition of the enemy.[2]

Everything in the army seems to indicate changes in commanders, positions, and plans of the coming campaign.[3] Nothing as yet can scarcely be regarded as definite, and the rumors you get in the papers [are] the same as I do.

Enclosed please find a check payable to your own order for two-hundred dollars. Send me a detailed account of the bills paid with the $1100 and an estimate of what you will require to finish the parlor, and furnish it with the two rooms up stairs. If we cannot do it all at once, a part can be done at a time, only do not go in *debt*.

Give my love to the boys and girls and kiss them for me.

My health is very good, and I would be perfectly happy if the war was over and I with my beloved family. With deepest & most abiding affection I am

Your true husband
J.W.G.

*   *   *

Head-Quarters, Second Division, Twelfth Corps
Bridgeport [Ala.]   Mar 21st 1864

My Dearest Mary

Your dear letter of the 11th inst. is received. The "Scab" has already been used and myself and several of my staff vaccinated. The vaccination a few days before I left home never took the slightest effect and if a like

---

2. Geary's report of this reconnaissance stated that no large bodies of the enemy were in the vicinity. The six prisoners came from Cleburne's division. See *O.R., 32*, pt. 1, 29.

3. During April, major changes occurred within the Army of the Cumberland in preparation for the Atlanta campaign. Consolidation of the Eleventh and Twelfth Corps into the Twentieth Corps affected most of the officers at the dinner Geary attended. Hooker would lead the new corps, and Geary the second division within it. Von Steinwehr refused to accept demotion to brigade commander under Geary and effectively thus ended his career. Howard was assigned to command the Fourth Corps, and Ward lost his division to lead a brigade in the 3rd Division of the Twentieth Corps.

result comes from this I will consider it proof positive that I am not likely to be effected with the disease *small pox*, of which there are now over thirty cases in the "pest camp" at this place. The soldiers are generally very healthy, and most of the cases are on the natives.

The enemy continues to move about as if he sometimes has the intention of attacking Our lines, but seems to be undecided as to *where, how,* or *when.* The busy hum of preparation is heard on all sides. The continued movements of troops indicate that sooner or later their marches must bring them into collision with the enemy, and a battle be fought. God grant that we may be victorious and the war soon terminated. If you could only see the horrors of war for a single day you would never desire to look upon its like again, and would not wonder why your soldier husband hates it so much, yet duty bids us stay and endeavor to bequeath peace at least to our children for their heritage. I often feel a desire to be translated back to the days of my romance, and enjoy the pleasure of air castles and gorgeous imagery of youth, but the facts, stern and frightful, that are continually surrounding us makes me feel that all is real and that true happiness mocks at us as we follow it like will-o-the-wisp, the puerile grasp at the ever fleeing rainbow.

Your letters my dear Mary, are always pleasant to me, and keep me in memory of the sweets of a beloved home and family. They ameliorate the influences of the moral malaria of an army, they make life more pleasant to know that I am not forgotten at least by one that loves my name. The prattle of the little ones is ever pleasant, and their *wise saws* are ever arousing.

Kiss all the children for me, tell them not to forget me, to be good and they will be happy.

Give my love to Mrs Church and Comfort, John and Lizzy, and Captain and Mary Lee.

Do not trouble yourself about my promotion, if I act well my part as a Brigadier General, it will be as honorable as if 'twere done by a Maj. Genl.

I will send the children some thing from time to time, but I want them to write me as often as they can.

Ever your loving husband
J.W.G.

* * *

Bridgeport, Ala   Mar 31st 1864

My Dearest Mary

Several days have elapsed since I have had the pleasure of receiving a letter from you. If you knew how highly I prize one of those beloved missiles, what an immense valuation I place upon it, and what a pleasant unction to the soul I consider it, you would not hesitate to communicate a little more frequently. I feel the loss of home much [more] sensibly this period of my absence than I have ever done before. The love and ease of home makes me long for its enjoyments. The duty devolving upon me as a parent to protect and prepare the children by education and otherwise to enter the world in a respectable manner is now one of the most important duties of life, and should not be too long deferred. This matter is of so much importance that I sometimes think seriously of resigning and giving my attention to private business and to my family. But we are now just in the opening of the most important campaign of the war, upon its results hangs the fate of our country for weal or for woe. To leave now, would therefore, subject me to many unjust aspersions, and I am compelled to defer it for the present. After some great victory will be the best time. Then in truth we can enjoy what little we have in true satisfaction and happiness, considering it a competence.

The day before yesterday I had a small skirmish with the enemy, and after pouring a few well directed shots from Knap's Battery into them they *skedaddled* with intense alacrity. You of course have heard of Forrest movements west of us in Ky. at Paducah. I have not heard any more of it than has appeared in the published accounts.[4] From the best information I can obtain, our column will be 80,000 men in the movement about to be made.

I desire that you will *not* breathe the subject of my contemplated resignation to any one. It would be injurious if bruited about.

4. Forrest took 2,800 men on this expedition into western Tennessee and Kentucky, from March 16 to April 14. He hoped to gather supplies, break up guerrilla bands, collect conscripts, and refit his men. While a portion of his force captured Union City on March 24, the rest covered the 100 miles to Paducah in fifty hours. Located where the Tennessee empties into the Ohio River, Paducah had been in Federal control since 1861. Forrest's men pushed Union soldiers from the town and into fortifications. Confederates held Paducah for about ten hours, then abandoned it, partly because smallpox afflicted many in the area. Later in this expedition came the attack on Fort Pillow (April 12), in which Forrest's men killed African American soldiers who surrendered.

I am in usual good health, and expect to go to Stevenson, Ala., to review and inspect the third Brigade of my Division which is located at that place, tomorrow.

Give my love to Capt Lee and Mary, Mrs. Church & Comfort, John & Lizzie, and any other friends you may deem proper.

Ever in loving devotion
Your true husband
Jno. W. Geary

Love & Kisses to all the children.

* * *

{The changes in the army's command and organization that Geary forecasted several weeks ago became public on April 2 when Sherman announced his intention to combine the Eleventh and Twelfth Corps into the Twentieth Corps. Major General von Steinwehr of the Eleventh Corps resigned, and Slocum of the Twelfth Corps accepted transfer to a smaller assignment on the Mississippi. Geary continued to lead the 2nd Division but reported to Hooker, with whom he enjoyed an acquaintance dating back to their days in California after the Mexican War. Promotion to major general—the rank granted to more capable division commanders—still eluded him. When telling Mary of the change on April 21, he stressed that he received great confidence from commanders in spite of "being one of the junior officers."

The transition bothered some of the men as well. One noted that the merger of the two corps created "dissatisfaction among the '{White} Stars' who were on not very good terms with the Teutonic crescents, from the days of Chancellorsville to that of 'Wauhatchie,' where they did not come up in time to assist in repulsing Longstreet's Superior numbers."[5]}

* * *

Head-Quarters Second Division, Twelfth Corps
Bridgeport, Ala.   Apr 9th 1864

My Dearest Mary

I have just returned from a trip over the late battle-fields of Lookout, Mission Ridge, and Ringgold. The tour occupied three days, and I assure you

---

5. [J.] A[ddison] [Moore] to "Dear Old Home," April 14, 1864, Moore Family Papers, MHI.

was very instructive and interesting. The weather still continues cool and wet, and of course, the roads are [in] such a condition as to preclude any idea of a movement or active hostilities until near the 1st of May, at which time I think it is probable that not only this but all the other armies will move simultaneously, and the grand crisis of the war will be upon us. We cannot tell of, or know how it will result, untill after the battles are fought, but I have an abiding faith, with God's favor, the campaign will be decisive.

The roads are constantly thronged with troops going to the front. The advance is principally made up of Cavalry, and I presume it will not be long until the infantry and Artillery begin to follow but I need not to make a record of anticipated events, when facts will so shortly present themselves. Suffice it to say, our column will move with about 100,000 men. Grant's column before Richmond will number about 200,000 men, and the South-West column will be about 100,000 men.[6] If some definite impression be not made upon the rebellion with these forces, I do not [know] when it can be crushed.

Your letters up to reasonable date are all received, and I beg to thank you for your promptitude in correspondence, and for the many expressions of love and confidence there in contained. Be assured my Dear Mary, that all your feelings are fully reciprocated in the fullness of love, and of every other regard, and that you absorb all my affections on earth, that in you are centred all my hopes of happiness on earth, and that you are in my eyes the one altogether lovely.

Our dear little pets I have no doubt are happy and are growing finely. Stimulate the boys as much as possible in their studies. Give them my kindest love. I would advise you not to make any mistakes in Comforts love affair. Let her and the Dr manage their own matters and if opportunity is afforded let them both understand that you are no matchmaker and that the responsibilities must rest upon themselves and as they fell the tree so it

---

6. For the first time in the war, the Union under Grant planned a coordinated advance in all regions of the South. Geary, however, overestimated the numbers available. The Union may have had 200,000 troops in the vicinity of Washington and Virginia, but that spring of 1864 the Army of the Potomac moved with roughly 120,000 men, and Sherman left for Atlanta with just shy of 100,000 men. The size of the forces in the southwest also did not approach the scale Geary mentions. Major General Nathaniel Banks had at most 35,000 troops available for his Red River campaign (March–May 1864), and only because he borrowed from the Army of the Tennessee under Sherman. The Department of Arkansas reported on March 31 as having roughly 15,000 men present for duty. This still meant a sizable advantage for the Union, but one that was needed to mount an offensive campaign into a huge territory where the enemy fought on the defensive.

must lie. The Paymaster has not been here yet, when he comes I will make remittance. Devoted love to yourself and all the family.

Ever in fidelity, love & truth yours

Jno W Geary

*   *   *

Head-Quarters 2nd Division, 12th Army Corp,
Bridgeport, Ala.   Apr 12th 1864

My Dearest Mary

Your kind letters are always welcome, but none was more welcome than that of the third instant, relating principally to our own dear family. That the little ones at home miss *me*, as well as yourself, is a pleasant and yet a somewhat melancholy reflection. How often is that stereotyped question asked by all who are absent, "Do they miss me at home?" Yes they miss me at home is the happy response, and I am convinced they consider me somewhat more than a *cypher* there.

I wrote you a day or two ago, after my return from Ringgold, which letter I hope you have received. Today at 12 m. I set out on a lengthy tour of reconnaissance down the river Tennessee. I go on Steam Boat, and will be absent several days. I have a strong armament and will I hope have a successful voyage on this my first naval expedition.

Enclosed find check for $150. 'Tis all I have at present.

Give any quantity of kisses and love to the children, and love to all kind friends.

I will write when I have an opportunity, while en-route.

I commit you and all the family to the care of Him, who is alone able to protect and preserve us all.

Your loving husband

J. W. Geary

*   *   *

Hd. Qrs. 2nd Div. 12th A.C.   Bridgeport, Ala.
April 16th 1864

My Dearest Mary

You have no doubt received my note written just as I was leaving on my expedition down the Tennessee River. I have returned as you may perceive once more from the field of conflict *unscathed*. I went down the river with the Steam Boat "Chickamauga" and two large barges. My force was 800 men, my armament 4 pieces of Artillery. I was absent 4 days, distance travelled 110 miles, and returned same. At Guntersville the extreme Southern Point on the river, I had a fight with the enemy, whipped him, captured Guntersville, drove back the enemy,[7] destroyed his boats (you know my *bump* for destruction is pretty good,) burnt the houses from which the enemy fired on my command, captured a large mail containing about 150 letters, a large number of bonds,[8] and other papers of value. I send a blank *bond* and a *ring* to Mary (my daughter,) in another letter.

I afterwards proceeded on my tour down the river and after several skirmishes succeeded in reaching Whitesburg where some Union Troops were encamped. There I learned that a large body of the enemy were in advance, near the town of Triana. I determined to see for myself. I proceeded about 8 miles when I have in sight of the enemy three times my number with Artillery. I immediately opened into his ranks a ferocious fire of Arty. and Infty., succeeded in breaking his lines, when to my surprise I discovered a body of the enemy approaching my right on the North bank, and another in my rear, finding [myself] nearly surrounded I laid on with might and main on all sides. We were soon enveloped with smoke so dense that we could scarcely see, the sun was just setting, and night coming on, I turned my boat up stream, drove back the rebels from my rear and reached Whitesburg after dark.[9] On our way we shelled several bodies of rebel

7. This "driving" Geary accomplished with skirmishers and artillery fire against a body of Confederate cavalry that picketed the town. The general estimated the total strength at 250 to 300. See *O.R., 32*, pt. 1, 663–68.

8. Seventeen $1,000 bonds of the Tennessee & Coosa Railroad.

9. Geary mentions little of these dramatics in his official report, which indicates no such battle. "We moved but a short distance and were near Triana," he wrote, "when we found on the north side a force fully equal to my own, in line of battle with skirmishers out, in a low, swampy, secreted place, densely wooded, and a force much larger on the hills on the south side, with a piece of artillery about being put in position upon them." He added: "They presented an insuperable barrier to the passage of so frail a boat, whose decks

cavalry on the South bank. As my reconnaissance was finished, I determined to return to Bridgeport, and as the enemy were erecting a battery for my special benefit at Guntersville, I determined to pass that point if possible before daylight, which I succeeded in doing. After one more skirmish at the mouth of Riley's Creek, I reached here in safety. I had three men wounded on the trip. The enemy's loss must have been severe. My reconnaissance was a perfect success. Thus ends my first naval expedition. I came very near being shot myself on one occasion. Thank God for this & every other mercy of my life. All the glory and the honor be to His holy name.

Give my love to all the children. Also a kiss.

I am as ever truly your faithful
and loving husband
Jno W Geary

*   *   *

Hd. Qrs. 2nd Div: 20th Corps.   Bridgeport, Ala.
April 21st 1864

My Dearest Mary

I am indebted to you for many valuable and very highly esteemed letters, which I assure you are all very highly prized. Your graphic description of the family group around your writing table with all the prittle-prattle was very interesting and pleasant, and nothing could have afforded me more pleasure than just to have dropped in "Paul pry" like, "hoping I did not intrude," and made one of the party. What a smashing of lips would have been there my countrymen! What a pressure of heart to heart! and interchange of soul and sentiment, but this dream of happiness cannot yet be, the stern realities of war are upon us, and they must be met.

I have been somewhat indisposed since my return from my maratime expedition down the Tennessee, but I am now rapidly recovering. Yesterday was the most pleasant day of the season. The sun shone brightly, the breezes blew mildly, and the birds, of which there [are] Legion sang sweetly. The trees are rapidly covering themselves with the expanding foliage of

---

threatened to give way even at the rebound of our own pieces, and with boiler and engine exposed. The men were necessarily huddled together, and there was no shelter for scarcely a single man." Because the ship could not force its way past, he turned it around and went back to Guntersville. He reported none of the exchange described to Mary. See *O.R.*, 32, pt. 1, 666.

summers, and every thing, the martial pomp around us excepted, was calculated to lull the mind into perfect tranquility, but experience teaches me that it is only that inexplicable lull which precedes a coming storm.

Maj Gen Thomas, the Department Commander, paid me a visit, and remained with me all day. We to-gether examined different regiments, the hospitals, the Steam boat yard, where 15 Steam Boats and numerous small craft have been built since I have commanded here. We also visited all the depots of subsistence, forage, and other quarter master's stores. The beauty and regularity of the camps, and the general cleanliness of the whole place elicited his most heart[felt] approbation, and I had the honor to receive his thanks for the faithful manner in which the trust confided to me has been fulfilled. He was also commissioned by Maj. Gen. Sherman, to "return his thanks to me, for the able and efficient manner in which my late reconnaissance had been made, and for my report thereof."[10]

So much for self. I do not tell the above for self gratulation, but for your information. God is entitled to all the honor, and I feel that I am only his instrument. He has so often preserved me from the dangers of perilous battle that I feel that I am an especial object of His care, and we cannot therefore be too thankful to Him, who is God over all, the Giver of every good and perfect gift, and especially that of the Lord Jesus Christ, the savior of mankind who taketh away the sins of the world.

My command now consists of 20 Regts, and 12 pieces of Artillery, and as you see, the compliment has been paid me, *being one of the junior officers,* that I am assigned to the command of a Div: in the 20th Corps, as the caption of this clearly indicates. May God give me wisdom and strength to fulfill the expectations of my commanders and of the government, and to do my part with ability, in restoring the tranquility of our disturbed and distracted country. I wrote Willie G. a long letter upon his birthday, I hope he has received it, and carefully read it.

When does Willie H's. birthday occur. I will give him a letter the[n] if I have the opportunity to do so.

Tell Mary Lee and Pet, I will write to them soon. Kiss little Maggie and all, the others. Give my kindest regards to Capt Lee, John & Lizzy, Mrs.

10. Ironically, the details in Geary's long report, written to advance himself, provided the Union command with useful intelligence. Thomas expressed "satisfaction at the manner in which Brig. Gen. John W. Geary conducted his expedition and the results which followed." Thomas continued: "From the information furnished by General Geary, and that derived from other sources, there seems to be foundation for the rumor that the enemy intend attacking our railroad communications from a southwesterly direction" (*O.R.,* 32, pt. 1, 668).

Church & Comfort, Col and Mrs Feeman, John Lee and wife, and do not forget my friend Mr. Eberly.[11] I feel under many obligations to him for his many kindnesses to me when I was at home.

Keep me advised of all that is going on at home in Pennsylvania. I observe the efforts to remove the Capitol from Harrisburg with deep regret. If it should be removed to Phila, Good bye to the future welfare and interests of the Commonwealth.[12]

I confidently commit you and our dear children to the care and protection of God. May He shield us all from every evil and danger and restore the union of our family and of our country.

Ever your true & loving husband

J. W. Geary

*   *   *

Hd Qtrs. 2nd Div. 20th A.C.   Bridgeport Ala.   May 1st 1864

My Dearest Mary

This day has been quite cool and pleasant, much more so than a number of its predecessors. The sun shines brightly and all nature is dressed in living green and decked with fairest bloom of roses, violets, and inexhaustable quantities of honeysuckles which perfume the air, (that is when you can get out of the stench of some dead horse, mule or some other animal that has fulfilled its destiny.)

The exuberantly fertile soil lies uncultivated, and the lazy, good for nothing *white-trash* live in their miserable excuses for houses, which usually consist of two pens and a shed connecting them, starving to death. Except such things as they can beg from the soldiers, they have nothing to eat.

The mountain scenery in this country is truly grand, sublime, and picturesque, the broad majestic Tennessee lies like an immense silver snake at

---

11. Christian Eberly owned numerous storefronts along Market Street in New Cumberland and was a friend of the Church family.

12. The impetus to move the state capital from Harrisburg to Philadelphia had to do less with the war than with a long-standing desire by legislators from the east to locate the seat of government in their section of the state. Some of this motivation came from the need for better facilities than the small town of Harrisburg could offer, and some came from the desire to add to the prominence of the Quaker City. In early April 1864, a senator from Philadelphia introduced a bill to accomplish this task, but opposition from Harrisburg residents, and from legislators from other parts of Pennsylvania, effectively stopped the measure by the end of the month.

their base, where they wash their feet in its pure liquid. The river abounds in fish of every kind, beautiful in appearance, delicious to the taste, and afford a nutricious article of food. Its bosom is filled with aquatic birds of almost every species, ducks of the largest kind predominate. The hills look like pyramids of expanding foliage, owing to the density of their forest clad sides. Upon them game abounds, deer, Wild Turkeys, and fox squirrels predominate. Of rabbits there are not a few.

For a week or ten days troops have thronged this thoroughfare, going towards Chattanooga and Ringgold. Every thing looks as the quiet, preceding the storm is about to be broken, and the impending strife commence. I am at present superintending the patrolling of the river with gun boats, and expect to leave here for the direction of Dalton for a few days.

Perhaps before this reaches you we will be on the east of Lookout Mountain, treading again the bloody and classic fields of last fall in search of new ones.

No one in the army can judge truly of the horrors of the Campaign which is probably to last for months, in so terrible a climate as the *"Sunny South."*

I send Willie Geary a paper with a beautiful piece of poetry marked. I wish you to read it. Every one who has ever commanded a regiment can feel and acknowledge its truth. *"The swords thirty-seven & the bayonets one thousand."* I wrote Willie a short time ago on his birthday, has he received the letters? I dreamed of you last night, and thought I saw you clearly. As usual in my dreamy effort at securing the fancy I awoke, and the phantom was lost. How often in life we mistake the shadow for the substance.

I expect a letter from you to-morrow morning when I will write again. Gen Sickles[13] called to see me to-day.

Give love to children and friends

Ever yours in love
truth and fidelity,
J.W.G.

---

13. Major General Daniel E. Sickles, who lost his leg at Gettysburg. Sickles also lost his command in a controversy with Union Major General George G. Meade over the subordinate's advance of the Third Corps to a position that left it exposed to Longstreet's assault on the afternoon of July 2, 1863. Active in the national Democratic Party, the New Yorker and Geary may have exchanged political news, although Sickles was in Chattanooga primarily to visit Joseph Hooker.

*   *   *

Hd. Qrs. 2nd Div: 20th A.C.
Pea Vine (10 miles west of Dalton, Geo.)   May 6th 1864

My Dearest Mary

Four days ago I wrote you two letters upon the same day. Since that period I had no opportunity to stop to write, and much less to send you a letter.

On the 3rd instant I concentrated my Command at Bridgeport and marched to Shellmound 6 miles. That is where the famous Nickajack Cave has its location. Very many of the officers and men visited and explored it, and enjoyed great pleasure while doing so. For my own part, I could not willingly go into it, and consequently did not go to it. When we advanced on Wauhatchie in October last on the night of the 27th of that month my dear Edward was with me, and we together explored it. Never shall I forget that night. I remember him more vividly in that cave than any where else, and when I wish to see his manly face, enlivened with all the vivacy which the scene *excited*, I have only to refer to Nickajack Cave, and his smiling face is with me. But he is gone, and is now a bright angel in Heaven. And perhaps may approve the honest endeavors of his father in crushing this most infamous rebellion. From Shellmound we started on the morning of the 4th up the same route we did in Oct last. But the scene was very different. Then it was cold, wet, & dreary, and we skirmished all the way. Now it is Spring, mild and clear. The balmy breezes were blowing, the roads dry and flowers blooming, and instead of shivering around fires as we did then, we sought the cooling shade, and still more cooling beverage trickling from the rocks of Sand, or Raccoon, Mountain. At one of those beautiful Springs we rested and while sitting by it, I discovered a large grove of the native *Shrub*, with all the delicious odors of the "Strawberry." This was the first time I knew they were natives of our soil. We passed over Raccoon Mountain's rocky summit into Lookout Valley, through Wauhatchie's bloody Glen, took a lingering look at the spot where Eddy breathed his last, and after visiting Maj Gen Hooker at his quarters a mile or so back, I marched my Divsn around the Lookout Mountain point, and encamped at the base of that ever memorable pyramid near where it laves its foots in the beautiful but serpentine Tennessee, having travelled 22 miles. My men having travelled but little for some months were both footsore and tired. A soldier, however, soon resuscitates upon a night's rest, and so it was in this case, for the command [marched] 16 miles and again rested for the night. During this march we passed the battlegrounds of "Mission Ridge", and "Chickamauga" and within 4 miles of that at Ringgold.

This morning, after a march of 6 miles, we reached this place and are now within 12 miles of the enemy. Tomorrow morning we set out from here—where? Towards the enemy at Dalton. A collision cannot long be delayed in this quarter now.

God bless my dear Wife and children. He will bless us and if we trust in Him, through the Lord Jesus Christ, and his mediation. Tell all the children I love them dearly. I commit you all [to] the care of God. With deepest love and devotion I am your faithful husband

Jno. W. Geary

*   *   *

{Ordered to dislodge Confederates from Dug Gap in Rocky Face Ridge—or prevent the enemy from joining forces that opposed Major General James B. McPherson at Snake Creek Gap six miles away—Geary's men attacked two regiments of Arkansas infantry and the 9th Kentucky Cavalry around 4 P.M. on May 8. The rocky, steep terrain helped 1,000 Confederates hold off 4,500 Union soldiers. Although the enemy retained the gap, Geary claimed success because McPherson took Snake Creek Gap.

After the war, Colonel W.C.P. Breckinridge, who commanded the 9th Kentucky Cavalry, wrote that Geary's report of this battle, although on balance correct, contained errors. According to Breckinridge, the Union general erroneously stated that Confederates had two lines of entrenchments; that the Northerners drove the Southerners from the first defensive position; and that losses were large (Geary claimed 252 Southern casualties)—when there were not more than a score killed and wounded, errors that made Geary's effort appear better than it was.[14]}

14. Albert Castel, *Decision in the West: The Atlanta Campaign of 1864* (Lawrence, Kans., 1992), 131–35; W.C.P. Breckinridge, "The Opening of the Atlanta Campaign," in *Battles and Leaders of the Civil War*, ed. Robert U. Johnson and Clarence C. Buel, 4 vols. (1887; New York, 1956), 4:279.

*   *   *

Babbs Gap 4 miles West, Dalton   May 9th 1864

My Dearest Mary

We have been engaged all day in fighting and manoevering. The loss in my command in killed, wounded, and missing is about 200. We occupy the battle ground and expect to advance to-day.[15]

Every thing looks as if we must whip Johnston's Army and you may look for stirring news soon.

I am well, but am very fatigued. I will write every opportunity. May God protect us all.

Ever your loving husband
Jno W Geary

*   *   *

Mill Creek or Dug Gap Geo. 4 miles from Dalton   May 10 1864

My Dearest Mary

I am very busy and I only write to let you [know] that *I am well*.

Enclosed, a *Something* called a "ten dollar confederate" bill, given to me by a loyal Georgian.

Every thing looks as if we will whip Johnston out of the "Buzzards Roost"[16] in a day or two.

Love and kisses to the children.

God bless you and them.

Your affectionate husband
Jno. W. Geary

---

15. Geary's mention that he occupied the battleground seems calculated to portray the engagement at Dug Gap as a victory. But his troops could not dislodge the Confederates, and when the fighting died they merely remained in the position before the pass.

16. Confederate General Joseph E. Johnston had established the main part of his force at this point.

*   *   *

Head-Quarters, 2nd Division, 12th Army Corps[17]
Mill Creek Geo. May 11th 1864

My Dearest Mary

I write to you as often as possible. I have been holding this place for 3 days since the hard battle I had here on Sunday afternoon. The fight took place within 4 miles of Dalton at Mill Gap, a part of the Chat*too*gata Mountain (accent the "*too*")[.] The enemys loss and mine was about equal. Their killed is greater than mine, while my wounded is great[er] than theirs.[18]

The object of the battle was to attack and hold the enemy here, while Gen McPherson passed through Snake Gap, 3 or 4 miles south of this toward Ressacca. My killed is 49. The enemy's 62. My wounded 278. The enemy's 190. John Guistwhite[19] was wounded in the right arm much as I was at Cedar Mountain. Dr. [Alfred] Ball [surgeon-in-chief] says he will recover without losing it.

I could say many things about this battle and the gallantry of my men, but have not time. Also the hair breath escapes of myself and staff. One of my black horses was hit in the foot, not much injured. The position of the enemy is almost impregnable, and we will yet have much hard fighting to dislodge them.

The news from Va. seems cheering this morning, and we all hope for the best, and that this terrible war will soon be over.[20]

Pray God for our safety and success, and if He goes up to the battle with us we will succeed.

My health is good, and my men generally well, but many are sick and have to be sent to our Depot at Ringgold.

---

17. Although Geary was now in the Twentieth Corps, he wrote this on paper bearing the typeset letterhead of his former corps designation.

18. The results were not that close. Geary lost 357 killed, wounded, and missing, while Confederates reported casualties of not quite "a score."

19. Sergeant John H. Guistwite, wounded at Rocky Face, Georgia, May 8, 1864. He survived and was mustered out with the rest of Company I on July 18, 1865.

20. Grant and Lee had fought a punishing battle in the Wilderness, May 5–6, which ended in a tactical draw. The Army of the Potomac turned the Army of Northern Virginia's right and moved south until blocked by Confederates at Spotsylvania Court House. Union troops temporarily breached the Southern line on May 10; Grant prepared a massive strike on May 12 that resulted in some of the war's most vicious fighting at the "Mule Shoe" salient. No one gained the upper hand in these battles, which Grant intended to hold Lee from sending reinforcements elsewhere while also exacting a heavy toll on Confederate manpower.

Tomorrow will doubtlessly be an important day with us here. There is scarcely a doubt but that the next ten days will decide the campaign.

I expect to receive orders to march to "Snake Gap" this evening. Just now about 6,000 rebels along the top of Chattoogata Mountain within 1½ miles of me in full view. If they expose themselves a little more I will open on them with 12 cannon. They generally keep in safe positions.

Give my love to Willie Geary and all the children. Kiss them for me. God bless you and them is the prayer of your

devoted husband
Jno W Geary

P.S.

Before the departure of the mail I have still a few moments I can devote to you. A Sabbath stillness reigns over field and camp; here and there [a] warbler swells out in full tones as merrily as if the benign influences of peace had thrown the rainbow over the bleeding wounds of our country. The flowers consisting chiefly of honeysuckles and native *shrubs* breathe their incense from the gale, rendering it perfectly aromatic. Every sound in the distance is the boom of cannon or perhaps an occasional shot from opposite pickets, which the imagination often may transfer into reconnaissance in force, battle &tc. &tc. Such is life here. The mail goes. I will close.

Ever yours.

*   *   *

Hd. Qrs. 2nd Div 20th A.C.   Near Resacca [Resaca] Geo.
May 14th 1864

My Dearest Mary

All day yesterday our army was engaged with the enemy, *"Buzzards Roost,"* The *"Chattoogata Mountain,"* and DALTON, are captured. The enemy are in force at Resacca and the battle even now roars upon our ears. This morning is foggy and I expect by nine a.m. the fight will become general. My Division is not—*mirabila dictu*—(i.e.) (wonderful to [be] told) in the battle. It is in reserve, and either we will have no fighting, or the hardest of it. Time will determine. I believe this is the 1st time I have written you in the midst of a battle.

The enemy will undoubtedly be driven over the Oostanaula River which is quite a considerable stream running south-westward to Rome where it has it[s] confluence with the Etowah River and forms the Coosa River.

I will continue to write you daily or as often as the mail departs.

My health is good and the army generally in good spirits.

I hope God will soon destroy this rebellion, for sometime I fear the wisdom of man in doing it. If left to man it will be a failure.

Thank God for all his mercies and wonderful deliverances without number. May we hope for their continuance, and humbly pray for the same. Give love and kisses to the children. Remember me in kindness to Capt Lee and all our friends. I will hope to hear from you frequently. This letter is written on my knee with cannon roaring all around me, and the rattling of musketry on our front. You must therefore, excuse its incongruities and imperfections.

With undying love I am very truly
your faithful and devoted husband

J W G

This place is 15 miles south of Dalton.

* * *

Near Calhoun Geo.   May 18th 1864

My Dearest Mary

The great battle of *Resacca* has [been] *fought* and *won*. Three days hard fighting with the blessings of Providence, has decided it in our favor. Loss in killed and wounded on our side is between four & five thousand, and that of the enemy, acknowledged by themselves, about ten thousand.[21]

We are now hotly pursuing. We were the first troops at Ressacca—we then took the road via Fite's Ferry on the Oostanaula, & McClure's Ferry on

21. As usual, Geary exaggerated enemy casualties. The battle of Resaca, May 14–15, cost the Union roughly 4,000 casualties (about 600 dead or mortally wounded) and the Confederates roughly 3,000. Although it is debatable who won the battle tactically, the Confederates withdrew when Sherman's men crossed the Oostanaula River, threatening Johnston's supply lines.

the Coosawattee river, thence to this place. We do not expect to fight any regular battle until we reach Al[la]toona, on a range of mountains between here and Atlanta, which is the present *goal* of our *ambition*. I hope we soon [will] be able to close the war in the south in the blaze of glory and victory. I captured 4 pieces of artillery at Resacca, which by a strange coincidence is the remainder of the identical battery from which I captured two pieces at Lookout Mountain.[22]

I am well, and in good spirits, with a firm reliance upon God, to whose tender mercies we owe every thing, even our lives. I recd your letter of May 1st, last night, upon reaching this place, and I assure you it was as much a treat to me as any of mine could have been to you and the children at home.

Give my love to the children with kisses. Also my regards to Capt Lee and other friends.

I commit you all to the care of the Great Father of us all. Pray God for my safety and success.

I will write you as frequently as possible.

Ever your faithful and loving husband
J W Geary

My command is in line.

*   *   *

Near Cassville Geo   May 20th 1864

My Dearest Mary

I have just rec'd. yours of 3rd inst. and am pleased to have you write in such good spirits. Also to learn the health of yourself and that of the children. We are fighting every day in hot pursuit of the enemy and have already driven them 45 miles into the interior in the direction of Atlanta. Rome, Kingston and Cassville have been taken, and we expect to march today towards the Etowah River, where the enemy will doubtlessly make

---

22. These four twelve-pounders were on the Confederate left and were seized on Geary's orders the night of May 15. Geary claimed credit for the action, which gained publicity in the North, particularly in *Harper's Weekly*. No one knew at the time that Johnston had ordered that the cannon be abandoned because they were not worth the casualties needed to remove them.

strong resistence. I am well, but fatigued. Such is the case with all. Love to children and yourself.

Ever yours
Jno. W. Geary

God and our country.

*   *   *

Head Quarters 2nd Division, 20th A.C.   Near Dallas, Geo.
May 29th 1864

My Dearest Mary

I know your solicitude about me, hence I embrace every opportunity to write you, even upon the battle field. Under the roar of many cannons, the rattling of miles of musketry, and whizzling of missiles I write this brief letter. It is now 26 days since we left Bridgeport, nine of which has been in actual battle. How our present engagement will terminate is in God's hand, undecided to mortal eye. We are now 5 days under fire *consecutively*.

I am a monument of God's mercy, unhurt, though I have had many hair breadth escapes. God will I hope give us continued victory.

I confidently place you and myself at Gods disposal, knowing He will place all things in such a manner as will redound most to His glory and our good.

Give my devoted love to the children. May God bless you and them. I am as ever

Your loving husband
Jno. W. Geary

Same to all friends

*   *   *

Near Lost Mountain Geo.   June 3rd 1864

My Dearest Mary

This is the evening of the 11th day's hard fighting, and we are now in possession of "Allatoona" and "Acworth" on the east side of the "Allatoona Mountains." The total casualties of my Division number over 1200 men. I am happy to state that my glorious old Division has maintained its previous prestige. I am well, but very much worn by constant care and anxiety. We are getting along very slowly but surely. The country is an almost unbroken forest. The weather has been very wet, and I am now seated on some wet leaves in the woods writing a note to you by candle light, which although it contains no intrinsic value, I hope will reach you.

I have received no pay for 3 months, as there is no paymaster with us, and I cannot therefore remit you any money now. You must draw on Mr. Wier[23] to help you out of the scrape, and as soon as I find a Pay Master will remit you {in} abundance.

I am in hopes of the final success of this campaign and from what I can hear from Grant's army, I think he will soon be in Richmond.

Kiss our dear little ones for me and tell them I love them all.

Give my love to Capt Lee and Mary Lee, Mrs. Church, Comfort and all other friends.

I will write to you as often as the mail leaves with safety.

As ever I commit you and the dear little ones to the care of Him who never sleepeth. His mercy to us all is indeed wonderful and beyond praise.

Truly your loving husband
Jno. W. Geary

*   *   *

Head Qrs. 2nd Div: 20th A.C. Camp near Acworth, Geo.
June 8th 1864

My Dearest Mary

I am in receipt since last night of your three letters bearing dates respectively 20th, 24th, and 26th, also one from Willie Geary. And now having a few leisure moments this morning, I hasten to give you and him my warmest thanks for your frequent and kind remembrances, and to assure you both of my continued love and affectionate regard. There is another thing however I beg to assure you of, and that is the difficulty of answering each and every one separately, from want of time and proper conveniences

---

23. James Wallace Weir served as cashier for thirty-one years in the Harrisburg Bank. (Geary misspells the name.)

for so doing. I am now sitting under the wide spreading branches of a huge Red Oak tree, and am writing this short epistle on my knee. Around me are at least 50 officers talking busily upon almost every subject, my troops are in line of battle, laying upon their arms. The enemy are also in line, a little beyond the range of our cannon, and to-morrow may possibly bring about a collision of arms. We had truly a victorious march and have pushed the enemy more than one hundred miles, still he is not yet whipped sufficiently to relieve him of his arrogance.

As we pass through the country, we leave it as though all the locusts of Egypt had been upon it. There is not a single blade of grass left upon the earth. Wheat fields are eaten to the ground, and the rising corn is beginning to yield its quota to the sustenance of our animals. The provisions of the people is also taken without compunction, and they are left in utter want. Sometimes they resort to every subterfuge to hide from the prying eyes of our men, their bacon and other dried meats[;] one which was found out yesterday caused no little merriment. Several families had clubbed together to "save their bacon," which they buried in several handsome *graves* near their houses. Somehow or other the soldiers smelt the matter, and resurrected about half a ton of the most excellent hams from the aforesaid *Graves*. The fame of the resurrectionists soon spread far and wide, and every grave was in danger of being opened, but the fourth attempt brought the business to a close, for the only thing extracted from it was the body of a dead rebel whom our skirmishers had just killed and buried.

As you are doubtlessly aware we have fought several important battles in the south. God in His mercy has vouchsafed each of them to be victories, how many more may yet have to be fought, He of Infinite wisdom alone can forsee and define their results. I trust that He will give us continued victory and crown our efforts with a speedy and a lasting peace.

You and Willie must consider this a joint letter for it will be impossible to write two just now. I will write to the Willies as soon as I can sit down to a desk and not be in the immediate presence of the enemy.

Relative to furnishing the house, I have funds sufficiently applicable for that purpose but for want of a paymaster cannot remit them to you at this time. I wish I could do so, so that you could make our house comfortable. I wonder if Mr. Wier would not advance you seven or eight hundred dollars, and hold my bonds as security for payment until I will be able to make you a remittance. Ask him. He cannot more than refuse. You may show him this paragraph.

The distance is so great that I fear my permission to visit the *Phila. Fair*[24] will not reach you in time for either you or Willie to go, nor do I suppose you can go without the necessary money. I wish you both to go.

My health continues very good but I must confess to being very tired.

Tell Captain Lee that I hope he will not take offence at my apparent negligence in not answering his letters. It is want of time, materials for writing, and a place to write, and not a desire to neglect it. Say to him I will yet make up for lost time, and that I hope to hear from him on the subject of politics, his opinion on the subject of the war, &c., &c.

Give love and kisses to all the children. Love to all our friends, and believe me, with prayers to Almighty God for your happiness and safety and of all of us. I am very truly

Your true and loving husband
Jno W Geary

P.S. Show what is necessary to Mr. Weir. Also give to Willie Geary to read. Adieu. *J.W. Geary*

*   *   *

Camp near Marietta Geo.   June 1864

My Dearest Mary

Since writing to you last I have gone through two terrible battles. One at "Pine Hill" and the other at "Pine Knob." The latter lasted two days and was fought principally by the "White Stars." My loss in killed & wounded is 519, of which 81 are killed. Captain [Moses] Veale of my staff is mortally wounded being shot through the lungs.[25] In the former battle my loss was light, artillery principally engaged during which Lieut. Genl Polk was

---

24. The Central Fair of eastern Pennsylvania, New Jersey, and Delaware lasted in Philadelphia from June 7 through June 28, 1864, matching New York's effort of roughly $1 million in contributions. Philadelphia's fair, however, was spread out over a larger area encompassing roughly two square blocks with Union Avenue, at Tenth Street, in the center. The effort was part of a massive benevolent campaign for soldiers' welfare organized nationally by the U.S. Sanitary Commission.

25. Veale survived this horrible wound and returned to duty later in the war, although he was shifted from staff responsibilities to an aide-de-camp.

killed by Knap's Battery. The result of these two battles is that the enemy is driven three miles nearer "Atlanta."[26]

Yesterday was a day of chase, of hard fighting, as usual I had a sharp round with a Division of the enemy's cavalry, in which I whipped them in twenty minutes, inflicting serious loss upon them. Immediately afterward, we encountered the main line of the rebel army. They opened a most tremendous Artillery fire upon us. I opened in return 12 guns upon them and utterly destroyed one of the rebel batteries. A desertee who escaped from it says the men and gun carriages were literally cut to pieces. We are fighting just now (when dont we fight) and the roar of musketry and artillery is terrific about 1 mile to my left. Our line of battle is about 10 miles in length. God in His infinite mercy has thus far spared me untouched. My health is as good as I can expect under the amount of labor and solicitude I have to undergo.

I often think of you and the dear ones at home when I am enveloped in the smoke of battle, and all the terrors of Pandemonium reign around me, and pray for you all *then*, and I often think how little you know of the terrors and horrors of war. God grant you may never hear it. Pray for my safety and I may yet return, but God only knows final results.

Give my love to Willie Geary and Henderson, and tell them how pleased I am to hear they are progressing well in their studies. Tell "Pet" I am delighted to hear how well she can spell and read, and that she is a good girl. As Maggie cannot talk yet, you may kiss her sundry times for me. Kiss Pet and Mary Lee. Give my love to Capt Lee, Mrs Church, and Comfort, John & Lizzie and Mr. & Mrs. Feeman. And give my kindest regards to my friend Eberly.

It is raining an Eastern storm here just now, and the rage of the battle gives it all the appearance of a *thunder storm*. We have not yet taken Marietta. It is defended by 100,000[27] rebels, and you know they fight with desperation.

---

26. On June 15, 1864, Geary's division participated with Butterfield's division in action against Confederates positioned just east of Gilgal Church. Both sides suffered large losses for little gain. Lieutenant General Polk was killed late morning while observing federal positions from Pine Mountain with Generals Johnston and William J. Hardee. The 5th Indiana Battery, not Knap's Battery, fired the fatal round.

27. Confederate effectives numbered closer to half of Geary's estimate of 100,000.

I must close this note. The paper is so damp I can scarcely write. My God bless us all, and keep us from every harm.

Ever your loving husband

J.W.G.

P.S. The country through which this great struggle is passing is entirely aband[on]ed and desolated. Scarcely a blade of grass remains.

*   *   *

Camp near "Noses Creek" Geo.   June 21st 1864

My Dearest Mary

I am still amidst the roar of artillery and the rattle of musketry and still I am unhurt and in good health, certainly I am a monument of God's mercy, and I cannot be too thankful to Him.

I am in receipt of your kind favor of the 9th inst. Your letters were always welcome, but never more welcome than now. It seems as if distance and difficulties of communication lends enchantment to our separation and in every respect brings the loved ones of home dearer and nearer to me.

Since my last we have fought the battles of "Mud Creek" and of "Noses Creek" two very difficult ones, where the enemy made stands and where severe actions occurred.[28]

Marching orders are this moment received, and I must move. So goodbye for the present. God bless you & all at home and May He preserve us from every harm.

Your true and loving husband

J.W.G.

It still rains incessantly and the roads are wonderful. I will drop a note from every possible point. The enemy are becoming more and more desperate.

---

28. Geary probably referred to skirmishing involved in getting into position across Noses Creek, June 20–21, as Sherman probed the Confederate left to find a way to flank Johnston and take Marietta. The Twentieth Corps faced forces led by Hardee and Lieutenant General John Bell Hood.

*   *   *

Camp, 3 miles from Marietta, Ga.   June 25th 1864

My Dearest Mary

I have just learned from Dr. Goodman of your safe arrival at Germantown, and the pleasure of the family at your coming, &c. &c.[29] I hope you will be able to enjoy your visit, but I am annoyed that there has been no paymaster here, and, consequently, that I have been so long unable to remit to you funds which you must urgently require.

I understand the fair at Philadelphia is a most magnificent *affair*, far eclipsing that held recently at New York, and, wonderful to be told, the New Yorkers acknowledge it.

The battle of Kulp's [Kolb's] Farm came off day before yesterday, in which the enemy under Hood were beaten with great loss.[30] Capt [William] Wheeler, chief of artillery on my staff, was killed, Capt [R. H.] Wilber, one of my A[ide].D[e].C[amp].s was hit in the left shoulder, and Capt [Thomas H.] Elliott A[ssistant].A[djutant].G[eneral]. recd contusion in the right thigh. My staff has suffered more than any other in the Army. My command has participated in ten battles during the present campaign without dimming the lustre of its glorious emblem, the "White Star." The total of our casualties will much exceed two thousand killed and wounded. If we keep on, the Division will soon be *"expended on the field of honor."*

A heavy battle is at this moment going on at Kenesaw Mountain about three miles on our left, the roar of artillery is incessant. I suppose it to be [Union Major General James B.] McPherson's command.

The enemy contests every inch of the way to Atlanta, with great obstinacy. And we have now been twenty eight days under fire since we left Bridgeport.

Amidst all the thunders of battle by which I have been surrounded, I am still untouched. The Mercy of God endureth about me, and I have been protected in the hollow of his hand. Praise God and give him eternal

---

29. Mary enjoyed a periodic correspondence during the war with an A. L. Goodman, sister of the surgeon who served with Geary.

30. The battle of Kolb's Farm on June 22, 1864, featured an attempt by Hood to push the Federals back along the Powder Spring road toward Manning's Mill, nearly two miles west of the farm that served as the main landmark between the two forces. The assault failed, costing Hood roughly 1,500 total casualties, while Union casualties were extremely light—numbering at most 250.

thanks. We cannot be too thankful for the past and we cannot too humbly beseech His protection for the future.

Relative to the Congressional nomination, it is almost impossible for me to give an opinion. In the first place I have nothing tangible to operate on. No nomination, nor an offer of any. Were a nomination offered me on the platform you mention, I would not decline it, but as to obtaining leave of absence and going home *to stump the District,* I cannot honorably do it. If nominated, however, I would address the people of the District by letter and remain in the field, leaving it to them to decide the question between me and an openly avowed Copperhead. You may give my views of the matter to Capt Lee, and take no part in it yourself.

Give love to all the children and relatives. Say to Capt. Lee to write me on the status of affairs generally. I am so busy I almost hate the sight of pen and paper.

Tell Willie G. to give me an account of the Fair in his next letter. Also Willie H. to give me a description of his *rural felicity* among the Allegheny Mountains.

I am sitting in the woods under a shady oak. The rains having ceased the sun pours down his rays on us in an unmerciful manner. It is extremely hot.

> Your almost melted
> but loving husband
> *J.W.G.*

*   *   *

> Hd. Qrs. 2nd Div. 20th Army Corps
> Near Chattahoochie River, Ga.   July 8th 1864

My Dearest Mary

I am the recipient of three letters from you bearing date at Germantown, and I assure you it afford me no ordinary pleasure to know that you have had the enjoyment of a congenial visit among friends and true hearted people. I sincerely trust that you will also enjoy your return home among the household jewels. I exceedingly regret that I have not yet been paid, (no paymaster having arrived) or I would have furnished sufficient funds for procuring furniture sufficient for the house. This was my intention had the P.M. done his duty. I am astonished to find there is nine hundred dollars to my credit in the Harrisburg Bank. Either Snodgrass or Mrs Brown has not collected the money due them and it still remains there on deposit, subject to my drafts which they hold. This is the only way in which I can account for that at present. If I could remit to you I would do so at once in sufficient amount to pay all our debts and furnish the house. I wish it was done.

We have had much hard fighting in Northern Georgia. The enemy has stubbornly contested every inch of ground. As fast as we drive him from one fortified position he simply falls back to another perhaps stronger, better, and more easy of defence aided by natural as well as artificial defences. The surface of the country is broken into an infinity of hills of the most irregular shapes and running in every possible direction. No two of them parallel. The valleys are deep ravines, and very marshy, being difficult to pass our artillery & waggons across them. It is almost universally covered with heavy timber with a dense undergrowth, and here and there *only* a field forms the exception. The country is well watered, and here in the vicinity of the river we find some cool springs which afford most delicious beverage. The inhabitants with but few exceptions have fled from before us as we have advanced in our victorious career. There is scarcely a man, woman, or child, or negro to be seen, not a horse (except the dead ones our cannon forced the enemy to leave behind) nor a cow, hog, or sheep is to be seen, even the very chickens, geese, and turkeys are driven before us as the enemy recedes, and not a living thing is left to tell the tale. Talking of turkeys reminds me of an incident a day or two ago. We were driving the enemy before us at a furious rate when near the head of my column a fine turkey mounted into the top of a hickory tree. It was very tempting, to think of the delicious meal it would make, so I drew my trusty revolver, and fired with deadly aim, down came the bird, and subsequently our agreeable anticipations were fully realized with a sumptuous repast.

The enemy are encamped partly on this side and partly on the south side. They are very strongly fortified and have an immense amount of artillery in position. They will undoubtedly make a stubborn resistance in this position. This Camp is about 1½ miles from the river, with the enemy between us and them. The only way to beat them here will be to outflank them as we have done heretofore.

The weather is excruciatingly warm, and it is almost impossible to perform more than half a day's labor in 24 hours. There is much remittant fever among the soldiers in consequence of the malarious influences arising from the decaying vegetable matter around us.

My own health, admist all my exposures, wettings, burnings, and dangers, is unusually good, and although death and sickness and every evil to which humanity is heir dwells around me, I am still by the mercy and goodness of Our Heavenly Father, a spared monument of His mercy. Let us devoutly and sincerely thank and praise Him for His manifold mercy to us.

We are now in full view of Atlanta (8 miles). Like Moses, we can find a high toped Pisgah, and from it view the promised land. *Geographically* speaking it is only 8 miles from us, but *militarily* it may be much further.

Kenesaw Mountain and the city of Marietta were taken on the 3rd inst. and since then we have fought our way here.[31]

I am pleased that the Philadelphia fair was so grand a success, and that you and Willie Geary had the satisfaction of visiting it. Such an occurrence may never happen again in a lifetime.

I long to see you and our dear ones at home once more. May God bless us and preserve us from every evil and soon restore our country to peace. Ever your true & loving husband

Jno W Geary

* * *

Hd. Qrs. 2nd Div: 20th A.C. Camp near Chattahoochie, Ga.
July 14th 1864

My Dearest Mary

Rumors of the invasion of Maryland and Pennsylvania reach us daily.[32] The statements concerning which, and the number of troops engaged in it, are so multifariously stated that we hardly know what to believe or what to imagine. The latter, imagination, is always busy and is always more ready to make things worse than they really are. If I could just be transferred suddenly to Pa [Pennsylvania], and light down amongst the invaders with

---

31. Kenesaw Mountain, June 27, was the scene of a bloody failure on the part of Sherman, who sent roughly 15,000 men against well-protected Confederates and lost roughly ten Union troops for every Rebel shot. Eventually, Kenesaw and Marietta fell as Sherman once again flanked the Southern army, forcing Johnston to fall back toward Atlanta.

32. After repelling a Union force from outside Lynchburg, Virginia, in late June, Confederate Lieutenant General Jubal A. Early swept down the Shenandoah Valley, crossed the Potomac, fought a battle at Monocacy Junction near Frederick, Maryland, and threatened the defenses at Washington, D.C. By this time, Early had recrossed the Potomac. The action concerned many in the North and forced Grant to send the better portion of two corps to Washington. The raid successfully fulfilled Robert E. Lee's objectives to preserve the valley's grain supply and divert troops that could be used against Confederates near Petersburg.

my Division, as it is, they would see such sights as they are not accustomed to witness, and the raiders would be soundly thrashed.

Give me the fullest information on this raid. I sincerely trust they will not molest our nest and little ones. Let me know what you have bought in the furniture line, and whether you have the house furnished. I received your letter of July 2nd in which I found you still remained in Philadelphia. How do you like the Goodman family? Is Billy Campbell crazy? If so, how long, and how does Mrs. Campbell take it?

We are still on the north bank of the river, although four Corps are over some distance above us probably with a view to turning the enemies flank. A few days will decide the course of new movements.

The weather is so warm we can scarcely move,— to keep from melting is about enough for us to do, without making it hotter by creating a battle.

There is a column of Federal troops numbering over 20,000 men, moving from the direction of New Orleans toward Mobile with a view to make an attack upon the latter place, in which a portion of our iron clad navy will co-operate, and if successful in capturing the place, Mobile will soon be our base of supplies and the movements will be onward.[33]

The picture of our beloved Eddie I think is almost perfection. To me it seems his dear face exactly. The baby's is very good except the mouth which she ought to be taught to keep closed under "photographic circumstances." Your picture like all others I have never seen certainly does not do you justice and in truth I must say I do not like it half as much as the original. I have given the pictures a place in my album, and thank you kindly for them as kind remembrances of loved absent ones.

Let me know who is nominated for Congress on the Union side in your District. Also on the Democratic side, and what the probable chances of success for the Union candidate will be. Give me also any other prospects you may have or know about political matters in general.

The destruction of the Alabama is a great triumph, and must more or less depress the ardor of the rebels.[34] I suppose Copperheads have new cause to lament.

33. Since March, the Union had been launching renewed and persistent efforts to capture the city of Mobile, Alabama, which resisted these efforts until nearly the end of the war, although David G. Farragut captured the port on August 5, 1864.

34. Constructed at the Laird Shipyards in England, the CSS *Alabama* fought a battle with the Union vessel USS *Kearsarge* on June 19, 1864, in international waters off Cherbourg, France. The *Alabama* sank after an exchange between the two warships that lasted roughly one hour. Thus ended a highly successful raiding career that spanned twenty-one months and resulted in sixty-four prizes worth more than $6.5 million.

Give my love and kisses to the children. Tell [them] I do not forget them, and I hope they will not forget me.

Remember me kindly to all our friends. I commit you and the children to the guardian care of Him who ruleth all things for the best. God bless and protect you all.

Ever and lovingly yours
Jno W Geary

* * *

{On July 17, Jefferson Davis could no longer tolerate the retreating of the Army of Tennessee and replaced Joseph Johnston with John Bell Hood. Knowing the political situation dictated an attack, Hood seized the chance to strike a portion of Sherman's force under Thomas that had split from the Union army and, in the battle of Peachtree Creek on July 20, exploited gaps in the line on both sides of Geary's Division. Candy's and Johnson's brigades panicked and fled, abandoning a four-gun battery. Hooker personally rallied Geary's reserve brigade to mount a counterattack that finally forced a Confederate retreat in that section of the line. Nearly half of Geary's losses came during this part of the fighting, which featured Ireland's Brigade. While substantially correct, Geary's account to his wife embellishes his role in the battle, while ignoring both the Federal chaos and Hooker's presence.}

* * *

Head Quarters, 2nd Division, 20th A.C., Near Atlanta, Ga.
July 24th 1864

My Dearest Mary

You have doubtlessly ere this learned of the terrible battle of "Peach Tree Creek," about 4 miles from Atlanta in which my Division acted so prominent a part. With less than 3,000 men I had advanced about 800 yds. in front of the main line of our corps and secured a lodgement upon a fine ridge, easy of defence, if fully occupied. I had the assurance that the 1st Divn would advance also and hold that portion of it which extended to my right. *This was not done*, and two entire corps. numbering at 30,000[35] men flanked us in that position. They soon reached the hill on my right and

35. The Confederates numbered roughly 19,000 total.

doubled round into my rear, thus enveloping my command on three sides, front right and rear. Under such a pressure I changed my front to the right, shortening my original line as much as possible, and with my second line at right-angles to my first, I succeeded in defeating the enemy. My command, being in the centre, sustained the main portion of the assault. After three and a half hours hard fighting the battle ceased at dark and we lay on our arms during the night. The loss in my Division was severe, in killed and wounded and missing amounts to 476. Capt Elliott my Adjutant General was killed, also, Col [George A.] Cobham of [the 111th] Pennsylvania—both very valuable and beloved Officers.

The battle of "Peach Tree Creek" occurred on the 20th. The 21st was occupied in burying our own, and the enemy's dead, and caring for the wounded.

On the 22nd our line advanced to this place driving the enemy to his fortifications around the city and within it. We are now within shelling distance of it, and the roar of several hundred pieces artillery is incessant night and day. Atlanta is a beautiful city, on a hill, well built, and contains 30,000 inhabitants. It is now being invested and beseiged. It cannot hold out long, although its frowning battlements meet us on every side.

The entire loss of the Enemy at Peach Tree Creek is acknowledged by them to be about 5,000, while the entire loss of our army was about 1,600.[36]

On the 22nd a battle occurred on our left in which our Gen McPherson was killed. On the whole it is said not to have been so favorable to our arms [as] the battle of "P.T. Creek."[37]

We are strongly entrenched and we have to lay close to our embankment to escape the shells and missiles of the enemy. They are no respectors of persons and would just as soon hit one person as another.

My health is reasonably good, notwithstanding the intense heat of the weather.

36. Current scholarship places Confederate casualties at roughly 2,500, and Union casualties at 1,700. Geary's men suffered greatly: the 476 casualties accounted for 28 percent of all the Federal losses, but Williams's 1st Division sustained even higher casualties. See Castel, *Decision in the West*, 380–81.

37. The battle of Bald Hill, July 22, east of Atlanta on the Georgia Railroad. Hood had attacked the left wing of Sherman's force, the Army of the Tennessee under James B. McPherson. During the fighting, McPherson had gone to check a gap in his line when Rebels emerged from the brush and demanded his surrender. He doffed his hat, wheeled, and tried to flee, but the Confederates cut him down. A bloody day of fighting accomplished little, but cost Hood about 5,500 out of 35,000 soldiers and the Federals about 3,700. Historian Albert Castel (ibid., 414) believes that the Twentieth Corps, in which Geary served, missed an opportunity to storm the city of Atlanta while this fighting went on.

God in His merciful Providence admidst so many dangers and battle has still preserved my life. We cannot be too grateful and thankful to Him for His mercies for they endure forever. To Him be ascribed all the honor and the glory for we are only His instruments to effect His all-wise purposes.

Give my love to Willie G and Willie H.—tell Willie G. I do not wish him to enter the ranks again as a private under no circumstances. It will be sufficient for him to take care of the family and let others take care of the *country*. I would like to have a letter from him soon.

Give my love and kisses to Pet Geary and Mary Lee. Kiss little Maggie a dozen times.

Remember me fraternally to Capt Lee and John Church. Also to Comfort and Mrs. C. I hope this campaign will soon terminate when I can go home and at least pay you a visit, and perhaps when I can do so *honorably* will quit the service.

Write me as often as you can. Your letters are always read, and heartily welcomed.

Pardon this hasty scrawl. It is written on my knee under a heavy bombardment from the enemy.

God bless you all.

Your affectionate husband
Jno W Geary

*   *   *

Camp near Atlanta   July 29th 1864

My Dearest Mary

Your two esteemed favors of the 18th and 20th inst. have been received. Accept my thanks for these and other similar favors. As usual I am writing to you under a heavy cannonade. This is the fourth day of the seige, and throughout the live-long day the bursting of bombshells, the booming of Cannon, the rattling of small arms, the dead and the dying are features of the day and the night. But there are still worse features than these. *War* and pestilence I have witnessed, but my eyes have been spared until now from witnessing the emaciated and languid form of their skinny twin sister *famine*. To-day I saw a young mother with a starving child so poor as scarcely to live, seeking bread at our home. Her husband was a conscript in the rebel ranks, and this is but a specimen of Davis' work. If there is one spot in hell hotter than another, why should it not be reserved for him who has brought such evils on his fellow man.

I cannot tell how long the seige will last, but Atlanta is not taken yet, and its frowning heights are very powerful.

Maj Gen Hooker took umbrage at the appointment of [Major] Gen [Oliver O.] Howard to the Army of Tennessee in place of Gen McPherson who was killed and has been relieved at his own request. There we are now without a Major Genl to command the corps. Who will be assigned I cannot tell.[38]

There is much hard fighting in this Campaign. My command has lost about 3000 men killed and wounded. The destruction of the enemy by us has been terrible.

My health continues good. The weather is very warm and I am sunburnt as yellow as sole leather, but that will wear off. When there arrives a time in which I can honorably do so I will go home.

Remember me in love to the children. Kiss them all for me. Give kindest regards to Capt Lee and all our friends. What about that Congressional nomination?[39]

May God, as in the past, ever be merciful to us and preserve us in safety. Ever your true husband

J.W.G.

The Pay Master has not come yet.

*   *   *

Camp near Atlanta   Aug 1st 1864

My Dearest Mary

Your kind letter of July 24th is received and I am thankful to hear that you are all well, and that the great raid scare is over, but I have later news by Telegraph, that is, that another invasion was going on, and that 40,000

---

38. Sherman chose Major General Henry W. Slocum to replace Hooker as chief of the Twentieth Corps. While Slocum made his way from Vicksburg, Alpheus Williams temporarily commanded the corps.

39. New Cumberland sat in the 15th District, which included the counties of York, Cumberland, and Perry. Democrat Adam J. Glossbrenner ran against, and defeated, a Republican named Bailey. Born in Washington County, Maryland—also the home of Geary's mother—Glossbrenner lived in York, Pennsylvania, and had deep roots in Democratic politics, having served as a clerk in the U.S. Congress and State Department and as a private secretary to President James Buchanan, whom Geary despised.

rebels are at Chambersburg.[40] This is a beautiful commentary on the military prowess and foresight of some of our rebels, both state and national. I feel under these circumstances as if I ought to be home to take care of the loved ones there and if needs be to battle my enemies there in defence of my altars and fireside, and the loved ones surrounding.

The siege of Atlanta drags its slow length along, and with the exception of some manouvering but little has as yet been accomplished. We have advanced our works near the city line, but Shermans great object is to outflank the rail-road which leads to Macon.

This will be done in a day or two, and then we hope to see the inside walls of Atlanta.

I am much worn down with constant fatigue, and the heat of the weather but hope to weather the storm safely with God's blessing. Otherwise my health is good.

Hoping this will reach you safely at home, and that we still have a home, though if half the stories of a present raid be true, it is hoping against hope to hope that we yet have a house for I verily believe the rebels will burn our house. Then if God spares my life you will see sights. I'll burn up every town which may thereafter fall into my possession.

Give love and kisses to all the children. Regards to friends.

This is written in the rain amidst the booming of cannon, bursting of shells &c. I hope you will therefore excuse its many imperfections. I am as ever your true husband with abiding love

Jno W Geary

* * *

Camp near Atlanta, Ga.   Aug. 3rd 1864

My Dearest Mary

I am in receipt of your valued letter of the 22nd ult. and I hasten to reply that I am about in usual health, and am trying to recuperate myself from the fatigues of the late terrible battles. Accounts of which you have

---

40. In retaliation for the burning of private homes in the Shenandoah Valley by Union forces under Major General David Hunter, Confederate Lieutenant General Jubal Early sent a brigade of cavalry under John M. McCausland to demand $100,000 in gold or $500,000 in U.S. currency, or else the Pennsylvania town would be burned. When the citizens refused to comply, McCausland followed Early's orders and destroyed a substantial portion of the town.

doubtlessly read from more than one graphic pen, but how truthful a tale may be told is hard to say. It is enough for me to tell you that on Wednesday the 20th ult. my command fought and whipped six times our own number. It was in reality a second Wauhatchie, occasioned by the failure (needless criminal failure) of the 1st Division to come into line on my right. I whipped Hood once more, and I think he will not wish to trouble the white stars again. The rebel loss could not have been less than 6000.[41]

Every thing has been very quiet here for several days, but is that kind of quietness that the tiger or the cat uses before springing upon its prey. Our troops are moving from our left to the right, where I think a battle will be fought to-day. The battle may take place on the left, however, as our enemy is very wiley, and as he sees our troops massing on the right, he may think our left weak and strike there. I am now in the left flank and in the latter event will be engaged. If the fight takes place on the right, I will push my command into Atlanta and endeavor to let my banner be the first to float over its battlement. God grant it may be so in victory and safety. At all events you may look for a battle here today or tomorrow.[42]

I hope Willie Geary will not again enlist as a private. If he must come into the service, I can take him with me as an officer, where I can take care of him, and see to his improvement and promotion. I hope the re-newed action of Grant in blowing up and assaulting the enemy's works at Petersburg will be productive of the final reduction of the city, and of recalling the Raiders from Penna.[43] I have had no news of the raid except the report alluded [to] in my last letter that 40,000 rebels were at Chambersburg.

41. Geary stretches the truth considerably here by making it appear that his division was the only one on the field. Confederates had roughly 19,000 troops. The 2nd Division probably contained about 3,500 before the attack on July 20. For the Southern force to be six times that of the 2nd Division meant that Confederates fought no one else that day, when in fact two other divisions from the Twentieth Corps absorbed heavy losses, particularly the 1st Division, under Alpheus Williams. These two divisional commanders obviously disliked each other. Just before the battle, Williams wrote home to complain of the self-serving claims that Geary distributed through the newspapers, adding: "I have been made exceedingly mad, I confess, to read the meanness which would rob another division of its well-earned reputation, to bolster up some ambitious fool to a major generalship" (*From the Cannon's Mouth*, 331).

42. No major battle occurred, but Sherman's men met stiff resistance as they crossed Utoy Creek and forced Confederates to extend lines south and west of Atlanta.

43. Geary referred to a mine dug by the 48th Pennsylvania under the Confederate line at Petersburg. Union soldiers packed explosives into the tunnel, and on July 30 the explosion left an immense crater that created a half-mile gap in the line. Because of incompetent leadership, the Union failed to exploit this opportunity. Nearly 15,000 Federal soldiers piled into the area, including U.S. Colored Troops, most of which provided easy targets when they funneled into the crater. Roughly 4,000 Northern casualties resulted; the South lost 1,500.

Let me hear from you frequently. I am very anxious about you and our dear home. Let me know without delay anything that menaces you.

Give my love to Willie Geary and the babies, and believe me very truly your faithful and loving husband

Jno. W. Geary

* * *

Camp near Atlanta Ga   Aug 10th 1864

My Dearest Mary

Yesterday was a day of continuous cannonading from 100 pieces on our side, from morning to night, inflicting terrible damage upon the houses and public edifices in the doomed city. I saw the gable end of an elegant house stove in by one of the shots. I cannot tell how many lives were lost but the casualties among the enemy must have been numerous. The great bulk of our army is on our right flank in the direction of East Point, which place is regarded as the key to Atlanta. At East Point the Rail Road diverges to Macon, and it being regarded as the key to the city it is deemed imperatively necessary that it be taken as that road is now the only one which furnishes the rebel army its supplies. It is expected that this point will be captured by tomorrow, after which we may look for the early capture or surrender of the city. Today I have been busy in superintending the erection of a battery in which I will place 6 forty pounders, with a view to the bombardment of the city. I assure you I will awake her up when I get them ready.

The siege is tardy, but we are hopeful of a speedy reduction of the city. I am again in the enjoyment of my usual health and am recovering from the fatigue of our recent Campaign.

The enemy's soldiers have commenced to desert and there is no more hopeful sign of the fact about to be that they will "give out."

It is now 12 days since the date of your last letter, and as I am conscious that you are menaced by the new raid I feel very anxious about you and our little ones. I feel confidence in God that He will in His good pleasure guard and protect us as in former days, if we will only put our trust in Him.

God bless you dear Mary and the children. May Heaven protect you from every evil.

Your loving husband

Jno W Geary

No Pay Master yet.

*   *   *

Hd. Qrs. 2nd Div 20th A.C. Camp near Atlanta, Ga.
August 11th 1864

My Dearest Mary

I have a few moments of leisure this morning and I hasten to devote them to you. Last night I dreamed sweetly of you and of the dear ones at home. The fact of seeing you all even in my sleep, in the fancies of the night was very pleasant and the vividness of the vision made it next to reality. The soldier's dream of home is one of the most delightful in which I have ever reveld in the stilly-night. The weather is exceedingly wet, and my clothes have not been dry for the last seven nights. Still I do not experience much difficulty in consequence of it. The noisey siege is still progressing. The battery of heavy guns placed in my lines was opened yesterday and during the night a gun was fired every five minutes. It was fearful to listen to the crashing of the shell through the houses as if they were so many egg shells, and finally wound up with a terrific explosion scattering the fragmentary remains to the four quarters of the globe. To bring the matter more particularly to your imagination just think of a 64 pounder passing through Harrisburg every five minutes, and you can have a just idea of the circumstances surrounding the doomed city of Atlanta.

I cannot give you any idea of the length of time it will require to reduce the city, but every thing looks hopeful and must yield under present prospects. I have endeavored to perform my duty in this war. Do you think it receives proper appreciation, among the real people, aside from politicians?

My health is reasonably good, and a little rest would soon restore me to full vigor.

Why don't Willie Geary write to me? He has plenty of time, and he should do it. Give my love to him and Willie Henderson. Kiss the girls for me. Give my regards to all kind friends. Tell Capt Lee I will wait anxiously for his political news.

With most ardent love and confidence in you, I commit you to the care of Him who alone can protect us from every evil.

Your account of the raid is thankfully received. I hope the burning of Chambersburg will teach the people of Pa how to take care of themselves.

As ever your true husband
Jno W Geary

* * *

Hd. Qrs. 2nd Divsn, 20th A.C. Camp one mile from Atlanta
Aug 15th 1864

My Dearest Mary

I am in receipt of your kind letters up to August 1st and tender to you my warmest thanks for the many fervent expressions of love and regard contained therein, and desire to renew my assurances that they are all more than reciprocated in my own breast. I assure you absence does not decrease my love for you and my devoted attachment to home and the tender ties contained therein, but on the other hand greatly increases it. If I ever get safely moored at home with the benign influences of peace around me, I will never again wish to rove from its sweet precincts, and would be disposed to live upon less rather than submit to a separation from all I hold most dear and loved. This war lasts so long that I sometimes fear you will have nothing left but the old soldier, who will be utterly useless for all else than "to shoulder the crutch and fight his battles over again." In other words, a *troublesome old fellow*, worn out in the service. However the bugles blast brings me to my feet yet with the ardor and strength of youth, and none leave me behind in the contest. Great God when will all these terrible battles cease. For one hundred days and nights consecutively I have been in the whistle of bullets and blaze of battle; even at this very moment more than 50 cannon are being fired upon the doomed city of Atlanta. This continues night and day with[out] intermission. Fires are frequent and of nightly occurrence in the city, a whole block was destroyed night before last, the houses are riddled with cannon balls or torn to pieces with shells & many of the inhabitants are killed. Still Hood holds out sternly, and we must content ourselves with a continuance of the work of destruction.

When the city will be taken I cannot tell. The works and defences around it are certainly equal to those around Richmond.

One of the best estimates we have of our ultimate success is that large numbers of the enemy are deserting and coming over to us, like *rats* deserting a sinking ship.

My health is good and I am in good spirits, and feel that the rebellion is tottering to its destruction. We must therefore persevere, and blessed will be he who endures unto the end.

Give my love to Wm G & H. I will devote some attention to Willie Geary's schooling if I have time when we reach Atlanta. Give love and kisses to all the children, respect to all friends, and accept for yourself my most devoted love

Your husband
J. W. Geary

*   *   *

Hd. Qrs. 2nd Div, 20th A.C. Near Atlanta, Ga.
Aug. 23rd 1864

My Dearest Mary

I am indebted to you for your kind and interesting favor of May 15th, just received and I hasten to acknowledge its receipt.

There is no change of any importance in our position relative to the enemy. Genl [Judson] Kilpatrick has just made a successful raid entirely around the army of the enemy in Atlanta cutting the Macon Rail Road in two places. This will undoubtedly be followed by a general movement on our part before many days.[44]

My health is good.

---

44. The night of August 18, Kilpatrick left with 4,700 men to sweep around the Confederate left to hit the Macon & Western Railroad at Lovejoy's Station below Jonesboro, south of Atlanta. Lawrence Ross's Texas Brigade of 400 men burned bridges, set ambushes, and provided other obstacles to slow the Union advance. Kilpatrick expelled Ross's Texans from Jonesboro, but had to cut his way out of an encirclement at Lovejoy's Station. He rode around both armies because the route offered the best way back. The Union forces accomplished disappointingly little, having torn up only half a mile of track at Jonesboro and some rails south of Lovejoy's. Most of the damage was repaired before Kilpatrick returned to the army on August 23.

Capt Lee's letter also received. I will answer it in the morning.
Give love to all the children and accept the Lion's share yourself.

> Your true and faithful husband
> *Jno. W. Geary*

P.S. The P. Master is on his way!

*   *   *

Hd. Qrs. 2nd Div 20th Army Corps   Paces Ferry Geo.
September 1st 1864

My Dearest Mary

I am indebted to you for letters up to August 24th, and you must
pardon me for not writing for a few days as we were in a position not at all
supplied with mail facilities. Sherman has been manouvering his army with
a view to induce the rebels to come out of Atlanta. Our Corps now guards
the fords of the Chattahoochie River 6 miles from the city, while the other
portion of the army are marching around the right of the city to cut off the
sources of supplies for the Rebels in it by destroying the West-Point and
Macon Rail Roads. I understand by rebel deserters just entering my lines
that the roads are both in our possession. If so, it is only a question of how
many rations they may have. Something will occur for weal or woe very
shortly here. So keep a lookout for breakers.

I have also a letter from Willie. He is desirous of entering the Army.
This must not be. We have already made many sacrifices in this war, and I
hope you will disuade him for any such purpose. He must not look to the
bounty as any inducement. It is my intention to send him to school ere
long, and he had much better await my decision in that matter.

The Paymaster has not yet paid off myself and staff, but he will be here
soon. I am informed that some money has been deposited to my credit at
the Harrisburg Bk. If so, see Mr. Wier, and he will pay to you five hundred dollars and charge it to me. I will write him to that effect.

Yesterday I wrote to Mary a brief letter, it being her birthday. I hope
she and all the rest are well. I will write to Willie Geary again very soon.

Write me as frequently as you can. Your letters are always a solace to me
above all others. They always receive the preference. May God bless and

protect the innocent ones at home, and may you be an especial object of His divine care.

I am well.

Ever your faithful and loving husband

Jno. W. Geary

*   *   *

Hd. Qrs.   Atlanta, Ga.   Sept 3rd 1864

My Dearest Mary

I telegraphed you the thrice glorious tidings of the capture of this far-famed city, and now from one of its most stately mansions, I have the honor to address you. As stated in my telegram of the 2nd, the city was occupied in the fornoon of that day, The 20th Corps being the 1st to enter. And the flags of the ever-a-head and glorious old White Star Division were the first to wave from the town Hall, and the battlements surrounding. The heaviest fighting was South of the city, and we entered from the north. About 3,000 prisoners are captured. Among the spoils are 17 pieces of heavy artillery, a large quantity of ammunition and small arms &c. &c. The rebels in their haste burned a large number of houses containing stores of various kinds. Also burned 81 rail road cars containing artillery ammunition. We also captured 3 locomotives and 7 partly burned, with many cars.

The city is a very pretty place, built much in northern taste and stile, and contained about 15,000 inhabitants. There is scarcely a house that does [not] exhibit in some degree the effects of the battle which so fearfully raged around it. Many of the best are utterly ruined, and many of the ornamental trees are cut down by our shells.

Here amidst the glories of victory which God has vouchsafed to give us, is the best place to witness the horrors of war, the wounded and the dying—the starving, ruined, people whose infatuation seems in many instances to be chronic, mope around the corners as if some unearthly catastrophe had occurred, and it brings to my mind a vivified scene of the times when it was said, "Babylon is fallen."

I will reserve a fuller account of the city for another letter.

Give love and kisses to the children. I wrote some days ago to Capt Lee,

and Mary Geary, & Willie Geary. I send you a few leaves and a rose bud
plucked in Atlanta.

With devoted love your faithful husband
Jno. W. Geary

Call on Mr. Wier for $500.

* * *

Hd. Qrs, 2nd Div: 20th A.C.   Atlanta   September 8th 1864

My Dearest Mary

In consequence of the raid now in progress in our rear under [Major
General Joseph] Wheeler of the Rebel cavalry, no mails containing either
letters or papers have for 3 or 4 days been received. Consequently I have
not heard from you for several days. Our occupancy of this city has thus far
been undisturbed. The inhabitants of the city who remained after its capture have been thrown into great excitement by an order of Gen Sherman
directing that all the inhabitants should leave the place within five days,
permitting them to elect whether they would go north or south. This is to
prevent them from becoming chargeable to our government and of eating
up the rations and subsistence intended for the army.[45] I have not yet had
time to give you a description of Atlanta, will do so at no distant day. I am
now engaged upon my report of the part *performed by* us in the brilliant
campaign just terminated by the capture of the city.

I enclose you a few of the printed orders of Maj. Gen. Sherman relative
to important transactions in Georgia. There is a short armistice agreed
upon between Gen Sherman and Gen Hood to terminate on the 22nd instant. There will probably be no fighting until after that time.

I regret to inform you of the death of one of my bravest and best Brigade
Commanders Col David Ireland [of the 3rd Brigade], died of dysentary this
morning, —a great loss to my command and to the service.

My health is as good as usual, though I must confess I am a good deal
worn down [by] the rigors of the campaign.

Kiss the dear little ones for me. Give my love to the Willies, to Capt Lee
and all our friends. And remember me to my friend Eberly.

45. Sherman issued this order on September 7. More than 400 families totaling roughly 1,600 people
were forced to leave the city between September 11 and 20.

I may not write you very fully until my report is finished, as it will be very voluminous and very important. I am as ever in love and affectionate regard your devoted husband

Jno W Geary

*   *   *

Atlanta, Georgia   September 18th 1864

My Dearest Mary

I have not written to you for several days. My whole time, night and day, having been occupied in writing my Official Report of the part sustained by my Division in the late memorable and glorious campaign. It embraces one hundred and twenty three days from the time we entered on the journey, May 2nd, to our entrance into the city during the present month.

During which time we fought ten pitched battles, three times as many skirmishes, and were under fire most of the time. It was indeed but one grand battle, one grand victory from beginning to its end.

The number of casualties in my command was 2700. I have punished the enemy whenever I could and from my Division he has suffered tremendous losses. He had better never have fought at Wauhatchie. Vengeance is sweet and the Lord has repaid.

The mails have again begun to arrive as usual and I am in receipt of your letters dated Aug. 28th, 31st, Sept. 4th and 10th, for all of which please accept my thanks. I am pleased to learn the good accounts concerning yourself and the children, and every thing seems more than usually cheerful, and consequently I am much more happy. Of course my family are my first care and love, and when they seem happy, I will be so as a matter of course. I am also pleased that Miss Goodman has at last paid you her long looked for visit. I hope you have enjoyed her trip and visit very much. Her brothers here are well.[46]

My report will occupy at least 200 pages of fools cap paper, closely written, and will take several days yet to finish it.[47]

46. H. Ernest Goodman, former surgeon of the 28th Pennsylvania who rose to Brevet Colonel and Surgeon-in-Chief of the Army of Georgia, and Samuel Goodman, who served as a staff officer with Geary.

47. The finished report is a monstrous effort that consumes thirty-five pages in the *Official Records*. To tell about his one division, Geary wrote five pages more than Sherman needed to record the movements of the entire army. See *O.R.*, 38, pt. 2, 112–47.

What Sherman has in store for us, I cannot tell. Every one is busy with reports and nothing else is yet spoken of. I would like to go home but must wait events. Give *love* and *kisses* to all the children. Tell the Willies their letters are truly welcome and I am looking for one from each of them. Remember me in love to Capt Lee & Mary.

I am in devoted love your truly faithful husband

Jno W Geary

6

Through Georgia and the Carolinas

September 1864–April 1865

{Although Atlanta was secured, the Union army inside the city remained vulnerable. Hood's 30,000 soldiers could not take the city but could disrupt supply lines stretching from Chattanooga to Atlanta and entice Union troops to pursue into Tennessee. For a while, this strategy worked as Sherman emptied most of the army from Atlanta to give chase. Only the Twentieth Corps, including Geary's division, guarded the city. The Confederates left an annoying trail of destruction, cutting rails for eight miles from Big Shanty to above Acworth, which severed the mail temporarily between Geary and home. Repairs required 35,000 new ties, six miles of iron, and 10,000 men working for seven days. This helped convince Sherman to sever his supply lines and conduct his march to the sea.[1]

In Atlanta, Geary's division busied itself with garrison chores and raiding for supplies. "We take every thing from the people without remorse," he wrote Mary on November 1. Shortly, he would have an opportunity to seize even more as Sherman's

---

1. As early as October 9, Sherman revealed in a telegram to Thomas at Nashville: "I want to destroy all the road below Chattanooga, including Atlanta, and to make for the sea-coast. We cannot defend this long line of road" (W. T. Sherman, *Memoirs of General W. T. Sherman: Written by Himself*, 2 vols. [New York, 1875], 2:152).

army traveled first to Savannah on the Georgia coast, then through South Carolina and into North Carolina. Geary's wartime journey nearly described a complete circle as his division proceeded from the Virginia theater of war through the western theater and back to the East.}

*   *   *

Atlanta, Ga.   Sept. 23rd 1864

My Dear Wife

I have this moment received your kind favor of the 15th inst. giving a description of your visit to Chambersburg, and of your sensations upon witnessing the scene of the ruins, and how the bereaved people must have felt when under orders to leave their loved homes for the purpose of their houses being burnt. Well this is war, and only a small portion of it at that. I would not like you to witness some of the terrible scenes through which I have passed. Your nerves would not stand it. Why even in this city women and children were crushed to pieces by our cannonballs and shells during the siege—houses torn to pieces—burned. The horrors of a single battle field must be seen to be appreciated. You have no doubt witnessed the scene of the conflict at Gettysburg and of course, out of compliment to me, you would visit the spot where I and my Division did battle. You saw there a small portion still imprinted upon the trees and rocks. Our old breast works, hastily constructed, before which lay 1200 of the enemy "stark and stiff" beside the wounded.

The crash of musketry and the sound of cannon you cannot hear—that is left for the imagination, but enough is there to teach you the dangers of a single battle, and to point us to the Great Mercy of God, who has so often, amid such scenes[,] preserved me still among the living. I hope you have returned safely, and that you will give me a full account of what your impressions of what a battle field is when viewed 15 months after the conflict.

I have written you many letters which had not reached you up to the date of your letter, doubtlessly you have recd them by this time.

Give my love and many kisses to the children.

My health is good and my time is still taken up with my report, which is quite lengthy.

The weather is very wet, and the equinoctial storms are prevailing.

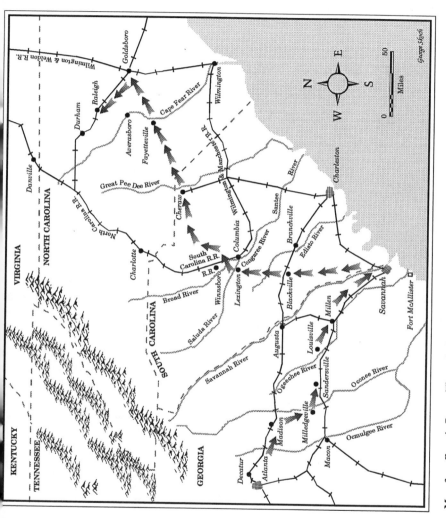

Map 3. Geary's Route Through Georgia and the Carolinas

The enemy are again reported in motion and it is probable some of us will be sent to watch his movement. Sheridan's victory was grand.[2] I commit you and all ours to the care of the great Creator. Your loving husband

J W G

*   *   *

Atlanta Ga.   Oct 1st 1864

My Dearest Mary

Last night I wrote a brief note to Willie which I suppose will reach him simultaneously with this to you. I gave him some of the current affairs of the times, and I suppose you would prefer yours dedicated to matters of a more personal character. The weather here has been as warm as at any period of the summer, except the nights are a little cool. It is now raining as if it had never rained before, and as though Noah's deluge was about to be reenacted, but the bow of promise appears in the lucid intervals and allays all fear (if there be any) of that dire catastrophe.

Atlanta is situated on high and very undulating ground, and why it was ever selected as a site for a town, has not yet occurred to my imagination. I suppose it was the result of some accidental start. 22 years ago it was a howling wilderness, and it is only 18 years since the first house was erected in it. Northern capitalists came here and built it up with taste. The situation is high and healthful, being 1050 feet above tide water, and I suppose that advantage over the low and unhealthy cities of the south has given its chief celebrity. For it has neither river or mountain or rich plain, surrounding, to make it a mart for commerce, mineral, or agricultural wealth, but since the days of Rail Road it has become quite a manufacturing place, and Foundries, Machine shops, Car factories are to be found in abundance. There [are] several beautiful churches numbered among its edifices, also, The town hall, three immense hotels, with several smaller ones, a masonic hall, Athenaeum, and many fine and tasteful private residences, with sufficient of a poorer sort to cover 15,000 inhabitants. In point of inhabitants it was about equal to Harrisburg, but covered much more territory, and was

---

2. On September 19, Sheridan's Army of the Shenandoah defeated Confederate forces under Jubal Early at the battle of Third Winchester, Virginia. Two days later, Early suffered another defeat at Fisher's Hill near Strasburg, some twenty-two miles south of Winchester.

by no means so compactly built. The lots are generally large, & [with] the house in the centre, surrounded with forest trees and shrubbery of all kinds. The streets are wide and straight but are angular like those of Washington City, all terminating towards the heart of the city. The cemetery is almost a wonder—it contains nearly 10,000 newly made graves filled principally by rebel losses in the late battles. The principal ridge which is its backbone, is the watershed which divides the waters of the Ocmulgee river, which empties into the Atlantic, and those of the Flint and Chattahoochie rivers, which at their confluence form the Apalachicola river, and carries their waters into Apalachee Bay in Gulf of Mexico. The climate is very mild, and ice is seldom formed as thick as window-glass. All the northern fruits grow well here, particularly the peach. Figs and grapes thrive, and could be produced in abundance if the energy of the white men was bestowed upon their production and culture. The Staple commodities are Cotton, Tobacco, Corn and Oats, but little wheat being cultivated. The native timber bears a remarkable resemblance to that of Penna, with here and there an additional variety. As the streams are small and filthy, I have not seen or tasted any fish. The only wild game I have seen is quail. Snakes are numerous and among them may be found some huge rattlesnakes, and others of a poisonous nature. Domestic grasses and clover are almost unknown. Domestic cattle are very scarce and of poor quality. In fine, the country has been cruelly "niggered." It might be made a paradise.

Pardon me for having spun out this uninteresting letter to so great a length, and I will not do so any more. Except the officers and soldiers of our army, there are but few remaining citizens, and they are daily decreasing.

A new system of fortifications, much smaller than those of the rebels, are being laid out, the completion of which will destroy many of the finest edifices in the city. Three divisions of our troops are sent back to Tennessee and Alabama to look after [Nathan Bedford] Forrest and Wheeler, who are trying to cut the rail roads behind us.[3]

How I would like to be at home and take a romp with you and the children. I would enjoy it well.

Time makes my feelings grow stronger to you, dear Mary and the little

3. To protect supply depots at his rear, Sherman sent Newton's Division of the Fourth Corps and Corse's Division of the Seventeenth Corps to Chattanooga and Rome on September 24. When it became clear that Confederates contemplated more than a cavalry maneuver, Sherman on September 29 also dispatched Major General Thomas with Morgan's Division of the Fourteenth Corps to coordinate matters in Tennessee.

ones at home. You need have no fears that time or distance will conquer love, it only sets it the more firmly.

Give love and kisses to all the family. Remember me to Capt Lee, with high regard.

Ever true & faithful
Jno W Geary

*   *   *

Hd Qrs. 2nd Div 20th A.C.   Atlanta Ga.   October 18th 1864

My Dearest Mary

You are doubtlessly aware that our communications by rail are cut by the enemy between here and Chattanooga, and consequently, no letters have been transmitted either north or south for several weeks. In this matter the rebels have had quite a success, but up to this time they have not injured us much except in the way of transmitting news. I understand the road will be open in a day or two, and I hasten to drop you a few lines to inform you of our welfare.[4] I have not had a letter from you for several weeks, but the "back numbers" will come in a bunch when they will be all the "welcomer."

I have just returned from an extended foraging expedition, of which I was in command. I took three brigades and a battery with me, and a train of 450 waggons. I ravaged the country thoroughly for a considerable distance south of this in the direction of Macon along the West Bank of the Ocmulgee River. The expedition was eminently successful and repaid Mr. Hood for the damage he did us to the Northward. All our teams returned laden to overflowing with corn and sweet potatoes.[5] The latter are very fine and abundant. I had two fights with the enemy and whipt him in both encounters, "Old Geary" is as much of a terror to the Georgians as he used to be [to] the Virginians.

We are engaged on new fortifications for the defence of the city by a

---

4. Repairs on the railroad began shortly after Hood failed to take Allatoona on October 5 and reopened the line just about the time Geary wrote this letter home.

5. As Sherman pursued Hood through the Chattooga Valley, the Union force drew supplies from the farms there. Sherman noted the irony: "General Slocum, in Atlanta, had likewise sent out, under strong escort, large trains of wagons to the east, and brought back corn, bacon, and all kinds of provisions, so that Hood's efforts to cut off our supplies only reacted on his own people" (Sherman, *Memoirs*, 2:157–58).

Fig. 7.   The general poses with his staff at Atlanta. The stars on their coats indicate the "White Star" division. The Twentieth Corps performed garrison duty in the city and stripped the neighboring countryside of supplies in preparation for the march to Savannah, Georgia. (U.S. Army Military History Institute, Carlisle Barracks)

much smaller number than was contemplated by the rebels when they constructed theirs. Our Corps is the only one in Atlanta, the rest having gone to rear after the rebel raiders. What will be the ultimate destination of our Corps. I am at present unable to tell. A few weeks will determine. There will no doubt, however, be some active work after a short time.

My health is good and the command is generally well. If I can I will obtain leave as soon as some of the fall campaign is over, as I am quite home-sick, and I am getting tired of what is called the "Sunny South." Give me the dear *Old North* in preference yet. Give love and kisses to the children. Give me your ideas of Gettysburg battlefield. I am ever your faithful and loving husband

Jno. W. Geary

* * *

Hd. Qrs. 2nd Div: 20th A.C.   Atlanta Ga.   Oct 19th 1864

My Dearest Mary

I have the pleasure to acknowledge the receipt of four letters from you, enclosing one from Willie G. They came in the midst of a very large accumulated mail which had been delayed at Chattanooga in consequence of Hood's raid in our rear. Our forces now have full possession of the road, and Hood is supposed to be retreating towards Tallidega, Ala.[6]

Our Corps hold this city alone, and there are no U.S. troops within 75 miles of us. The enemy has still some troops in our front with whom we have an occasional skirmish merely to keep our hands in.

The weather is quite cool, and we have frost nearly every night. We have not heard a word of the Pennsylvania election yet and it is now being looked for with considerable anxiety. Nine-tenths of the soldiers in this Army will vote for Lincoln.[7]

You must excuse my brevity this morning in consequence of so many letters awaiting my attention. I of course gave yours the preference and opened them first.

Kisses and love to the children.

Your true and affectionate husband
Jno. W. Geary

---

6. Hood marched his force toward Decatur, Alabama, and amassed supplies at the Alabama-Tennessee border before pushing northward toward Nashville.

7. This was the first time soldiers from Pennsylvania could vote for state and federal offices while away from home. In the summer of 1864, the legislature passed the final amendment to the state constitution that allowed men in the army to cast these ballots. When news of this circulated in the spring, a person in the 147th Pennsylvania noted: "The expression in the army is nearly universal for Lincoln for the presidency, at least in our Div. and our boys of Penna. are exul[t]ant over the idea of having a vote in the field. The Copperheads will receive a terrible rebuke from the army on election day" (J. A. Moore to R. A. Moore, April 26, 1864, Moore Family Papers, MHI).

* * *

Hd Qrs 2nd Div. 20th A.C.   Atlanta Ga.   Oct 24th 1864

My Dearest Mary

I have the gratification to acknowledge the receipt of your letters of the 1st, 3rd, 6th, & 10th instant and thank you warmly for the many kind and loving expressions contained therein. Always thankful to God for His kindness in preserving the health of my loved ones at home amid the convulsions of this wonderful period in our national existence. The break in our communication has been fully repaired and the cars are expected to run through to Chattanooga to-day.

The weather here is clear and cool and to all intents and purposes, is what we would call in Penn[sylvani]a an Indian summer. The country around this city is perfectly devastated for twenty miles by our foraging parties. My own reputation in Georgia is not secondary as "von terrible man."

The news of the elections have just reached us[8] and are satisfactory, and sufficient to assure us that the Union Party will be successful in November at the Presidential election. The rebs here are much chapfallen at the disaster to their political friends in the north. They seem to consider it worse than a disaster in the field, and a death blow to their dearest hopes of success in their infamous secession schemes. So [may] it be. How does Samuel B. like the looks of things now? Perhaps the scales may fall from his eyes and he may see more clearly that there are some generals, some patriots, and some "pumpkins" generally all over the country who have not, nor will ever, bow the knee to Baal or any political Juggernaut the so called *Democrats* can scare up.[9] When you see him again tell him the day is not far distant when the *true* & *pure* democracy with "full eyed truth" will come forth unfettered & purified, into eternal youth like a Phoenix from the fire. Then and then only will she be successful. Then and then only will her gallant sons return to the fold, and *democracy* shall be like *truth*, "The eternal years of God are hers."

Give love & kisses to the children. Respects to friends. God bless all my home jewels.

Very lovingly yours

J.W. Geary

8. Pennsylvanians voted on October 11.

9. The comment about Democrats and generals refers to George B. McClellan, former Union general and Democratic candidate opposing Lincoln in the 1864 presidential campaign.

＊ ＊ ＊

Atlanta Ga.   Nov 1st 1864

My Dearest Mary

I have just returned from a foraging raid of which I was in command, and upon which I have been absent several days during which time no opportunity was afforded to me to write to you, and hence a considerable vaccuum in my letters to you. Upon my return I found three from you awaiting me in the Division P.O. I have perused them with pleasure and care. There was also one from Willie G. I thank both you and him for your kindly and constant remembrance of me.

Upon my energies and exertions has depended in a great degree the subsistence of the horses & mules, not only of the 20th Corps but of a large portion of the army, during the recent raid of Hood upon our line of communications. I have procured from the enemy over 2,400 wagon loads of corn, and ravaged the country for 25 and 30 miles around the place. And besides the corn, the spoils captured in cattle, hogs, sheep and horses has been large. We take every thing from the people without remorse. Among the articles should be enumerated "Sweet Potatoes" of the largest and "*best-est* kind." On this last expedition I obtained 3 waggon loads of them for my Staff-mess. This business is neither pleasant nor a safe one, it is attended with much solicitude and danger. I have had a number of skirmishes with the enemy on these expeditions, but I not only *whipped* but "spoiled" them. But I suppose it is excusable, as necessity is said to be entirely unacquainted with *law*. Would to God this war was over, and that these things cease, for, verily, I have no pleasure in them.

I was engaged slightly with the enemy on the 28th of Oct. and I could help thinking all the time that it was the anniversary of our dear Eddie's death: it made me exceedingly sad, but God's will be done. He gave, and He hath taken away, blessed be his name.

This night seven years ago we were affianced and tomorrow will be the anniversary of our marriage. I will then write you. Would I were with you tonight.

Enclosed you will find a brief letter for Mary our dear little pledge of love, it contains some cards with scriptural sentiments upon them. I hope she will appreciate them. I will send, per Adams & Cos Express, tomorrow a box containing some books which are too heavy to transport during our coming winter campaign. Some of them are of my military library and some were given to me in this city. There is a small globe for Willie

Henderson, it will assist him to study geography. I will send you the receipts in my next. May Heaven protect you and the little ones is my devoted prayer.

Ever yours
Jno W Geary

* * *

3 miles south of Atlanta   Nov 5th 1864

My Dearest Mary

We are just about evacuating Atlanta and are now moving upon Macon. We are entirely cut off from the rest of our countrymen. This is not by compulsion, but our own voluntary act. Atlanta will be destroyed and all the Rail Roads leading into it.

May God prosper and speed our mission is my humble prayer.

This will, as a matter of course, be the last letter you can possibly receive from me for several weeks. I commit you and the children to the care of Almighty God and humbly entreat His blessing upon you. Where we will turn up I cannot tell.

Give my kindest regards to our dear friends.

Kiss the little ones for me, and believe me ever your true and loving husband

Jno W Geary

* * *

Hd. Qrs 2nd Div 20th A.C.   Atlanta, Ga.   Nov 8th 1864

My Dearest Mary

Once more there is a prospect of a departure of the mail before we evacuate this city, and strike more deeply into the heart of Rebeldom, and once more I hasten to drop you a note to assure you again that notwithstanding the hum of busy preparation for our departure you are still fondly and ardently remembered.

It is possible that we may not leave here prior to the tenth inst, but in my opinion it will not be longer deferred. It will at least be 30 or 40 days before another letter from me can possibly reach you. You had better, therefore, hereafter direct your letters to Washington City, to be sent to me where I may turn up. I know you will indeed be very lonely without my letters, but you must trust in God and pray Him to guide me safely through.

You must watch rebel sources for news of our whereabouts for some time, but do not rely upon them for facts.

We are all in good spirits, and hope to make the grandest campaign on record.

Give my love to all our friends. Write to brother Edward, he complains that he has not heard from you for 6 or 7 months.

Kiss all the children and believe me your devoted husband

J W Geary

*   *   *

Atlanta Ga.   Nov 10th 1864

My Dearest Mary

We are not gone yet. Don't know the hour of starting. Had a fight with [Brigadier] Gen. [Alfred] Iverson's command at daylight yesterday morning. He attacked my lines with a view of carrying them by *surprise*. He was beautifully repulsed with considerable loss, viz: 8 killed and about 20 wounded. He had 4 pieces of artillery. I had not a man killed, wounded or missing, which is wonderful as they fired over 100 shells at us. We drove him in the direction of Jonesboro. It does me much good to whip such "old rips" as Senator "Iverson," whom you doubtless remember in the U.S. Senate the winter we were in Washington City.[10] Thank God for His mercies, for although I was in the whistle and blaze of the fight, I came out unscathed. His mercy is ever enduring and to His name be all the glory.

I have just now received your letter of the 28th ult. The anniversary of our dear Eddie's death, and translation to heaven. It seems but a few days since that awful night. It can never be effaced from my memory.

Our army will be under the immediate command of Major Genl Sherman, & will consist of four Army Corps of about 15,000 each. It will be divided into two wings. The right will be composed of the 15th and 17th

---

10. Geary made a common mistake in thinking that the junior Iverson was the father who served in the U.S. Senate from 1855 until resigning in 1861. Alfred Iverson Jr. led a brigade of cavalry in Martin's division of Joseph Wheeler's cavalry.

corps, and will be commanded by [Major] Genl [O. O.] Howard. The left wing will have the 14th and 20th Corps under Maj Gen [Henry W.] Slocum. We will take with us about 75 cannon, and a considerable number of cavalry under [Brigadier] Gen [Judson] Kilpatrick. The whole movement is understood at Washington & will doubtlessly be cooperated in by Gen Grant. Of these things do not let the public know for a short time.

I am delighted with your descriptions of dear little Maggie. I have no doubt she is interesting and I would like to get home to nurse her for a while. Kiss them all for me. I can make no choice among them. God bless them all, and my prayer is for their future usefulness and goodness. I have written this in great haste, and I hope you will excuse its many imperfections. If there be another mail before we leave I will write again. If not I will trust in God for your protection, and for my own safety. Remember no matter what distance separates us, and however long communications may be cut off, that I am always the same confiding, faithful and loving husband.

I think I told you in my last to direct your letters to *"Washington City,"* *care War Department.*

Let Mrs Church have the house. I can see no better purpose to which it can be applied. Give my love to Mrs. Church and Comfort. Also to Capt Lee & Mary, to John & Lizzy, and such other friends as you may include.

The mail is ready to depart and I must say good bye.

Your true husband
Jno W Geary

P.S. Mr. Wier will let you have two or three hundred dollars ($300) if you require it.   *J.W.G.*

* * *

{The army prepared for the march to Savannah by systematically purging the sick or less hardy men and limiting wagons and artillery to the most essential. On November 15, the vanguard left Atlanta while the remainder of the 62,000 infantry, artillery, and cavalry filed out the following day. Sherman ordered the men to forage liberally off the countryside, for his purpose was to "make Georgia howl." They met with little opposition; the Confederates had only militia and cavalry under Joseph Wheeler to face a seasoned army.

The Twentieth Corps took the northern route to Madison, then cut through the state capital at Milledgeville before going on to the coast through Sandersville and Millen. Geary's division alone accounted for the destruction of 2,700 bales of cotton, fifty cotton gins and mills, eleven flour mills, fourteen sawmills, and three factories.

When Sherman cut his supply lines to begin the march, he could not communicate with Union command, nor could soldiers receive or send mail until they arrived at the coast near Savannah nearly a month later. One of Geary's first acts was to write home.}

* * *

Hd. Qrs. 2nd Div: 20th A.C.   2½ miles West of *Savannah*, Ga.
Dec. 16th 1864

My Dearest Mary

Once more in the providence of God, I have the pleasure of addressing you, though it is again upon the battle field. As usual my command is the nearest to the city and in full view of it. The enemy have a strong line in our front, well defended with swamp dykes, rice-field marshes &c. &c. and are very defiant. We are therefore in the midst of the thunders of a siege.

We left Atlanta, after utterly destroying it, and its communications, and travelled via Stone Mountain, Yellow river, Ulcofauhatchie, & Ocmulgee rivers to Milledgeville. Thence over the Oconee River and via Sandersville crossed the Ogeechee. We then took "Millen" and came on to this city. We subsisted chiefly upon the resources of the country. My health is good, but after thirty days hard toil in the swamp and pines of Georgia we are a hard looking family. I hope will soon be in Savannah, when if possible I will pay you a visit.

Give my love and kisses to the children. May God continue to give us victory and health and soon restore us to peace. Please excuse this note. I write it on my knee sitting on a log with *only 12* of the enemy's cannon firing over my head. You would think all pandemonium was loose if you were here. Write soon.

Your true and affectionate husband
J.W.G.

* * *

Near Savannah Ga.   Dec 1864

My Dearest Mary

Yesterday was a day racy and rare, and under all the circumstances long to be remembered. We had been thirty-one days cut off from the world and "the rest of mankind," during which period we had not received a single word concerning the affairs of the North, except occasionally through the unreliable and lying *sheets* of the South, but yesterday we had a carnival of letters and newspapers. From you I acknowledge favors of Nov 10th, 13th, 15th & 17th. Also two from Willie G. and one from Mary Lee. Of course I proceed to write to you first, and at a more convenient season I will reply to theirs. The news of the presidential election was all fresh to us, although we had learned, through rebel sources, of Mr. Lincoln's election. I hope the friends of "little Mac"[11] are satisfied now. They certainly understand by this time that they are making a very large sized error and that their dogmas are not in keeping with the progress of the age, in which our lots have been cast, away up in the noon of the nineteenth century. They seem [to] be antiquated fossils, and like the Jews in the Christian era, cannot discern the signs of the times. It is now certain that the United States must be all *free* or all *slave*, and the momentous question has been decided in favor of freedom by the edict of the people in November. The rebellion is certainly much crippled by the result, and as Mr. Lincoln has had so great a triumph, he can afford to make *peace* by the offer of most generous terms.

This last campaign of Sherman's has almost disembowelled the rebellion. The state of Georgia is about as badly destroyed as some of the tribes of the land of Canaan were by the Israelitish army, according to Biblical record. One hundred millions of dollars would not restore it to its former condition.[12] But I will come at once to our present condition. We are in sight of the "promised land," after a pilgrimage of three hundred miles, and we are also once more beseiging a city of huge proportions, and a huge and defiant army,[13] with whom we have to contend for its possession by force of arms, which seems to be the only arbitrament left, as they have just refused Sherman's demand for the surrender of the city [issued December 17]. The

---

11. George B. McClellan.
12. Sherman estimated the damage at $100 million. Of that, the soldiers used roughly one-fifth; the rest was waste.
13. The "huge" army consisted of a garrison of roughly 10,000 soldiers.

place is a great prize, and like all things of great value, very difficult to obtain.

There will therefore be some hard fighting, but I think it must yield. My troops are now engaged throwing up immense batteries from which we expect to commence the bombardment of the city on next Tuesday. Being in good shelling range we will soon knock it to pieces. As I intend to write you frequently, I will not anticipate results, but will wait to chronicle each in its turn as it occurs. The climate is very warm here now, and every insect is creeping about. Butter flies are dallying in the sunshine, and even snakes of every kind are creeping about. Shad are most abundant in the rivers, but the luxury of fish or oysters has not yet been tasted by us, as the fishing waters are covered by the enemy's cannon. Almost every breeze bears the hostile blast of the trumpet, and the thunder of the enemy's guns answers loudly to the thunder of our own. But I think our success is certain.

Although our "Cracker Line" is open,[14] still through the laziness of some party our fresh supplies have not yet reached us. Though we look for the first installment almost hourly. We are now on very short allowance.

I do not recollect whether I told you, in my last, about the death of my famous black horse, "Charly." He died near the city of Milledgeville, *full of honor*. He was a noble *charger* and carried me safely through a score of battles. I miss the old fellow very much, and I hope ere long to find one as good, but probably never will find one with so much nobleness of character.

John Brooks (my servant) while out foraging was captured a few days ago.[15] He was in company with a Captain Geary[16] of one of my batteries who was also captured.

Give my love to all the children. Remember me most kindly to Captain Lee and Mrs Church and Comfort, and be particular not to forget my good friend Eberly.

Hoping that God will stand by me during this struggle and preserve me from wound and death, and restore me again in health to my family to enjoy repose in its loved society. I am as ever

Your loving husband
J. W. Geary

14. As his first priority upon nearing Savannah, Sherman on September 13 had troops take Fort McAllister to open communication with the Union fleet, which could then ship supplies via the Ogeechee River.
15. An African American body servant Geary had hired in Georgia. See letter of April 2, 1865, for Brooks's return to the North.
16. No relative of the general, Captain William Geary served in Company A of the 109th Pennsylvania.

* * *

Savannah Geo.   Dec 23rd 1864

My Dearest Mary

My eventful career is still upon its everlasting whirl. I am now the *Commandante* of the City, in honor of its capture by me, and of the surrender to me.[17] My command was in the city five hours earlier than any other troops. We captured by ourselves alone about 75 Cannon with ammunition, 30,000 Bales of cotton, 400 prisoners, and liberated many of our own soldiers who had languished for months in the southern dungeons. Oh how pleasant it is to bid the captive go free, none but those who do it can taste its exstatic pleasures. God has vouchsafed me so many blessings that we will give all the glory to His great name.

This is a beautiful city and is well preserved.

I am well, but as usual almost smothered with business and responsibilities.

God bless you and all the little ones, and grant us soon a joyful and happy meeting.

Kiss the children for me. Give my love to all friends.

I long to hear from you. Let me hear from you at once.

Ever your loving husband
Jno. W. Geary
Brig Genl

* * *

Hd. Qrs.   City of Savannah Ga.   Dec 27th 1864

My Dearest Mary

As *Commandante* of the city and my Division, I am almost overwhelmed with business, and of course I am unable to write long letters, but I will try to make up in numbers and frequency what I may lack in quantity. The weather is pleasant and all nature looks gay. The city will be filled with

17. Just as with the towns of Leesburg and Winchester in Virginia during 1862, Geary's "capture" of Savannah came less through any effort on his part than because Confederate Lieutenant General William J. Hardee withdrew his force under cover of darkness on December 21, leaving it open for Federal troops to march in on December 22.

reviews every day this holy week. Our army is in splendid condition and is already making full preparation for a campaign in South Carolina. I enclose you daily Papers, from which you can glean what is daily passing within the city.

I am well, and I am not certain that I can obtain leave of absence just now, but you may rest assured that I will come as soon as the good of the service will permit, and I can honorably do so. The churches were all open on Sunday and Divine Service was performed in each. Officers, soldiers, and citizens mingled in quiet as though nothing had occurred. A good anecdote was perpetrated by Gen Sherman when asking permission to preach. After some "heming and hawing," the Clergyman said, well Genl, the diocess of Georgia requires us to pray for certain persons. Will that be objectionable, to which the Gen replied, yes, certainly, pray for Jeff Davis. Pray for Jeff Davis? Certainly pray for the Devil too. I dont know any two that require prayers more than they do, pray for them certainly. The gent preached but did not pray for Jeff Davis.

Give love and kisses to the children. Your loving husband

Jno W Geary

*   *   *

Hd. Qrs.   City of Savannah   Jany 1st 1865

My Dearest Mary

I am in receipt of your two favors of the 11th and 16th ult, the latter containing a letter from Mrs. Moore,[18] containing the detailed account of her family affairs. The whole family seems to be doing all they can to increase the population of the country. But I am afraid the "stay at homes" will produce as mean a race as themselves. The good and the noble are all absent and of course in some respects the future generation will be sadly deteriorated. *We* must stir ourselves or we will be behind in these matters. A truce to these wars[;] they destroy much of the enjoyment of life.

The people of this city present a spectacle of humbled aristocracy. Many of the families are almost in a starving condition, having to subsist on rice almost exclusively. My position as "Commandante" affords me an opportunity of seeing much of southern life unveiled. Like the veiled prophet of Khorassaw, they have deceived the world with its dazzling splendor, which

18. Probably Hetty W. Moore, sister of Geary's first wife.

being now torn off exhibits itself in terrible ghastliness. My health is good, but I am almost run down with work, downright hard work of mind and body.

The climate is very pleasant, there having been no snow yet and very little weather which can be called *cold*. The dampness of the atmosphere, however, renders fires necessary about half of the time. Oysters are abundant on the coast and are now beginning to come in plentifully. Shad and other fish are beginning to make their appearance. They are delicious.

I will remit to you some money in my next letter as I expect to be paid off soon.

Every thing seems to be in course of preparation for the further prosecution of the campaign in South Carolina.

Give love and kisses to all the children, and kindest regards to all friends of the family.

Little Pet's picture came safely to hand. I think it very pretty and I prize it very highly. I carry it in my breastpocket right over my heart, and look at it frequently. O how I would like to be home, where the wearied soldier might find some rest from his toils of body and mind, and have the society of those he loves most dearly, but God's will be done, I hope the war will soon be over.

Ever your true & loving husband

J.W.G.

*　*　*

City of Savannah, Ga.   Jany 6th 1865

My Dearest Mary

I sit down to write to you only a few lines, after a very fatiguing duty, viz. the preparation of my report of the part of the campaign just terminated by the capture of this City, by my Division.

These documents are always very laborious and difficult to prepare. And now I feel so tired I can scarcely write a line even to you. I am very well, but am much worn down with severe and arduous duties.

Enclosed you will please find a draft for $200, endorsed by me to your Order. It is a New Year's present, and with it I tender you all the compliments of the season, and the wish that you may witness many returns in health, happiness, and prosperity.

Last night I was present at an officer's party, and Maj Gen Sherman's. It consisted of the Generals of the Army, and of the Officers of the Navy, among whom was Admiral [John A.] Dahlgren.[19] There were no "niggers" in the party. It was a most brilliant meeting as all were in full uniform.

I wish I could get home for a short time only, but I fear my application will not be granted.

I am in receipt of your kind and loving favor of the 23rd ult. for which I thank you. I hope your next will be in answer to news from me here.

I am of the opinion that our campaign is not yet completed. A portion of our troops are already in South Carolina and it is believed pretty generally that we will soon follow.

Kisses and love to all the children including Mary Lee.

Remember me kindly to all our friends, Capt Lee of course is first on the list.

My prayers are always for your safety and that of the dear ones at home.

We will trust in God and He will never desert us, but will be our everlasting protection.

Your true & loving husband
Jno W Geary

* * *

Savannah, Ga.   Jany. 8th 1865.

My Dearest Mary

Your letters have pretty generally been received up to the 30th of Dece. I thank you kindly my Dear Mary for your faithful and loving letters, so oft repeated. They are a solace to me amid the difficulties and trials of a soldier's life and while away the tedium of long absence.

Gen Sherman I think will not consent for me to remain in this city, on his alleged reason that I am too valuable a soldier in the field and, therefore, cannot be spared. This may be very complimentary to me as an Officer, but I confess I cannot see any propriety in it. But of course I must obey and that is the end of it. If I could have obtained the assurance of remaining here, you would have received orders to join me here without delay. I would also have asked Frank to come here for business purposes.

19. Dahlgren, inventor of the rifled artillery piece that bears his name, commanded the Washington Naval Yard at the beginning of the war, was promoted to chief of the Ordnance Bureau in 1862, and from 1863 on led the South Atlantic Blockading Squadron.

We expect to march in a few days, two Corps, the 15th and 17th, have already moved to Beaufort. South Carolina will be the field of action.

I am well but much pressed for time. My letters are brief, but when you know how many I write you will excuse their brevity.

Give my love to all the family. God bless you all.

Your loving husband
Jno W Geary

*   *   *

City of Savannah, Ga.   Jany 15th 1865.

My Dearest Mary

I am in receipt of your three letters bearing date respectively Dec 31 and Jany 4th & 2nd. I thank you kindly for them, and the one from Willie H. is received also. They are all sweet as "sounds from home" can be, and are valued accordingly. Willie's will be answered in due time, yours just now. I am at a loss to know why my letters are so very tardy in reaching you. I wrote you on the same day Dr. Goodman[20] did to his sister, and sent it by the same mail. The delay and carelessness is probably chargeable to the Distributing Office at "Hilton Head" S.C., as I am just now informed they are very careless there. It is likely such delays will not again occur. But whether they do or not, you must not suppose you are forgotten for a single moment.

Every thing is moving quietly along in Savannah. I do not know yet who will remain in it as commander. There is a bare possibility that I may be that person, but as it is not determined upon I cannot even make a suggestion upon what I will do about the subject. "Sufficient unto the day is the evil thereof."

Savannah is a beautiful city built upon a level sandy plain upon the South bank of the Savannah river. The streets are wide with small squares at each intersection. Two rows of live oaks or other evergreen trees fringe the Curb stone, and some of them have four rows, which gives the city a fresh appearance even in the coldest weather. We have had but very few days that could [be] called cold since we have been here, and only a few frosts. Flowers are blooming beautifully in the gardens, and there are many beautiful ones here. There [are] two or three fine roads to the southward for

20. Surgeon H. Earnest Goodman.

driving or riding and where timber exists. It is mostly evergreen. The river daily yields us a portion of its luxuries to gratify our palates. Oysters, Shad, and Sheepshead are the staple commodities of the concern. The inhabitants are very needy for food and are now subsisting principally upon rice. I hardly know what is to become of them. It is probable we shall move in ten days at most.

I have been brevetted *Maj General* [effective January 12] but have not yet been assigned to duty as such. When that is done I will receive the pay of a Major General.

Give my love and kisses to the children.

Remember in kindness to all our friends. Business of all kinds as far as I can see will be overdone in every respect.

My prayers are for your health and happiness.

I am most affectionately

Your true husband
J.W.G.

* * *

Savannah Ga.   Jany 19th 1865

My Dearest Mary

Your two letters of December 18th and January 5th are received.

You will observe your letters are coming in by degrees and it is possible they will arrive in due time both back and late numbers. I am pleased to hear of the progress and growth of the children, and from what you say of Maggie, she must be a wonderful baby for beauty.

We will of course excuse the frailties of maternal fondness and suppose that she is at least passible. Tell Mary Geary if she will be able to read by the time I get home I will buy for her some beautiful picture books & some nice candies too.

I hope Willie H. will improve in his writing somewhat. I think he will make an admirable correspondent.

Willie G. has improved much in writing and spelling lately, and I am much pleased in consequence of so doing.

I am now under orders to proceed to South Carolina with the rest of the Army, and expect to leave tomorrow. I am relieved by Maj Genl Grover in

Fig. 8. John W. Geary as major general. Promotion to major general eluded Geary for much of the war, but he achieved his goal on January 12, 1865, by brevet, or honorary rank. (U.S. Army Military History Institute, Carlisle Barracks)

command of the city.[21] He is from Maine, and may be a little more aboli-
tionized than I am. I enter the field once more in hopes that the soldier's
toils will soon be recompensed with a glorious peace, and a joyous return to
his loved ones at home. The honors of a *Major Genl* set easy upon me, as I
have been performing the duties of that rank for more than two years. I am
assigned by the President according to my rank.

I am very actively engaged preparing my troops for the field, but it is
raining very heavily and it bids fair to be wet for some time. The Savannah
River is rising and overflowing the rice field on its banks, and our departure may be delayed for several days.

Give love to our friends. Kiss the children, and believe me ever and truly
your faithful and loving husband,

J.W.G.

* * *

Savannah, Ga. Jany 23rd 1865

My Dearest Mary

Your letters of the 6th, 10th, 13th, & 8th. are just received, and I beg
you to accept my kindest thanks. I sent you a check some time ago, I think
near the 1st of this month, for which I am not in possession of an acknowl-
edgement from you. It was a Treasury Draft for $200. Let me know as soon
as it comes to hand. I always feel somewhat uneasy until I hear my checks
are received. I wish you would be a little more particular in acknowledging
any of my letters by date or something they may contain. If they [are] not
worth that much, they must be very worthless.

I have been under marching orders for several days and am only prevented by the rains and consequent high waters of the Savannah and
Ogeechee rivers. Their waters actual[ly] intermingle and form one grand
river west of the city. We are therefore stormstaid.

To-day I have been trying to arrange my papers and to write my correspondence up to date, and now as twilight begins to draw the curtains of
night around me, my thoughts naturally turn to the home fireside and
mentally I am among the little ones at the feet of her I love. The hat is

---

21. Brevet Major General Cuvier Grover's 4th Division of the Nineteenth Corps replaced Geary's men in
garrison duty at Savannah.

doffed, the buckle is undone, the sword and sash are thrown aside, and the soldier's unbending neck yields with love and devotion around the family altar where all is confidence and love. The little prattler on my knee looking perhaps with strange surprise to see how such a bearded monster could be so wondrous kind.

Those more advanced with joyous accents are leaping about almost jealous that they cannot monopolize the whole amount of attention. Then more than there sits with joyous rapture the partner of my bosom, who I often think married me when fortune had deserted me, when *friends* looked askew, and some of them as fearful of political contagion as they would have been of one who had the small pox or some contagious disease. And now after years of faithful service to my country when the *sun* begins to shine once more upon us, in fame, in position, and I may add pecuniously, does she not love me more than then. I think I am right in thinking so, for I judge of you by myself, my own love being increased tenfold. Let but a few more months pass over our heads, with the blessing of God and perhaps it shall be with us as it is stated in Holy Writ: "The stone which the builders rejected the same is become the head of the corner." May God be pleased for to Him we are indebted for every protection for every glory and honor. We will praise His name forever.

Kiss the little ones. Give love to all the family, and believe me ever and truly faithful and loving husband

J.W.G.

*   *   *

{Grant agreed with Sherman that the army should not remain at Savannah, but march to Virginia to further "disorganize the South, and prevent the organization of new armies from their broken fragments." The men itched for this campaign—even though winter made the swampy terrain more difficult—for it allowed them to take vengeance on South Carolina, which most blamed for the start of the war. "I have never burned a house down yet," one Union soldier wrote his sister, "but if we go into South Carolina I will burn som down if I can get a chance." Major General Alpheus Williams noted that orders to spare homes and private property were ignored, adding: "Our 'bummers' . . . put the flames to everything and we marched with thousands of columns of smoke marking the line of each corps."[22]

22. Glatthaar, *March to the Sea and Beyond,* 79; Williams, *From the Cannon's Mouth,* 374.

Geary's division again formed part of the Left Wing, which traveled through Blackville, Lexington, and Winnsboro, then crossed the border and arrived at Fayetteville, North Carolina. Joseph Johnston organized the opposition, although there was little he could do but retreat as Union soldiers bridged swamps and corduroyed roads to march an average of ten miles a day. Two minor brushes came in North Carolina at Averasborough on March 16 and Bentonville on March 19– 21, before the generals on both sides began conducting surrender negotiations that closed at Durham Station on April 26.}

*   *   *

Sisters Ferry Ga.   Jany 30th 1865

My Dearest Mary

I am indebted to you for letters bearing date respectively 14th & 15th inst, I am gratified to know the condition of yourself and family—that you are all well.

You can perceive from the place named above that I am again on the warpath. I left Savannah on the 27th and am now 45 miles up the Savannah River, on the Georgia side, we are constructing a bridge and road to South Carolina and expect to cross on the 1st of February. A large portion of the army is over the river now, but I was sent here to deceive the enemy by making a feint on Augusta, to checkmate one Genl Iverson and [Brigadier General William Wirt] Allen [who] are above this place 12 miles at Brier Creek with two Divisions of Cavalry. I have whipped them before and do not feel alarmed at them, and after coquetting a little with them I will pass to the other side, and leave them alone on the south. Every thing is being destroyed in South Carolina as far as our troops have advanced, and I am of the opinion that the state is doomed to utter destruction.

The new Commander at Savannah does not seem to get along very well. An awful conflagration occurred there the 2nd day after I left. The people, almost frantic, ran about the street, crying if Gen. G[eary]. had been here this would not have occurred.

There is no such idea as dividing the (2nd) Second Division, or of breaking it up, it renders too much good service for that.

My health is very good. Except a sore nose, which is hacked by the cold weather. It has been very cold here several days.

I regret exceedingly that I cannot write to you as frequently as I would wish, but I will do so as often as we will have mails to carry the letters away.

May God protect us on the impending campaign, destined doubtless to be the most important of the war.

I commend you and those dear ones at home to His care, with confidence that He will [protect you].

Kiss the children for me and give my love to all friends. I am as ever your faithful and loving husband

Jno. W. Geary

*   *   *

Hd Qrs. 2nd Div 20th Corps   Sister's Ferry Ga.
Feby 2nd 1865

My Dearest Mary

Your kind favor of Jany 23 has just been received, and I hasten to reply before the return mail departs. We have been stopped for several days by natural obstacles which we are using every effort to overcome. The swamp on the north side of the Savannah River at this place is about two miles wide and in some places about fifteen feet deep. It is a very difficult matter to overcome, and would not be attempted by men of less energy than Sherman's Army. We expect to commence crossing about tomorrow evening, and then we will not cease day or night until all get over to South Carolina. No one can tell the impediments the southern swamps are to locomotion, except those who have seen them, and I fear we shall have many of them to overcome in S.C. and perhaps they will give us as much trouble as the people themselves.

I am sorry to learn that there are so many colds in the family, but I hope they will only be temporary. Do not expose yourself unnecessarily, as in the first place there is really no necessity for it, and in the second, we are informed of the extreme cold weather with you. The weather here has been unusually cold for the latitude, and still continues unpleasant. At present we have strong indications of rain. I hope we will get across the river before another rise takes place.

You do not write much about the prospects of peace. What do the people north think about negotiations pending? Or are they only mithical?[23]

23. On February 3 aboard the Union steamer *River Queen* at Hampton Roads, Virginia, President Lincoln and other Northern officials met with representatives of the Confederate government for four hours to discuss an end to hostilities. Lincoln's demands included surrender of the South, recognition of national authority, and abolition of slavery. The Confederacy could not accept such terms, and the war continued.

There is much hope expressed here by union men in Georgia, that peace and reunion will soon take place, but strange to say, they all desire to see South Carolina scourged first, because they say she is the cause of the sufferings already heaped upon the south. They will soon be gratified in this latter respect I hope.

I am getting very anxious for a visit home, and indeed I sometimes begin to think that I am afflicted with "Nostalgia," and you know it is cured only by going home. It is now over one year since my last leave, and I think it should not be refused much longer. Give my love to the Willies. Kiss the girls a dozen times each for me, and believe me ever and truly your loving husband

Jno. W. Geary

* * *

Near Fayetteville N.C.   March 12th 1865

My Dearest Mary

An order has this moment reached me stating that a mail will leave town at 5 P.M. for the North. I hastily scratch you a line by the way side, simply to inform you that in the Providence of God, I am once more permitted to inform you that I am well and that I have escaped the rigor of a wonderful campaign of 375 miles. Love to the children and all friends. God bless you all.

Your soldier husband
J.W.G.

* * *

Camp 4 miles East of Fayetteville   March 14th 1865

My Dearest Mary

Yesterday we arrived at this place, and finding that there might be another chance of writing you, I hasten to drop you a hasty note, hoping that it will reach you. I have so much to tell you that it will be impossible for me to perform that duty until some time or other when we meet. I can do so by word of mouth during the long nights of winter. Suffice it to say that this has been a terrible campaign and one such as I never wish to be repeated.

Fayetteville is an old town pleasantly situated on the South bank of Cape Fear River. The buildings are mostly of an old fashioned character. The Government arsenal was a beautiful place, but is now destroyed. In it we found the *Government machinery* that was taken by the rebels at Harper's Ferry.[24]

We have at this moment a rumor that Richmond is evacuated, and that Lee with his army is moving south. If so, he will be after Sherman's Army, which they hate so much.

It is probable we shall move very soon. If so, I cannot communicate with you for a few days, until we reach some new base, possibly Goldsboro, or Washington. The weather has been very wet but is now quite warm resembling our May.

I hope the war will soon be over, and I feel almost like a *real* "Know Nothing" for we have not heard from home, or seen a newspaper from the North since we left Sister's Ferry.

Give my love to the Willies and Marys. Kiss little Maggie, and be assured that my prayers are ever for your safety and protection, and I trust the blessing of God will ever rest upon you and the loved flock at home.

Your loving and faithful husband
J.W.G.

*   *   *

Camp Near Goldsboro N.C.   March 26th 1865

My Dearest Mary

In the kind and tender mercies of an All Wise Providence I am again permitted to address you, and from a point originally intended 455 miles from Savannah, crossing all the rivers and almost innumerable swamps and streams of South and North Carolina. Much of the swampy road had to be "corduroyed" with heavy timber, to make it at all passible with our wagons and Artillery.

Upon the mud and swamps the people of South Carolina depend mostly for its defence, but Yankee ingenuity and stout arms have accomplished

---

24. The U.S. arsenal at Harpers Ferry offered an early target in 1861 for Virginia soldiers who stripped the facility of all that could be used by the Confederacy. Some of the material ended up at Fayetteville.

what Southern impudence and imbecility pronounced *impossible*. The people of South Carolina are the meanest, lowest, most contemptible, whining curs I have ever seen in any state. With the exception of a few sharp skirmishes, they seemed anxious only for their lives and all said it was not they who brought this accursed war upon the nation, but somebody else was always to blame. Sherman's trace across that state may hereafter be appropriately traced with a large sponge saturated with ink and drawn around in the shape of a horse shoe, beginning on the coast at Savannah, and on the Atlantic Coast about 50 miles wide, through the interior of the state via Columbia, Winnsboro, and Cheraw. In many places there does not remain a single dwelling, and the inhabitants are in a state of starvation many of whom must die of hunger. In this general devastation, in many instances disgraceful to humanity, you may rest assured that my hands are perfectly clean. I am desperate in battle you know, but no foe man has ever been crushed or insulted by me after the fortune of battle had thrown him into my hands, but on the other hand the kindest treatment has always been extended to them. This position will certainly be awarded me by the historian.

Hello! Here comes a mail! Stop writing. The loved missiles from the dear ones at home must be read and then we'll finish this communication.

Six hours have elapsed since the above was written, and out of 65 letters recd, I have the pleasure to acknowledge the following from you, viz: one of November 25th, 1864, per Dr. Mish. forwarded by mail from Wauhatchie, Tennessee. I also acknowledge the following of more recent date: Jany 25th, & 31 and 27th. Feby 1st, 5th, 6th, 12th, 15th, 20th, and March 15th, making 11 in all. I also received one from Willie Henderson and two from Willie Geary all of which I will endeavor to answer soon.

From your letters I observe you have had a hard winter with much snow. The sleighing must have been excellent, and I have no doubt it was enjoyed by many.

I have just read a long account in the newspapers of the great flood in the Susquehannah river and of the immense damages to the bridges and other property, public and private, along the river. There was nothing said about New Cumberland, and I infer that you are safe there. Though there must have been *high water* in the lower part of town. I am now closely engaged on my report of the part taken by my Division in the late campaign. It will require several days to complete it. Gen Sherman has gone to New Berne and it is reported to Fortress Monroe, and I cannot tell any thing about "leave of absence" until his return, as he is the only one who can grant leave to General Officers. My intention is, however, to pay you a visit, if only for a few days, provided the exigencies of the service will permit the leave.

Our late campaign seems to be well appreciated, both in this country and in Europe. It will occupy an honorable space in history.

Your description of little Maggie makes her very beautiful. I am therefore prepared for a big disappointment when I see her, as we do not all look through the same eyes. Give love and kisses to the two Marys and to the little One. Give love to the Willies and all our Friends. I will soon write to Capt Lee.

Rest assured of my continued ardent love and deep regard for yourself, it knows no diminution, nor is it conquered by absence or distance. It remains fresh and vigorous as it was on the day of our nuptials, and is only ripened into harder and more solid maturity.

God bless you and all the children.

Your true husband

J W Geary

P.S. My health is very good.

*   *   *

Hd. Qrs. 2nd Div. 20th A.C. Camp, near Goldsboro, N.C.

March 28th 1865

My Dearest Mary

Another mail from the "land of steady habits and love" has just reached, bringing welcome letters from you bearing dates as follows, viz: March 1st, 6th, 8th and 12th. All of them were carefully read, and as usual, fearing they might pass inspection of unworthy eyes, I committed them to the *flames*. Accept, I pray you, my most ardent thanks for your ardent and devoted affection and continued love. And I hope you will always be satisfied that it is duly and properly appreciated, and what is more it is fully reciprocated. I feel assured, however, of the long continued deprivation of each other's society.

But you are aware, at a time when it tried the stoutest nerves, I had to decide and take my position upon this great national question of the day I could not, & did not, hesitate to declare for my country, regardless of the scoffs and sneers of party.

Four long years have nearly passed, and you can better judge perhaps than I whether that decision was right or wrong. I would not change it if I could. How much better is it to hear the land resound with the plaudits of a patriotic hero, than to have my name associated with secret bands of traitors of the baser kind, seeking cowardly, and merely to destroy our nation. Oh, Shame! Where is thy blush? Where can some of our friends show their heads? Only am'g *traitors*. What will the iron pen of history say of them? They have lived for the hour, and verily, they have their reward. They may have a few more paltry dollars than we, but riches have wings, and often flee away, and I am much mistaken in my beloved Mary if she would not prefer to lean on her old battle scarred veteran's arm, *penniless*, than to enjoy the full fruition of all their ill gotten gains, *with a traitor's name attached*, and a *traitor's doom awaiting*, to carry down a worthless fame to the grave, and be "unwept, unhonored, and unsung." I am not much mistaken in Old Buck, Big-Black, or Buck—6 of one and half a dozen of the other.[25] And all so mean that devils will not associate with them when they go hence.

The work of crushing the rebellion "goes bravely on" and I sincerely hope will soon be over. I have labored long and hard, but not grudgingly, for my country. My sacrifices have been great, but still I love my country so much that I am still willing to honor "Old Glory," our starry banner, as long as I possess the power to do so, and will assist to place it, and lead the way, at the top-mast and forever flaunt in proud defiance of every foe, and in the future remind all traitors of their everlasting infamy who may dare to oppose its onward progress.

It is very natural that you should be lonely and desire my return, for we have been a long time separated. But I trust the time will soon come when Our Heavenly Father will permit our reunion together in happiness.

You say you are not growing any older in appearance. I am sorry to inform you that I am of the opinion that I am. These eternal solicitudes, night-watchings, and exposures will make any one an old man. Perhaps animated by your juvenile presence I may be again revivified and re-juvenated. Who knows, Or as the Spanish say "Quien sabe."

Willie Geary desires to enter the army. Persuade him at once from this.

---

25. "Old Buck" referred to James Buchanan, the Democratic predecessor to Lincoln; "Big-Black" was Jeremiah Black, a noted Pennsylvania jurist who served in Buchanan's cabinet; and "Buck" was Charles R. Buckalew, U.S. Senator from Pennsylvania from March 4, 1863, to March 3, 1869. War Democrats like Geary joined with Republicans in accusing these three Democrats of conspiring with Southerners—none of it true, but the allegations made for good politics.

If [he] must come, I will get him a commission, as aid and take him on my staff which will please him to ride and be a gentleman more than to [be] a foot soldier.

Give my love & kisses to all the dear ones, and believe me ever

Your loving husband
Jno W. Geary

P.S. I will remit you some money when the pay master arrives.

* * *

Hd. Qrs. 2nd Div: 20th A.C. Near Goldsboro N.C.
April 2nd 1865

My Dearest Mary

It is with extreme pleasure that I acknowledge the receipt of your two valued letters of the 21st and 25th of March 1865. In one you give an account of John Brooks[26] arrival, pilgrimmage &tc. I am very glad to hear of his safe arrival. I had almost given him up, but he of course, is satisfied I have tried hard enough to get him as we have followed up so far. I think for the present he had better remain a short [time] at home or until we reach a new base towards which we expect to march in a few days. Tell him I am glad he is out safe, and that I will write to him when he can join me.

I have applied for a commission for Willie Geary. I expect it in a week or two. As soon [as] it arrives I will send for him and John to join me. I am induced to do this for many reasons which to me seems good and sufficient, and which I will hereafter explain.

Another thing Willie will be company for me, and can act in the position of a staff officer, and I think he will improve as much under my tuition as he would with that of any one else.

My health is good, and I have not been sick one day this winter. I am in hopes our next base will be nearer home than this place. I trust we will reach it safely, and that the war will soon be over. I am, indeed, anxious to get home. I have been so long absent that all of you seem much dearer to me as the length of time increases.

I intend to write to one of the Willies next, and then to Mary G. and I hope she will write me a letter in return.

26. Geary's servant captured near Savannah near the end of December 1864. See note 15 above.

I have not been paid off yet, and, therefore, cannot send you any money, but will do so as soon as the paymaster arrives.

Excuse this hasty letter, for I cannot write. A Brass Band is serenading me, half a dozen officers are in my tent awaiting my leisure. I wish they were at home, and I could write you a longer and better letter.

Your truly affectionate husband
Jno W Geary

* * *

Near Goldsboro, N.C.   April 6th 1865

My Dear Little Daughter

I have been promising to write to you for a long time, and I am now determined not to put it off any longer, for fear I may have to march after Joe Johnston or Bob Lee, those two naughty rebel Generals. Today we have heard of the capture of Richmond by Grant's army and we are all much gratified, but as Lee and Johnston may get to-gether they may give us some hard fighting yet before the war will be over.[27] I have several times written to your mother since we arrived here, and I have received a number of letters from her. Also one from Willie Geary and one from Willie Henderson, but none from you or from Mary Lee. Now I think you girls might write me one dear, sweet letter. It would be so nice to hear from you.

Some time ago I heard you were learning to read very fast, when you write you can tell whether that is true or not. If it is true, I will be much pleased to hear you read some pretty story for me when I come home.

I send you some rebel money. You can give one note to Mary Lee, one to Willie H., one to Willie G. and keep one for yourself. Little Maggie is too small to know any thing about such things, and therefore I do not send her any as she would only tear it up. Kiss little Maggie for me, and give my [love] to the Willies, Mary Lee, and your mother.

Since we have been in North Carolina I have seen some very terrible things. The people here are nearly all in a starving condition, food is so scarce that many people are starving. And I have just been informed that

27. Lee evacuated Richmond on April 2, 1865. Grant and others feared that the Army of Northern Virginia, which fled to the west for supplies at Danville, would join with Johnston's force to prolong the contest. The Union army, however, caught the Confederates at Appomattox Court House; on April 9, surrender terms were signed.

some black women when trying to escape from slavery have thrown their babies into the swamps, where they died. Poor little black children, what a pity it is for them that they are so cruelly treated.

Our army is resting a few days here, but we expect to march again on Monday next. Write to me soon, and give me all the news about home.

Your Affectionate
Father

Miss Mary C. Geary
P.S. The money is not worth anything.

*   *   *

Hd. Qrs. 2nd Div 20th A.C. Near Goldsboro, N.C.
April 8th 1865.

My Dearest Mary

I came near dating my letter on the 28th, as yours was lying before me of March 28th, which was received yesterday. We have the full news of the glorious success at Richmond against Lee. Every body in the army of course is rejoicing, and at this moment every thing is [in] motion to march early tomorrow morning in the direction of Raleigh, with a view to intercepting the Rebels in their westward flight.

God grant that this war may soon be over. Every thing looks well here, and the blessings of heaven seem to rest upon our cause. A few blows of that kind will not only *scotch* but KILL the snake. What's the price of Copperheads now? Very small I suppose.

Thank God, who has given us, who have stood the brunt of this war, such cause of rejoicing and hopes of speedy and glorious success.

We leave at once for the interior. May God bless our mission, and preserve us from death or casualties.

I commit you and our dear children to the care of Him who is omniscient and can preserve [us] from every ill.

Ever yours in love & fidelity
Jno W Geary

*   *   *

Raleigh, North Carolina   April 14th, 1865

My Dearest Mary,

After four days of very hard marching and considerable skirmishing our army has reached this city, the far-famed capital of N.C. The roads over which we passed were swampy and tortuous, and were frequently barricaded by the enemy for the purpose of retarding our progress. Smithfield was taken on Tuesday, the day after we left Goldsboro. This city was taken on the 13th, being the 2nd day after the taking of Smithfield.

We are going to pursue Johnston's Rebel Army until we can overtake it. He is now fleeing before us, and with his defeat the war will be closed. Gen Sherman will pursue him until a collision takes place which may again try our temper & steel. Further than this I cannot give you any information at present of our prospective movements. One thing is very certain, however, that this war must be closed soon, and the harder we work to close it, the sooner we will get through. And then we can go home (sweet home). To ask for leave at this time, and under such circumstances would be sheer nonsense. *The work must be finished at once.*

My health is good, but this retrograde movement is a little grating upon my feelings personally. You know I preferred a visit homeward.

Raleigh, like most of the old towns of the south has seen its best days, and it is now considerably dilapidated. It is pleasantly situated, has finely shaded streets, and abundance of good water. The principal public buildings are the state house, Asylum for the "Deaf, Dumb, & Blind," and the Asylum for the Insane, both of the latter have many inmates. The inhabitants of the state, I am assured (by the leading men of this place) will vote *two to one* to return to the Union, as soon as the rebel army is driven away. I have no doubt that this will be true.

Give my love to all the children and kisses to the Marys and little Maggie. I am so exceedingly busy I can hardly write a letter any more, and, therefore, I hope you will excuse the hasty manner in which my letters are scribbled. But I can assure you my devotion to you, home, and family is as warm and ardent as it is possible for husbands, and fathers to be. I am ever truly your loving husband,

Jno. W. Geary

I cannot tell when or where I will be able to write to you again, but I hope you will continue to keep up your correspondence, it will reach me somewhere.

Remember me most kindly to Capt Lee and Mrs Church & Comfort. We left Goldsboro on the 10th.

* * *

Raleigh, N.C.   April 19th 1865

My Dearest Mary

I have just received your two letters dated 2nd and 5th inst respectively. I believe I always acknowledge your letters by date, and I regret that you nearly always omit that essential requisite in answering mine, by this omission, I am often left in the dark concerning what letters have reached you, and what ones have failed. A hint to the wise is said to be sufficient. I am happy to hear of your health and welfare, and that of our dear children. I also rejoice with you in the grand successes of our arms, and of the eminent hope for speedy peace, which I hope and trust will soon be fully consummated. Our army is lying still at this place much in the attitude of a tiger couchant, about to spring upon his prey. If Johnston's army surrenders as we now Confidantly hope it will, the war will cease, and *we* will return to our loved homes without delay. God grant that moment will soon come. It cannot come too soon for me. But as to going home at this stage of the game, as the phrase goes, we cannot think of it. The game must be played out, when it is so near a successful termination.

We have just learned the assassination of the President, his untimely loss has created a profound sensation in the entire army, and if we have to fight anymore, woe be to Rebeldom! The cowardly assassins are only exhibiting the same *phases* which so greatly embittered me towards them ever since the Kansas affair, and no one understands better than I their nefarious designs.

This most dastardly affair meets with decided disapprobation from the citizens of this place, as you will see from the enclosed paper.

Since writing the above I have received official information that the negociations between Gen Sherman and Gen Johnston, are of such a nature as to require the sanction of the Government at Washington. For that purpose a messenger was sent to that city last night and I have just received notice to make myself and my command as comfortable as possible for ten days to

come. Rumor says the negociation contains the surrender of the entire remainder of the Rebel forces both the army in our front and of that west of
the Mississippi in Texas and elsewhere. Thus you observe that peace will be
permanent, admitting that all goes well.[28]

I had hoped that Willie's commission would have been here by this time.
He is to be commissioned a Lieut in the 33rd New Jersey Regiment and from
that he is to be detail[ed] as Aid de Camp on my staff. So much for him. Give
him my love. I will send for him as soon as the commission arrives.

Remember me in love to all the children, and with kisses. Also to Capt
Lee and Mrs Church and Comfort.

Hoping soon to return home. I am ever and truly.

Your loving husband
J. W. G.

* * *

Raleigh, N.C.   April 23rd 1865

My Dearest Mary

Your very kind letter of the 11th instant is received, and I hasten to
reply. In the first place I will dispose of the matter relative to the com-
mandership of the 20th Corps. You are doubtlessly aware that there are
three Divisions in the Corps, and the three commanders Rank in the following relative order, viz: [Alpheus] Williams, [William T.] Ward,
Geary. Williams proved to be unsatisfactory to Gen Sherman. Ward &
Williams both drink too much, and neither could be trusted. Nor could an
inferior be placed over them. Consequently Gen [Joseph A.] Mower was
placed in command simply because he ranked them, and no injustice was
done to me. Except that the kind feelings of my friends in the Corps much
preferred my advancement to that position.[29] I am not outraged and have

28. Sherman and Johnston met on April 17–18 about five miles outside Durham Station in a house
belonging to James Bennett on the Hillsboro Road. Here Sherman framed a highly controversial document
that went well beyond his military authority. He drew up terms for the entire Confederacy that ordered all
arms be delivered to arsenals, recognized existing state governments and federal courts, and guaranteed
political rights to all individuals as long as they promised to obey the law. Both generals forwarded the
agreement to their respective civil authorities.

29. Brigadier General Alpheus S. Williams, not Geary, was the more popular choice for this promotion
among the easterners in the army. Sherman chose Mower, a westerner, because he wanted a more aggressive
commander for the final campaign. The move upset many of the men within the Twentieth Corps. See
Glatthaar, *March to the Sea and Beyond*, 23.

nothing to complain of. It is glory enough for me to know that I have served *well* in whatever capacity or position I have been placed, and perhaps my advancement has been as rapid as my merits would warrant. Let us be satisfied.

We are awaiting the results of the proposed surrender of Joe Johnston's army, and it is expected if the authorities at Washington approve and confirm the propositions, we will march for home by May 1st, that we will march via Richmond and encamp somewhere near the Potomac River and be mustered out. The march will require about 30 days, and it will take near a month to complete the other business of the army before our departure for our respective homes. Should this plan be carried out, you will be afforded the unusually favorable opportunity of seeing the greatest army now on the planet. This I believe would be pleasant to you as you have often expressed the desire to see a large body of men together, and I will endeavor to have you meet me at the proper time, of which I will give you notice.

The murder of the President creates a most profound sensation among the better class of the people of this state, and the act is most bitterly denounced. Andrew Johnson was born near this place, and is known to be a more determined and implacable man than Mr. Lincoln, they also feel that they have now a *Rowland for an Oliver*, and that they are not now so safe and so perfectly secure as they were under Mr Lincoln's administration.[30] Some of the stipulations with the Rebels do not meet my approval, and I fear things will not be set at rest so fully as might be expected.

My health is good and that of the army generally is in the same condition. Believing the war to be over and danger consequently past many officers and soldiers are joining their commands who were never there in the hour of danger. This is a good way to get glory without paying the price.

Give much love and many kisses to all the young ones, and also kindest regards to other friends.

Keep me advised to date of all that is going on in the political world.

---

30. "Roland for an Oliver" technically meant exchanging a blow for a blow, referring to the hero Roland in Charlemagne's court who battled for five days in combat with Oliver without either being the victor. But Geary's usage indicates that he believed Southerners feared the substitution of Andrew Johnson—who had promised vengeance against traitors—as less acceptable than the Roland-like Lincoln. Events would prove otherwise, as Johnson's policies in Reconstruction proved friendly to the South and anathema to Radical Republicans, who moved to impeach him in 1868.

With ardent and devoted love

Your true husband
J.W.G.

*   *   *

Raleigh N.C.   April 29th 1865

My Dearest Mary

Four days ago our Corps started after Joe Johnston. We went only about 15 miles when he agreed to surrender, and did surrender.[31] So we marched back to this *most beautiful city*. Peace, sweet peace is made and to-morrow we set out for Richmond and Washington City on our way to home, sweet home.

And now we can truly say, "Johnny comes marching home" in the language of the song. Thus you see I had the honor to participate in the last campaign of this ever memorable struggle.[32]

All is joy and gladness here among all classes.

The glory and honor be to God, to whose great name we ascribe all praise.

May He protect us during the march homeward and give us a joyful and happy meeting.

Kiss the children. Give love to friends.

Ever your loving husband
J.W.G.

*   *   *

{Sherman's men went to Washington, where on May 24 they participated in the Grand Review of the Armies. Although the administration quickly scaled down the size of the army, Geary and his men remained in the service until July 19. Within

31. Sherman received word on April 24 that Union officials rejected his terms. He was also told to end immediately a truce between the armies and to give Johnston forty-eight hours to surrender or resume hostilities. Final capitulation came on April 26 with terms similar to those that Grant gave to the Army of Northern Virginia. Troops were given paroles in exchange for their pledge not to take up arms; officers retained side arms and private horses; all men could return home.

32. Two more Confederate forces remained in the field: E. Kirby Smith's in the Trans-Mississippi, and Richard Taylor's in Alabama. On April 30, Taylor agreed to a truce with Union Major General E.R.S. Canby that effectively ended matters in Louisiana, although final surrender waited until May 4. Terms for Kirby Smith's army were drawn up May 26 and accepted by him on June 2.

a year, the Pennsylvanian used his military record to run for governor of the state. He first announced his availability to the Democrats, then threw in with the Republicans when recruited by Simon Cameron, who used the election to defeat his rival, Andrew Gregg Curtin, and gain control of the Republican machine. Geary served two terms as governor of Pennsylvania, acquiring a reputation as a headstrong opponent of the legislature. Geary harbored presidential aspirations when his second term expired, but fell ill and died on February 8, 1873, only weeks after leaving office.}

Index